THE RENAISSANCE

Its Nature and Origins

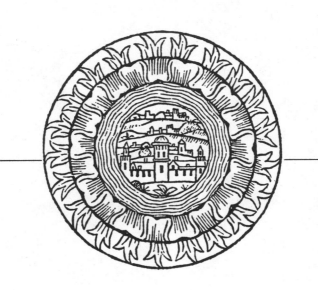

GEORGE CLARKE SELLERY

THE RENAISSANCE
ITS NATURE AND ORIGINS

THE UNIVERSITY OF WISCONSIN PRESS

Published 1950
The University of Wisconsin Press
Box 1379, Madison Wisconsin 53701

The University of Wisconsin Press, Ltd.
70 Great Russell Street, London

Printings 1950, 1962, 1964, 1965, 1969, 1972

Printed in the United States of America

ISBN 0-299-00644-1 ; LC 50-4422

PREFACE

This is an essay on the Renaissance, not a history of the Renaissance. It omits mention of many interesting details of that vast transformation in an effort to determine, through a broad survey of its more salient features, the fundamental nature of the movement and the sources of its power. The final chapter presents the conclusion, which the survey convincingly yields, that the Renaissance was not a revolution, set off by the Revival of Learning and its concomitants, but an evolution, based on the same forces, generally speaking, that are at work in the world of today.

It is a duty as well as a pleasure to acknowledge my obligations to former students, to Mrs. June Stalker, the skilled compiler of the index, and above all to my learned colleague, Professor Gaines Post, who has criticized the manuscript and read the proofs. The book owes much to all of them.

G. C. S.

MADISON, WISCONSIN, OCTOBER, 1949

774099

CONTENTS

CHAPTER I: THE PROBLEM

The Renaissance is still a baffling concept. The achievements of our European ancestors which ushered in modern times have been frequently and variously listed; but how are they to be accounted for? That is another question. Jacob Burckhardt of Basel gave a most impressive answer in his *Die Kultur der Renais-*

sance in Italien, which saw the light in 1860.[1] Here he argued that it was the Italians of the later Middle Ages who had freed themselves and, by precept and example, had subsequently freed the other Europeans from the varied restrictions of the Middle Ages. The Italians had done this through their own talents and the support they had drawn from the renewed study of the ancient classics, the masterpieces of Latin and Greek literature. "We must insist upon it," Burckhardt says, "as one of the chief propositions of this book, that *it was not the revival of antiquity alone, but its union with the genius of the Italian people, which achieved the conquest of the western world.*"[2]

Now it happened that in 1859 Georg Voigt had published his masterpiece on the revival of classical antiquity, *Die Wiederbelebung des klassischen Alterthums.* Burckhardt did not see it in time to use it; but it reached the learned public virtually with his own book and augmented the importance he ascribed to the revival. In short, the two books were read together as attributing overwhelming importance to the Revival of Learning[3] —a weight which the title of Burckhardt's book seemed designed to carry. John Addington Symonds's *Renaissance in Italy,* which began to appear in 1875, is indeed massive evidence of the truth of the observation which

1 Translated into English as *The Civilisation of the Renaissance in Italy* (first edition, 1878; reprinted frequently).

2 *Die Kultur,* p. 129; *Civilisa-*

tion, p. 171. Italics mine.

3 *Cf.* Goetz in *Historische Zeitschrift,* XCVIII: 30–54; Brandi in *Deutsche Rundschau,* CXXIV: 416–30.

Carl Neumann made in 1903: Since the appearance of Burckhardt's celebrated book, "the opinion has quite generally prevailed that the Renaissance was the mother of modern civilization, that the Italians were the first-born people of the modern world, and that all this was due to the passionate zeal with which they overleaped the Middle Ages and sought, with success, to link themselves again to the ancient world."[4]

Scores of illustrations, wearying the flesh and the eyes, could be given to back up Neumann's statement of the situation. Only a few will be selected. George Burton Adams, in his—for the time—very useful *Civilization during the Middle Ages,* put it thus in 1894: "It was the work of the Renaissance . . . to awaken in man a consciousness of his powers and to give him confidence in himself; to show him the beauty of the world and the joy of life; and to make him feel his living connection with the past, and the greatness of the future which he might create." "Men began to realize that there lay behind them a most significant history, and that the men of the past had many things to teach them. When men became conscious of this, the revival of learning began"—"that intellectual and scientific transformation of Europe which we call the Revival of Learning or the Renaissance."[5]

More than forty years later Conyers Read, in his in-

---

4 Munro and Sellery, edd., *Medieval Civilization,* p. 524.

5 Pp. 364, 356, 357. The entire chapter, "The Renaissance," from which the foregoing is taken, is substantially a paraphrase of Burckhardt.

formative book, *The Tudors,* reflects some though little
change in the Burckhardtian concept: The Renaissance in its essence was "a changed attitude of mind to-
wards man and his environment, substituting for the
medieval conception of man as a miserable sinner striving against the world and the flesh, man as an interesting and beautiful creature in a beautiful and interesting
world . . . . It was in short the impulse which set in mo-
tion the whole modern world . . . . Man turned to the
ancient models, not so much out of any reverence for
the Greeks and the Romans *per se* as because they
found in the classics the most satisfactory expression of
what they themselves were trying to express . . . . But
the impulse was universal and those who felt it merely
turned to Italy as they turned to the classics for further
inspiration and guidance."[6]

A little later, Frank Jewett Mather, the art historian,
in an address on "The Spirit of the Renaissance," put
the matter thus: "But the genius and insight of the pioneers of the Renaissance were shown in the perception
that the ancients had a truer knowledge of nature and
human nature than was elsewhere available. So in dis-
covering and reviving the ancient books and studying
the ancient marbles the men of the Renaissance were
merely pursuing the best beaten of several roads to self-
knowledge and to understanding of nature."[7]

Only the other day Roger B. Merriman, the histor-

6 Pp. 46–47.   7 *Historical Aspects of the Fine
                                    Arts,* pp. 45–46.

ian of the Spanish empire, paid his tribute to Burckhardt. He opened his *Suleiman the Magnificent* with
these words: "Few periods in history possess such fas-
cination as the first half of the sixteenth century. All
over Western Europe the spirit of the Renaissance had
triumphed, and was wakening the human mind to ever
greater activity . . . . Italy became at once the intellectual guide and the political prey of ruder and stronger
powers . . . . The spirit of the Renaissance was above all
individualistic. . . ."

The most sweeping commendation of Burckhardt in
English was pronounced by the English encyclopedic
author, G. P. Gooch: "No [other] historian has seized
and interpreted the psychology of an epoch with such
power and insight. In the Middle Ages, declares the
historian, one was a member of a class, a corporation,
a family; society was a hierarchy, tradition was supreme. With the Renaissance man discovered himself
and became a spiritual individual. The fetters of a
thousand years were burst, self-realization became the
goal, and new valuations of the world and of man became current. Dazzling personalities of the type of the
Emperor Frederick II had been witnessed but once or
twice in the Middle Ages. The complete man, *l'uomo
universale,* now became common in the world of action,
of thought and of art. 'The fifteenth century is, above
all, that of the many-sided man.' The soil from which
these wonderful human plants grew was composed of
many elements—the intense life of the City State, the
revival of the art and philosophy of antiquity, the weak-

ening of authority, the disintegration of [Christian] belief. The Tyrant and the Condottiere, despite their ruthlessness, were political artists, men cast in a gigantic mould . . . . With all its glaring faults, the Renaissance was the spring-time of the modern world."[8] These are strong words.

The Burckhardt-Voigt theory of the Renaissance (we shall for convenience call it the Burckhardt theory) did not enjoy such general acceptance as the foregoing comments would suggest. The main lines of hostile criticism have been two. First, it has been argued that many of the so-called Renaissance characteristics—for example, individualism, love of nature, and secularism or the concentration of human interest upon the affairs of this world—are to be found in broad reaches of the Middle Ages; and secondly, that many of the so-called medieval characteristics—submissiveness to authority, supernaturalism or interest in the transcendental, and superstition—were common in Renaissance times. These lines of criticism stress the evolutionary rather than the revolutionary nature of the Renaissance, and they imply or assert that Burckhardt's knowledge of the Middle Ages was defective and his colors too uniformly dark.

In 1885 Henry Thode published his charming study of St. Francis, *Franz von Assisi und die Anfänge der Kunst der Renaissance in Italien.* Here he argues cogently that the lovable saint, by his preaching of the

8 *History and Historians in the Nineteenth Century, pp.* 581–82.

human Christ and of flower-bedecked nature as a revelation of God to man, really inspired the artistic and
poetical achievements of the Italian Renaissance, while
the art of classical antiquity had merely contributed formal and technical aid.

It was Carl Neumann who pushed Thode's attack
closer home. In an article, "Byzantinische Kultur und
Renaissancekultur," published in 1903, he undertook to
demolish the principal support of the Burckhardtian edifice. Comparing the unprogressive civilization of the
Byzantine empire, in which antiquity reigned supreme,
with the progressive civilization of Western Europe, he
reached the conclusion that it was not the revival of antiquity but rather medieval Christianity and the realistic
Teutonic "barbarians" that had made possible the rise
of true modern individualism. "We must firmly grasp
the idea," he wrote, "that the medieval-Christian training and the so-called barbarism were the life-strength of
that which is traditionally called the Renaissance, and
that the revival of antiquity was a productive and benefi-
cent element only as long as it remained contented with
the rôle of companion, with its pedagogical rôle."[9]

Still more sweeping was the attack of Johan Nordström in his *Moyen Age et Renaissance,* published in
1933. In this little book, the author compares the cultural achievements of the Middle Ages, down to about
1400, with those of the Italian Renaissance. In the

9 Munro and Sellery, edd., *Medieval Civilization,* pp. 545–46.
Quoted in free translation from
Historische Zeitschrift, XCI:
215–32; in Munro and Sellery,
pp. 524–46.

light of his examination he declares that medieval Western Europe, under the guidance of France, had anticipated all the achievements attributed to Renaissance Italy, including the revival of classical learning, that the debt of Italy to the North, especially to France, was overwhelming; in short, that the modern age evolved out of the medieval.

Nordström's own statement of his thesis is given in his preface: As medieval studies develop, "it is clear that we must revise completely the traditional conception which makes us see in the Italian Renaissance the matrix of our civilization. That which we have been taught to regard as the great contributions of this renaissance to occidental culture is more and more seen to be, in its principal lines, a simple continuation, or a transformation under the influence of the ethnic Italian character, of the traditions of the Middle Ages. These traditions were mainly formed north of the Alps, during the first centuries of the second millennium [A.D. 1000–1300], in the bosom of that civilization which embraced nearly all of the West and of which France had been the most glorious artificer. Thus, before the relatively tardy appearance of Italy as the nation guide of civilization, we can speak of a 'European Renaissance,' which laid the strong foundations upon which were to be erected the multiple forms of the high civilization of our part of the world."

Nordström's attack on the Burckhardtian thesis was most vigorously met by Italo Siciliano in another little book, *Medio Evo e Rinascimento.* He totally rejects all

Nordström's arguments, frequently with disdain, and ends his own analysis with an impressive list of the great personalities of the Italian Renaissance and this sweeping claim: "When we think of all these we have no need of the astrologer to see why the Italian renaissance issued from Italy to conquer the world, and why it is for modern civilization what Greco-Latin civilization was for antiquity." Phrased a little differently the claim is this: "In the Middle Ages one spirit and one universal culture nourished various peoples; *in the Renaissance it is the élite of one nation which dominates and directs the whole world.*"[10] Burckhardt would not have put it quite so arrogantly.

Siciliano defends the Burckhardtian thesis with improved weapons. Burckhardt's watchwords—revival of antiquity, individualism, the discovery of man and of nature—lack "differential character." For example, there was undoubtedly a classical revival in twelfth-century France. The real question is "how did the twelfth century understand antiquity?" So too there was no dearth of individualism in the Middle Ages, both of the brutal nobles and the saints, of kings and popes. But how profoundly different was the individualism of the Renaissance Italian, educated and disciplined by ideals of the Renaissance!

The transition from Middle Ages to Renaissance, which took place in Italy, Siciliano explains, was marked by the entrance of "the intellectual or classical facul-

10 Pp. 147, 107–08. The italics are mine.

ties," which substituted artistic and intellectual vision
and elaboration for the fantastic and emotional vision
of the Middle Ages. What are "the intellectual and
classical faculties," and whence do they come? Siciliano's answer, in brief, is this: In the nature of the
Italian people there has always been a living classical
tradition, an innate "classical" quality, "and in Italy the
plant man has always grown better than elsewhere."[11]
But this answer is incomplete.

This natural endowment "escapes naturalistic investigation"; but naturalistic influences also operated: the
climate, the possibility of life in the open, and the beauty of the land. Political and social developments also
made their contribution. But it was not the successful
reaction of the mass, in the commune, against feudalism
that helped to release "the intellectual or classical faculties"; on the contrary, it was the detachment of science
and doctrine from the spirit of the populace and their
creation of the signory, the personality, the power of
the individual king, pope, tyrant, or Humanist.[12]

The Renaissance Italian, an aristocrat of the spirit,
did not blindly reject the Middle Ages. He studied all
that was of value in the Fathers and the doctors, in
Arabs and Jews, in St. Thomas and Siger of Brabant;
but the search gave no very satisfactory results. And
so, of necessity, the creators of the Renaissance re-
sorted to the great fountains of pagan antiquity, and

11 Pp. 119–20. Perhaps we should
recall the conditions in Italy
at the time (1936) Siciliano

expressed this thought.

12 *Ibid.,* pp. 107–10.

set to work to restore those liberal studies which, Boccaccio affirms, were totally abandoned in Dante's youth.
The fever was propagated, and the movement seized
the multitude.[13] Thus the Renaissance educated and disciplined the individual, fed him with its ideals and satisfied his spiritual needs, and formed a man profoundly
different from his medieval ancestor.[14] This new man
will continue to beat his breast and perform acts of con-
trition; but he also collects antiques and seeks fame,
study, and culture. The Virgin, the Christ, the statues
of saints and prophets are above all works of art, com-
positions that express an aesthetic more than a religious
ideal, before which one may pray, but which one should
in particular admire.[15] "These men are neither pagans
nor Christians, but scholars and artists."[16]

The spirit of the Italian Renaissance, Siciliano declares, is a fever of research, of discussion, of criticism,
a veritable frenzy for the new and the better, a mania
for discovery, and a capacity for synthesis, which en-
rich the personality and refine the taste. These, the
Middle Ages lacked; and these, the *élite* of Italy gave
to the world.[17]

The clash of opinion between Nordström and Siciliano can easily be paralleled, although on a much more
modest scale. E. F. Jacob, writing in the English periodical, *History*, says that "the result of the broadening

13 *Ibid.*, pp. 122–24.

14 *Ibid.*, p. 129.

15 *Ibid.*, pp. 133–37.

16 *Ibid.*, p. 140.

17 *Ibid.*, pp. 127–28, 146–47.

of Renaissance study is that we can no longer speak
with the old confidence of a separate and closed Renaissance period with a civilization and mentality of its
own, but must look for a gradual transformation of values, a process in which the scholastic and institutional
past is not rudely deserted, but is worked into the new
system and even brings that system to birth." A. S.
Turberville, writing in the same volume of the same
periodical, disagrees. "I still believe," he says, "that
the generally accepted view of the Renaissance, though,
as I have readily admitted, needing considerable modifi-
cation, in the main withstands the assaults of criticism,
and remains substantially intact."[18]

George Santayana, the Spanish-American philosopher, in his *Genteel Tradition at Bay,* remarked that
the Renaissance "simply continued all that was vivacious
and ornate in the Middle Ages."[19] And Alfred North
Whitehead, the English philosopher of Harvard University, writing of new, large-scale opportunities for
progress in 1942, ruled out the Renaissance: "I put
aside the Italian Renaissance, for it concerned only a
fortunate minority. It was the last spurt of the Middle
Ages. Thomas Aquinas would have enjoyed it."[20]

Whitehead's contention that the austere St. Thomas
would have enjoyed the Italian Renaissance is a bit
startling. On the other hand, Burckhardt would surely
have appreciated the tribute which Roger Merriman

18 *History* (N.S.), XVI (1931–   20 *Atlantic Monthly,* February,
32).   1942.
19 P. 9.

was to pay to the influence of his *Kultur* eighty-four years after its publication.   Meanwhile H. O. Taylor's modest pronouncement, footnoted in his *Mediaeval Mind,* continues to sound in one's ears: "A part of the serious historian's task is to get rid of 'epochs' and 'renaissances'—Carolingian, Twelfth Century, or Italian. For such there should be substituted a conception of historical continuity, with result properly arising from conditions . . . ."   The term Renaissance "seems to have been applied to the culture of the *quattrocento,* etc., in Italy sixty or seventy years ago . . . and carries more false notions than can be contradicted in a summer's day."[21]

The problem of the Renaissance should not be regarded as insoluble. It cannot, of course, receive a mathematical solution; it is a question of ideas and of movements in which ideas are necessarily imbedded, and statistics are inapplicable. But an impartial evaluation of the individuals, movements, and achievements that have usually—since 1860—been considered as significant for the so-called Italian Renaissance, and for the European Renaissance which accompanied and followed it, and also of some important individuals, movements, and achievements that have hitherto been disregarded or slighted, should yield considerations which, taken as a whole, will be sufficiently persuasive. It is therefore proposed to consider economics, government, literature and learning, history, philosophy, philology

21 I: 211 n.

and criticism, the fine arts, and discoveries and inventions, with the growth of science, during the so-called period of the Renaissance, enlarging its conventional frontiers whenever it proves helpful, and to draw such conclusions as the evidence will support. It is the hope of the writer that these will be of a sort to win the acceptance of those who are competent to judge, and that with their aid an end will be put to the contradictions which plague the student who wants to understand the past which underpins the present.

CHAPTER II: ECONOMICS

The economic well-being which underlay the advance in
literature, learning, the arts, and the other phenomena
of civilization in the fourteenth and fifteenth centuries
—the early "Renaissance epoch"—was not a recent development. Its beginnings antedated the first Crusade,
and its solid foundations were laid during the twelfth
and thirteenth centuries. The creators of this economic
progress were the merchants and industrialists, the pro-
moters of commerce and industry, who founded or
developed the towns and cities in which these were cen-
tered. These towns and cities were to be found throughout western Europe, but they were most numerous and

strong in northern Italy and in the Netherlands, where the province of Flanders was pre-eminent.[1]

In Italy the great urban centers were Venice, Genoa, Milan, and Florence. In the Netherlands they were Ghent, Ypres, Douai, Brussels, Louvain, Liége, and Bruges. Early in the fourteenth century Bruges became the chief commercial city of the Netherlands, the exchange mart for northern wares, on the one hand, brought down by the vessels of the Hanseatic League, and the southern and oriental wares, on the other, brought up by the fleets of Venice and Genoa. The Netherlands did not develop a carrying trade; they were content to concentrate on production and allowed the foreigners to come and carry away their products. It was only later that the Dutch took to the sea, where, for a time, they outdistanced all rivals. The great Italian cities were both commercial and industrial, and they led the rest of Europe in all phases of economic activity until after the time when the geographical discoveries relegated the Mediterranean to the second place in world commerce. The central position of Italy in the Mediterranean and its easy access to Constantinople and the Moslem lands go far to explain Italian economic leadership.

The commerce of the Italian cities was not restricted to imported and manufactured goods; it included

1 For details see Pirenne, *Economic and Social History of Medieval Europe* and *Medieval Cities, Their Origins and the Revival of Trade;* Chey- ney, *The Dawn of a New Era, 1250-1453;* and Chapters xiv and xv of *The Cambridge Medieval History,* Vol. VI; all with bibliographies.

money. The chief banking center of the period was Florence; Genoa was second. As time passed the cities of southern Germany, enriched by trade with Italy, developed a large-scale banking business, established branches in the Netherlands, and, shortly after the discovery of America, took over the leadership in the lending of money. Meanwhile the other countries of the West followed suit on a modest scale for more local purposes.

The growth of commerce and industry was not favored by the Church. This great supernational institution believed that devotion to the getting of wealth distracted men's attention from divine things. "It is easier," says the Gospel of St. Matthew, "for a camel to go through the eye of a needle, than for a rich man to enter the kingdom of God." "*Homo mercator vix aut nunquam potest Deo placere,*" decreed the Church. That is one reason why the Church authorities frowned on the transformation of the growing urban centers into the self-governing communes which in Italy and Germany became virtually independent republics, and in the remainder of western Europe became in large part autonomous, governed by the great merchants and industrialists.

The Church frowned especially on the trade in money and strictly forbade the lending of money at interest, which it dubbed usury. This prohibition was not effective, for with the growth of trade and industry it became more and more obvious that borrowed money, invested in commerce or business, produced wealth. Indeed, the productive use of money compelled the canon lawyers and the theologians, as early as the thirteenth century, to refine their interpretation of the legislation of the Church and to specify several ways in which a lender might legally secure compensation for the use of his money.[2] These ways, though legal, lent themselves to misuse, and the lender was always in danger of church censure. It was not until the sixteenth century that the trade in money became entirely reputable; secular legislation took control and contented itself with the prohibition of excessive rates of interest.

The fears of the Church that the growth of industry and commerce would lessen the devotion of the well-to-do to their eternal interests were well founded. Venice had gained its early wealth largely from the traffic in slaves, captured or bought on the Balkan coasts and sold to the harems of the Moslems in Egypt and Syria. The Church's prohibition of this unchristian business was ineffective; it was too lucrative. But the traffic in slaves is not a fair illustration. The average business man—let us get used to his technical name, the average *bourgeois*—was content to handle reputable and honest wares, and with his gains he built a comfortable and seemly life for himself and his family. It was not easy for him, living in a town which he and his fellows had created and adorned, to regard work as a penalty for sin or this good earth as a place of exile, a vale of tears, as the preachers taught. It was the bourgeois,

2 See Thomas Aquinas, *Summa*   *quaest.* 87–88.
  Theologiae, Vol. X, especially

not St. Francis or Dante, who was the first medieval man to recognize this life as good. Homesickness for the other world inevitably became more rare.

Walter Lippmann, writing of recent times, has noticed the same phenomenon. "The deep and abiding traditions of religion belong to the countryside. For it is there that man earns his daily bread by submitting to superhuman forces whose behavior he can only partially control . . . . He is obviously part of a scheme that is greater than himself, subject to elements that transcend his powers and surpass his understanding. The city is an acid that dissolves this piety."[3]

F. M. Powicke, in his impressive essay, "The Christian Life," introduces another factor to the problem, when he argues that the majority of people have always been pagans. "Our paganism," he writes, "so far as it is unsophisticated, is the paganism of our forefathers, less crude and violent, but equally natural, equally consistent with a life of Christian conformity . . . . By paganism I mean a state of acquiescence, or merely professional activity, unaccompanied by sustained religious experience and inward discipline . . . . It is confined to no class of persons, and is not hostile to, though it is easily wearied by, religious observance . . . ."[4] Was the proportion of such pagans increased by the development of city life? It would seem so.

The bearing of the growth of cities and of urban

3 *A Preface to Morals*, pp. 62–63.

4 Crump and Jacob, edd., *The Legacy of the Middle Ages*, p. 30.

wealth upon the origins of the Renaissance is not simple.
The old idea was delightfully easy: The growth of
wealth made possible the existence of a leisure class
whose members, or some of whose members, devoted
their attention to literature, learning, and the arts; the
Italian cities were the most wealthy; therefore the Renaissance was at first an Italian affair. According to this
view the producers of wealth had something of the rôle
of coral insects in the creation of islands, which men
were to adorn and beautify. But what of the intellectual grasp required for the development and mainten-
ance of the export trade, the calculations of supply and
demand, the insuring of risks, the invention of instruments of exchange, of bookkeeping, etc.? What of the
mental stimulation of contacts with men of strange
faiths and points of view? What, too, of the contributions of the *bourgeoisie* to parliamentary institutions
when, as the third estate, they participated in the work
of government in England, France, and Spain—to say
nothing of their control of the government of the communes? Do these activities develop intellectual power
and wisdom less effectively than literature, scholarship,
and the arts? How is it today? These questions do
not require an immediate answer; but it will be well to
keep them in mind as we continue our survey. They are
raised not to diminish but to broaden the reader's appreciation of the importance of urban life in the development of the civilization of the Renaissance.

CHAPTER III: GOVERNMENT AND POLITICS

Government is of great importance to civilized life. An understanding of its place in our period and of the contemporary political theories ought to cast some significant light on the nature of the Renaissance. We shall, therefore, study the ideas of a series of thinkers, beginning with Dante and ending with Machiavelli, but first we must sketch in a serviceable background. The career of Pope Innocent III will provide this background.[1]

Innocent III, pope from 1198 to 1216, was the greatest administrator who ever wore the triple crown. An Italian nobleman, educated at Paris, Bologna, and the papal court, he became pope at the early age of thirty-seven years. He was dominated by a mighty and noble ambition for the papacy, to organize Christian

[1] Luchaire, *Innocent III; Cambridge Medieval History*, Vol. VI, especially Chap. 1; both with bibliographies.

Europe as a great Christian commonwealth with the pope as its head, directing Christendom in both spiritual and secular affairs. Law, literature, philosophy, the fine arts, and all the other elements of civilization were to be "welded together in the synthesis of religion." No one questioned the pope's authority in the spheres of religion and morality. In purely secular matters, the states of Europe were conceded to have independent if inferior authority, but their rulers were subject to the pope as Christians; he could rightfully correct them for departures from Christian conduct or orthodoxy. Moreover feudal principles might enable the pope to secure and perhaps to exercise final control in the secular sphere. The Kingdom of Naples and Sicily had long been a fief of the Holy See, and Spain, Portugal, Hungary, Bulgaria, England (under King John), and lesser states became vassals of Innocent III. Germany bowed to his authority and accepted his ward, Frederick II of Sicily, as king and emperor. Only France, of the great states of the West, held out; but circumstances might well bring her round. The universities, then at the very beginning of their careers, were obedient to the papal behests. It was to be their part, as Innocent and his successors believed, to promote not only religious but secular knowledge, in harmony with the teachings of revelation as interpreted by the Church. There could not be, Innocent and all the other popes were sure, any clash between the two sorts of knowledge, for God, the author of revelation, was also the creator of the human reason. Innocent favored the plans of St. Francis and St. Dominic to organize two great armies of friars to evangelize the world, in close reliance upon the papal leadership. Early in his pontificate, he promoted a great crusade to drive the Moslem from the holy places.

Innocent III's magnificent plan, which St. Augustine and Gregory VII would have endorsed, was not fully realized. The English were angry at King John's surrender; Philip II of France only evasively bowed to Innocent's orders that he live with his wife and abandon his mistress; the Fourth Crusade was diverted, mainly by the greed of Venice, into an attack upon the Christian city of Constantinople; the Albigensian Crusade got out of hand and became little more than a worldly struggle for the lands of Count Raymond VI of Toulouse; and Italian communes repeatedly rejected intervention by the papacy. Looking back, it appears that Innocent III was checkmated by national feeling just beginning to manifest itself, by human greed, and by the unwillingness of men to become the passive instruments of authority. The broad idea that in the long run a supreme centralized authority directing all human activities would cripple human initiative and retard the advance of civilization had not yet been conceived.

Pope Innocent III's great plan, then, was not fully realized in his lifetime, but his successors might put it through. He had done much, and at the Fourth Lateran Council (1215) the fathers there assembled had bowed to his will and unhesitatingly endorsed his solutions of many important problems of church and state.

Innocent III was easily the most powerful ruler of his time.

The vigor and, broadly speaking, the success with which Innocent III had dominated Europe inevitably encouraged the canon lawyers to work out more completely their conceptions of the nature of the papal authority. The contests between the emperor, Frederick II, and a series of popes, which culminated in the deposition of the emperor at the Council of Lyons (1245), at the instigation of Pope Innocent IV, heightened the discussion and the pamphleteering. Frederick II had denied the validity of the decree of deposition and had appealed to the other kings to rally to his defence. "With us," he wrote, "it would begin, but you may hold it for certain that it would end with other kings and princes." The other kings declined to intervene, although it is noteworthy that in his courteous reply the saintly Louis IX of France gave Frederick all his imperial and royal titles. The death of Frederick II in the midst of his campaigns against the pope and the rebellious Lombard cities (1250) was followed by the destruction of his dynasty. This was achieved by the French troops of Charles of Anjou, brother of Louis IX, to whom the pope had transferred Frederick's kingdom of Sicily (and Naples) in fief.

Innocent IV had not explicitly asserted that he had jurisdiction over kings in temporal matters, that is, in the ordinary government of their countries; but his declaration that he derived his authority over the empire not from the "Donation of Constantine," but from Christ, and that it existed in the very nature of things and potentially from the beginning, was capable of that interpretation. The canon lawyers made no bones about it. The Cardinal of Ostia, one of the best of them (died 1271), wrote a very influential opinion on the theme, "And we ought to have but one head, the lord of things spiritual and temporal, since the earth is his and the fulness thereof."[2]

The canon lawyers did not have everything their own way. In France and Spain and England the kings were at work. In France, the most powerful state of the thirteenth century, a swarm of royal agents, usually lawyers who were trained in civil (Roman) as well as canon law, were busy checking the encroachments of the church courts and extending the authority of the king at the expense of the feudal lords. Even in the days of the pious Louis IX this had been going on; Joinville, later his biographer, had complained of it. Under Louis IX's son, Philip III, and his grandson, Philip IV (1285–1314), the progress had been more rapid. The king's agents, the legists, elaborated their ideas of the royal rights with the aid of the Roman law as codified by Justinian. It had been expounded at Bologna from the end of the eleventh century and soon after at Orléans and Montpellier in France. Now the Roman or civil law exhibited the empire as a secular state in which the state, in the person of the em-

2 Quoted in McIlwain, *The Growth of Political Thought in the West*, p. 237. See Chap-ter VI for the development of canonical opinion on the topic we have been discussing.

peror, was supreme over the (Christian) clergy as well as the laity.[3]   The importance of the renewed study of the Roman law may be judged by the magisterial words of F. W. Maitland: "Indeed there are [those] who think that no later movements,—not the Renaissance, not the Reformation—draws a stronger line across the annals of mankind than that which is drawn about the year 1100 when a human science won a place beside theology."[4]

Thus the development of the theory of the pope's jurisdiction over kings in temporal matters was paralleled by the assertion in theory *and in practice* of the secular authority of the king in his realm.   The inevitable clash came when Pope Boniface VIII (1294–1303) secured the papal office. He was a canon lawyer, a man of imperious and resolute temper, and he was determined to assert the authority which Innocent III and Innocent IV had exercised.   Yet the situation called for great caution.   The Sicilians had revolted in 1282 ("Sicilian Vespers") against the French dynasty of Charles of Anjou, and had called in Peter, King of Aragon, the husband of Emperor Frederick II's granddaughter, to rule over them.   The papacy supported

---

3 Vinogradoff, *Roman Law in Medieval Europe.* It is instructive to realize that the French legists of the later thirteenth century were essentially operating on the basis of the modern theory of the state: that the right of the state to act for the common good, when the public welfare is endangered, is superior to all other rights. Machiavelli, two centuries later, merely carried this doctrine to the logical extreme of amorality.

4 Maitland, *English Law and the Renaissance,* p. 24.

the Angevin dynasty (which it had established), now reduced to Naples; it even preached a crusade against Peter and financed an invasion of Aragon by Philip III of France. This was all in vain; Philip IV of France (1285–1314) made a peace which left the King of Aragon in possession of all his dominions, including Sicily, even though the papacy forbade it. Another event, the fall of Acre, the last foothold of Christendom in the Holy Land (1291), without any real papal effort to save it, also hurt the prestige of the papacy. Equally if not more important was another problem. French aid had made it possible for the popes to overthrow the Hohenstaufen. Who could supply the papacy with the necessary military force in case France should be the opponent? The empire was crushed. And France became the opponent.

Only the essential features of the contest between Boniface VIII (1294–1303) and Philip IV of France (1285–1314) need be considered here. The details are set forth in the histories of the period.[5] The trouble began over the matter of the taxation of the clergy by the secular governments, especially those of France and England. Boniface, in his bull, *Clericis Laicos* (1296), peremptorily declared that the canon law forbade, under penalty of excommunication, the levying of taxes on, or their payment by, the clergy without prior papal consent. Then Philip's prosecution of a French bishop for treason injected the issue of the other immunities

5 For example, in *The Cambridge Medieval History*, VII: 311 ff.

of the clergy. This issue, however, was soon engulfed in the broader matter of the right claimed by the pope to coerce the king into reforming certain abuses in the conduct of the government; for example, the depreciation of the coinage. Then tension became so great that Philip summoned representatives of the clergy, the nobility, and the townsmen to help him maintain what he regarded as the rights of the state. The meeting constituted the first Estates General of France (1302), and each of the estates sent letters of protest to Rome in defence of the independence of the king in the conduct of the temporal affairs of his kingdom.

Boniface's reply was drawn up at a synod in Rome, attended by French prelates, and took the form of a bull, addressed to all of Christendom, entitled *Unam Sanctam* (1302), which roundly asserted the supremacy of the popes over kings, and concluded with this sweeping statement: "Moreover we declare, we affirm, we define, and pronounce that for every human creature it is absolutely necessary for salvation to be subject to the Roman Pontiff." Now, it is clear that this categorical claim may be construed as affirming or not affirming the jurisdiction of the pope over monarchs in temporal affairs and that circumstances would determine which interpretation would finally prevail.

Boniface followed up the issue of *Unam Sanctam* with a demand that Philip agree to respect the rights of the pope and the clergy in certain specified matters, most of them of a financial character; and Philip, shaken by the defeat of his army at Courtrai and the death in battle of his adviser, Pierre Flote, expressed a willingness to negotiate. But Boniface insisted on Philip's complete submission and threatened excommunication and worse.

At this juncture Philip was persuaded by his new adviser, another civil and canon lawyer, William of Nogaret, to give up defence for offence. Accordingly, before a great gathering in Paris, Nogaret openly charged Boniface with heresy, simony, gross personal vices, and illegal possession of the papacy. The last charge was based on the fact that Boniface had been elected during the lifetime of his predecessor, the saintly Celestine V, who, it was said, had been coerced into resigning and had undoubtedly died shortly after in the custody of a partisan of Boniface. Nogaret ended his speech by calling upon Philip, as "the eldest son of the Church," to come to the rescue of the Church and to bring Boniface to trial before a church council, which the king was to summon to meet at Lyons.

Philip IV accepted the advice of Nogaret and dispatched him to Italy, with letters of credit on a Florentine banking house, to seize the pope and carry him to Lyons. (In their contests with the papacy the Hohenstaufen emperors had employed tremendous armies!) Arrived in Italy, Nogaret got into touch with enemies of Boniface, raised a force of a thousand men, proceeded to Anagni and captured the aged pontiff in 1303. But the people of Anagni rose and rescued the pope, who then returned to Rome but died before he could fight back. The "Attack of Anagni" was a profound shock to European sentiment. It left Nogaret, and by implication Philip, almost certainly excommunicated.

The College of Cardinals, anxious to end the perilous quarrel, elected as pope a conciliatory prelate, who took the friendly title of Benedict XI. He exculpated all those involved in the attack, with the exception of Nogaret, and granted Philip three years' taxes on the French clergy. Benedict died, however, in less than a year, and Philip used all his influence to secure the election of a sympathetic successor. Such a one was finally chosen in the person of the Archbishop of Bordeaux.

The new pope, Clement V (1305–1314), more than lived up to his name. Nogaret continued to serve his king, although still unabsolved. On behalf of Philip, he demanded that the dead Boniface should stand trial for his offences; a heretic does not escape trial by dying. Clement sought to escape the painful quandary by annulling the bulls *Clericis Laicos* and *Unam Sanctam*. But Philip IV insisted on the trial, and promoted Nogaret. He became *custos sigilli,* in effect first minister of the crown (1307). A month later Philip IV struck another blow at the prestige of the papacy by ordering the arrest of all the Templars in France on charges of sacrilege and vice. It was Nogaret who appeared with a group of crown lawyers before Clement, in Avignon, and opened the prosecution of the charges against Boniface. Clement postponed the trial from time to time; but it continued, to the scandal of the devout. It now seems certain that the trial of Boniface was pushed in large part to secure the destruction of the Templars and the vindication of Nogaret.

The settlement of the quarrel between the French monarchy and the papacy was embodied in a series of papal bulls. In the first of these, Clement V exonerated Philip from all personal guilt in connection with the affair of Anagni and recognized the purity of the motives which had actuated him in that matter. In another bull Nogaret was absolved from the excommunication which he had presumptively incurred. In a third bull Clement abolished the Order of the Temple, substantially on the ground that its usefulness had been destroyed by the charges made against it, and with King Philip IV seated at his side he announced his action to the Council of Vienne (1311–1312), which he had summoned together partly to determine the fate of the order. It was neither condemned nor exonerated. The trial of Boniface was tacitly dropped; but Clement canonized Celestine V in 1313. All the pages in the papal registers adverse to Philip were ordered expunged. Clement had never even gone to Rome, and in 1309 he had settled down in Avignon, across the Rhone from French territory. There his successors were destined to reside until 1376, and the cardinals were predominantly French, giving to the suspicious world the impression of subservience to France.

The quarrel between the papacy and Philip IV[6] had lasted almost twenty years. Its reverberations had pene-

6 See Scholz, *Die Publizistik zur Zeit Philipps des Schönen und* *Bonifaz VIII;* Holtzmann, *Wilhelm von Nogaret.*

trated all Europe, and its issues had given rise to fierce arguments and many publications. The earlier contest over the Investitures had not resulted in so much historical investigation and intellectual activity; but its importance is great, for it marks the end of the papal effort to realize the magnificent plan of Innocent III. Professor McIlwain's estimate may well be kept in mind: "As a whole the historic struggle between Boniface VIII and Philip the Fair stands out as one of the most significant in all the middle ages. In it we find the first important reaction on men's thoughts about political relations—particularly the relations of the *regnum* and *sacerdotium*—of the new national states whose further development accounts for the greatest difference between medieval and modern history."[7]

Pierre Dubois.—One of the most active of the pamphleteers for Philip IV was Pierre Dubois (*ca.* 1250–*ca.* 1321). He was trained in civil and canon law, was one of Philip's many local officials, served as deputy in the Estates General of 1302 and of 1308, and had a profitable private practice. Edward I of England (and Aquitaine) was one of his clients. His most important writing was a compact little book which he finished in 1306, *De Recuperatione Terre Sancte (The Recapture of the Holy Land)*. The title was doubtless designed to exploit the interest current at that time in another crusade (which never came to pass). The

7 McIlwain, *The Growth of Po-*   pp. 269–70.
   litical Thought in the West,

book advocates a sweeping series of reforms, all plausibly geared into the promotion of a crusade.[8] It is these reforms that demand consideration. Dubois did not himself think up these proposals; they were in the air. He was "a cistern rather than a fountain." They are therefore significant of the progressive ideas of his times, provoked, we may be sure, at least in part by the contest between Philip and the popes.

Dubois urged that the lands and possessions in Italy and elsewhere—the temporal power—of the pope and the Church at large should be transferred to the king of France in exchange for modest though adequate pensions. This would permit the clergy, high and low, to escape from wars and lawsuits and to concentrate their attention upon their spiritual duties. The monastic orders were to be united and thus end the rivalries which had contributed, for example, to the loss of Acre. The king of France was to assume his rightful position as temporal head of Christendom, the other kingdoms being led, by various devices, to accept his suzerainty. Wars between Christians were to cease, after a peace conference of all rulers, presided over by the pope, had agreed to the judicial settlement of all disputes. Anyone daring to break the peace was to be boycotted into submission and then sent to the Holy Land, there to slake his lust for battle in the front line of the army fighting the Moslem foe. Since the multiplicity of jurisdictions—ecclesiastical, feudal, and royal—and the pro-

8 *De Recuperatione Terre Sancte;* Power, in *The Social and* *Political Ideas of Some Great Mediaeval Thinkers.*

longation of lawsuits contributed to unrest and a great waste of money, Dubois recommended that all the laws be reduced to a single code, written in simple, untechnical language which the ordinary man could understand—one law for all—and that the procedure of trials should be speeded up, that oral arguments before the judges be replaced by written briefs. Education, too, was to be radically reformed: Girls' schools were to be established, the textbooks were to be simplified, and practice was to supplement theory in all subjects. There was no danger, Dubois was sure, that life would become static; there were endless fields for investigation, and the laws themselves would have to be steadily altered to suit changing circumstances.

This summary does not by any means exhaust the list of ingenious reforms which Dubois advocated, nor do justice to the arguments with which he supported them. He was not emancipated from all the fixed ideas of his age. He believed, for example, in the influence of the stars and in the malignity of the devils who were so numerous in the Holy Land, making its conquest difficult. Later ages will undoubtedly smile at some of our superstitions. Nor need we be disturbed by the circumstance that the recommendations of Dubois seem to have received no effective hearing; reformers still find it hard to secure more than minor changes in the *status quo*. The thing to note, the thing that is significant, is that long before the Revival of Learning the experience of living in the actual, workaday world was giving birth to ideas which today we find progressive.

Dante.—The first important effort to reassert the unity of Christendom, which Philip IV had so forcibly and successfully denied, was made by Dante in his *De Monarchia,* which he probably wrote some time between the years 1310 and 1313. The great poet had been exiled from his native Florence in 1302, along with other leaders of his party, through the machinations of Boniface VIII. Dante's hatred of Boniface was matched only by his scorn for Clement V—both are consigned to hell in the *Divine Comedy.*

It is Dante the poet and philosopher, not the exiled politician mindful of facts, who conceives of the solution of the world's ills. This he finds in considering the peace which Augustus gave to the world, the empire which Christ consented to be born into and whose legal jurisdiction he recognized by submitting to the Roman census. Clearly the empire was for the peace of mankind, and it should reassert its supreme legal and territorial authority, leaving to kings and princes the subordinate activities of their secular governments. In a similar way the pope should exercise his divinely ordained authority over the spiritual affairs of mankind. Emperor and pope (reason and the Faith?), each commissioned by God to ensure the welfare of humanity, were to aid each other; and the emperor would recognize the higher importance of the spiritual by reverencing his colleague, the pope.

In his preoccupation with theory Dante forgot, or considered of negligible importance, the brute fact that the empire of his day had been shattered by the overthrow of the Hohenstaufen and that its ability to exercise real jurisdiction over the young and lusty states of Europe, to say nothing of the German princes, was altogether imaginary. Dante dwelt in the realm of fancy, not of fact.   Nevertheless, his passionate craving for a central secular authority which would maintain peace in the world strikes a sympathetic chord in modern hearts. Indeed there are those who argue that Dante's ideal emperor possesses the attributes which lovers of peace still seek to embody in a world organization.[9] "Dante's book," says J. W. Allen, "was a fine piece of imaginative construction; but it was off the point.   It was not, really, what it has been said to be, the swansong of something dying: it was, rather, an attempt to resuscitate the dead. Some ten years after the *De Monarchia,* came the *Defensor Pacis.*"[10]

Marsilius of Padua.—At the very end of his chapter on "Political Theory to *c.* 1300" in the *Cambridge Medieval History,* W. H. V. Reade concludes that "the irregular boundary between the medieval and the modern is crossed as soon as the conception of Christendom, embodied for Dante in the Roman Empire, gives way to the belief that the largest autonomous community should be the territorial or national State." Surely this boundary was crossed by Philip IV and by Edward I of England. In any case, it was consciously,

9 See Ramsay, *The Imperial Peace.*
10 *The Social and Political Ideas of Some Great Mediaeval Thinkers* (edited by Hearnshaw), p. 170.

explicitly crossed by the author of the *Defensor Pacis*.

The *Defensor Pacis* was a militant book; it abandoned the apologetic and defensive arguments of the opponents of the supremacy of the Church in temporal affairs and attacked the enforcement of its spiritual authority. Even Philip IV had thought it expedient to fight the papacy with spiritual weapons: the Templars were heretics, Boniface VIII was a heretic, and Philip himself was "actuated by religious motives." All this is over with in the *Defensor Pacis,* and the state stands forth as the exclusive claimant to all earthly authority.

The principal author of the book, Marsilius of Padua (1270?–1342),[11] grew up in the Italian commune of Padua, which was Ghibelline—that is, antipapal—in politics. He had gone on to the chief university of Europe, Paris, where he became a professor in the faculty of arts and won the rectorship of the University for a term in 1312. At Paris he was in touch with the anti-clerical legists of Philip IV and the campaign against Boniface VIII. Later he was again in Italy, studying medicine, and then served as a diplomatic agent in France for the anti-papal tyrants of Verona and Milan. About 1320 he returned to Paris, where, in 1324, he completed his book, the *Defensor Pacis.* Two years later, along with his collaborator, the eminent Aristotelian scholar and professor in the

---

11 *Defensor Pacis;* Previté-Orton in *Proceedings of the British Academy* (1935), 137–83; McIlwain, *The Growth of Political Thought in the West,* pp. 297–315; all with excellent bibliographies.

University, John of Jandun, he fled for refuge to the
court of Ludwig of Bavaria and joined the group of
pamphleteers who were defending that emperor against
the attack of the Avignon pope, John XXII. The
group included the celebrated English philosopher,
William of Ockham, and the deposed head of the Franciscan order, Michael of Cesena.

The contest between Ludwig and the papacy was no
world-shaking affair; the papacy was no longer seeking
to assert its authority over all kings in temporal affairs,
but was merely trying to control the selection of the
emperor, the nominal head of the shattered Holy
Roman Empire. The papal motive appears to have
been chiefly to prevent Ludwig from exercising imperial
authority over the Italian lands of the absentee papacy.
The contest was in reality a petty, though protracted,
squabble. It ended with the death of Ludwig in 1347
and the election of his rival, Charles IV of Bohemia,
who renounced in advance any exercise of effective imperial authority in Italy. Thereafter, the claim of the
papacy to control the secular affairs of the governments
of Europe gradually faded away. Indeed, the con-
cordats made by the restored papacy with different rulers, after the close of the great Councils, was a clear
admission that nothing but the bare theory of the indirect power over kings remained to the pope.

The *Defensor Pacis* is divided into three parts. In
Part I, Marsilius discusses the organization and functions of a well-developed state, with particular attention to the functions which affect the position of the

priestly class.   Here he leans heavily on Aristotle's
Politics, the book which Thomas Aquinas had made
use of in his political writings, and on the Roman doctrine of the sovereignty of the people.   In Part II,
Marsilius examines and refutes the claim of the clergy
to an independent position within and above the state
and assigns to them their proper functions under secular law and divine law as revealed in the New Testament.   Part III summarizes the conclusions of the
whole argument in a series of forty-one propositions or
theses.[12]

The supreme authority in every state, according to
Marsilius, is the General Assembly of the people or the
dominant part *(valentior pars)* thereof.   This is the
Legislator.   "In every case," says Marsilius, "the establishment of the authority of human laws belongs
solely to the body of citizens, or the dominant part of
it which stands for *(repraesentat)* the whole, because
it is seldom possible for the entire body to meet together."   The executive authority of the state, which
Marsilius calls the ruling part *(pars principans),* is
the creature of the *Legislator.*   It may be and usually
is entrusted with wide powers to direct subordinate
officials, enact laws, and judge offences against the laws.
It is preferably elective and may consist of one person
or a committee, but all its authority is derived from
and revocable by the *Legislator.*   In other words, the
people are sovereign.

12 Translated into English in   *Source Book For Mediaeval*
   Thatcher and McNeal, edd.,   *History,* pp. 317-24.

The clergy are appointed by the state or its subdivisions to preach, teach, and administer the sacraments of the Catholic Church. The divine law, which they expound, is laid down in the New Testament. Violation of its provisions involves penalties, but only in the future life, since only God knows the secrets of the human heart. The clergy have no coercive authority, no right to enforce obedience to the divine law. Canon law has no validity, and the powers it assigns to the officers of the church, especially to the chief bishop, the pope, are a usurpation and the chief cause of war among Christians. The destruction of these usurped powers of the clergy is the chief purpose of Marsilius's book and furnishes its title, the *Defender of Peace*. The state may, of course, punish a serious breach of the divine law, such as heresy, as an offence against public order and a danger to the commonwealth; it may authorize excommunication, with its civil consequences, but with such punishments or any punishments the clergy have nothing to do.

The highest organ of the church universal is the General Council, composed of clergy and laity. It defines the faith and interprets obscure passages in the Bible. Theoretically its composition is the same as that of the *Legislator*. Presumably it may be called together by the authorities of the various states—Marsilius is in difficulty here—or possibly by the emperor, acting on their behalf, but only the states may use force. The authority of the General Council is purely moral.

For a scholarly appraisal of the continuing influence

of Marsilius upon religious reformers of various sorts, particularly upon Cranmer and the defenders of the Church of England, as well as upon the later political revolutionists, the reader is referred to Previté-Orton's British Academy paper (note 11). Here it is enough to observe that the withdrawal of coercive authority from the clergy and its monopoly by the state is characteristic of all advanced countries today, and that the sovereignty of the people and the delegated power of the executive and the legislative have likewise been accepted in every civilized land. Modern governments, confronted by religious revolts or dissidence, have found in the separation of church and state a more satisfactory solution of the great problem of the Middle Ages than Marsilius knew. Nevertheless, he has sufficient honor. Scrutinizing the life of the communes and of the larger states of his time, and studying the political facts and the conclusions of Aristotle's *Politics,* the medieval radical arrived at solutions of current dilemmas that anticipated the settlements of modern times. Unless a man is to lose credit for foreseeing by a long stretch of time the results of human experience and is to receive recognition only if his solutions immediately prevail, then the conclusion is inescapable that Marsilius of Padua ranks as one of the great thinkers of mankind, his *Defensor Pacis* as the greatest and most modern political treatise of the Middle Ages.[13]

13 *Cf.* Laski in *The Cambridge Medieval History,* VIII:626–30.

Machiavelli.—Marsilius of Padua's solution of the great political problem of the Middle Ages, the relation of the Church to secular government, was to strip the Church of all coercive authority and confide it to each of the states of Europe. Machiavelli, another and more famous Italian, went further and laid it down that the state is utterly untrammelled, not only by the Church, but by religion or morals, and is free to do anything it finds necessary to strengthen itself.

Machiavelli (1469–1527) was a Florentine, educated, it would seem, for the civil service; he was not a Humanist. He knew Latin, of course, but did not write it, and was content to express himself in his native Italian. This he did with masterly skill. He got his chance at administration after the defeat and execution of Savonarola in 1498 and soon became chancellor and secretary of the Ten, the committee of the government of Florence specially entrusted with war and foreign affairs. He was not an executive, but rather a high-grade civil servant, and was sent on diplomatic missions to Louis XII of France, to the emperor Maximilian, to Caesar Borgia—the sinister son and political deputy of Pope Alexander VI—, and to Pope Julius II.

Machiavelli's official activities came to an end in 1512 when the Medici, supported by Pope Julius II, overthrew the republican government of Florence, which had been set up in 1494, and made the city in all but name and harshness a tyranny under the old family. Thus divorced from his post, Machiavelli meditated and wrote, always endeavoring to persuade the Medici to make use of his talents. In this last he was substantially unsuccessful, for it was only in the last few years of his life that the Medici commissioned him to write a history of Florence. (This will be considered in the chapter on history.) If Machiavelli had not been excluded from office it is unlikely that we should have the writings to which he owes his fame.

Machiavelli's chief political works are *The Prince (Il Principe)* and the *Discourses on the First Ten Books of Titus Livius*.[14] *The Prince* was written during the first year of his enforced leisure (1513) and was dedicated and presented to the Medici cardinal who ruled over Florence. The time seemed most propitious, for in that year the Medici had obtained the papacy in the person of Leo X. Machiavelli was convinced that the helplessness of the Italian states before the might of Spain and of France was due to their disunion, and he blamed the papacy for being too weak to unite the peninsula and too strong, diplomatically, to permit any other Italian state to do it. The underlying causes of this sad situation were the lack of unselfish patriotism and the vogue of mercenary armies. How awaken the Italians from their indolence and supineness? How enable Italy to emulate England, France, and Spain and become a national state, strong enough to expel the "barbarians," the foreigners, who had been battening on the carcass of the peninsula ever

14 Both conveniently published in English in a single volume of   The Modern Library, *circa* 1940.

since the invasion of 1494? Machiavelli was persuaded that the end could be achieved only by a patriotic and ruthless prince who by force and craft, emulating the behavior of Caesar Borgia in the Romagna,
should reduce the whole peninsula to his sway. *The
Prince* explains how this can be done and attempts to
persuade Lorenzo de' Medici, the "boss" of Florence,
to undertake it.

The Prince is a small book. Its precepts may be summarized as follows: The strong man takes the world
as it is and men for what they are; he does not ask
what men should do, but only what they actually do do.
Among so many rivals who are not good, he has learned
how to be not good. He knows that since he cannot
possess all the qualities, he ought as a statesman to
have only those defects which will not cause him to lose
his state. He is deliberate, is not easily frightened,
and does not push confidence to the point of imprudence
or defiance so far as to make himself unbearable. He
would prefer to be both loved and feared; but as that
is hardly possible, he chooses to be feared, for men
love as they please, whereas they fear as it pleases the
prince. It is an honor to keep one's sworn word, but
history proves that those who have not scrupled to violate it have won against those who have stood by it.
The generality of men being bad, the statesman should
not inconvenience himself for them. He should discipline himself not to depart from the good if that be possible, but to be resolute to do evil when it is necessary.
It is much more advantageous to appear to have certain

virtues than actually to have them, since to have them
and to practice them might be injurious. The essential
thing for the prince is to maintain and augment his
state; if he succeeds in doing that, there are no means
which are not to be considered honorable, for the vulgar see only the surface of things, and the world is
made up of the vulgar.[15]

The Prince, an argument for despotic measures, does
not express Machiavelli's complete thought. That is to
be found only by adding the *Discourses,* a much larger
and a more deliberate work, from which *The Prince*
may be regarded as an excerpt, colored or spiced up
to win over the master of Florence. In the larger
book Machiavelli makes it clear that he prefers a democratic republican government, resting on the support of
the citizens, and it is his hope and belief that the despotic prince, having achieved the unity of Italy and
fortified it by means of a native army, the people in
arms, will then surrender his power to the people and
thus permit the republic to be established. There can
be no doubt that Machiavelli was sincere in this, and
that, as the last chapter of *The Prince* clearly shows,
he was an Italian patriot. Nevertheless, whether despotic or republican, Machiavelli's state is exempt from
the obligations of religion or morality.

Not that Machiavelli despises religion. Far from
it; religion is a very important prop to the state. But

15 Adapted from Benoist in *Académie de droit international,
Recueil des Cours, 1925,* IV:
136–137. See also footnote 3,
above.

Christianity, as taught, is far inferior to the old pagan Roman religion. The former, Machiavelli declares in the *Discourses,* "places the supreme happiness in humility, lowliness, and a contempt for worldly objects, whilst the other, on the contrary, places the supreme good in grandeur of soul, strength of body, and all such qualities as render men formidable . . . ."

It is well nigh impossible to escape from the conviction that Machiavelli has a strong bias toward ruse and cunning and that he thinks of the successful state primarily as the product of artifice. His chapter, "Of Conspiracies," in the *Discourses*—by far his longest chapter— is professedly written "so that princes may learn to guard against such dangers, and that subjects may less rashly engage in them." Yet the chapter is largely devoted to offering advice on how to conspire successfully: "The conduct of a conspiracy then is exposed to all such dangers . . . and to avoid these perils the following remedies present themselves." On the whole this chapter will give the hurried reader the quintessence of Machiavellism.

In dedicating *The Prince* to Lorenzo, the son of Piero de' Medici, Machiavelli makes the comment: "In my desire, however, to offer to your Highness some humble testimony of my devotion, I have been unable to find among my possessions anything which I hold so dear or esteem so highly as that knowledge of the deeds of great men which I have acquired through a long experience of modern events and a constant study of the past." Here Machiavelli places first his experience in the tragic years which followed the invasion of 1494. In the *Discourses* he selects his illustrations chiefly from ancient history. What, then, is the relation of his experience to his study of the history of classical times? The question is of some importance and requires an answer.

The reader may recall that Pierre Dubois attempted to capitalize on the contemporary interest in the Crusades by entitling his treatise on desirable reforms *The Recapture of the Holy Land*. For his part Machiavelli wrote in an age when the Revival of Learning had given the classics great repute, an age in which it was customary for a writer to pay his tribute to antiquity. Montaigne, the great French essayist, who wrote toward the close of the sixteenth century, states explicitly that he decorated his *Essays* with classical quotations out of deference to the taste of his time, but that he did not intend them to cover or hide him. Indeed, when the first installment of the *Essays* was criticized for a deficiency of classical quotations, he accepted the criticism and in the second edition inserted additional ones. Let us look at Machiavelli's situation. He had served Florence in terrible times. For fourteen years he had been apprenticed to the statecraft of his city, in a society of Italian states which were fighting for their existence with meager forces and above all with craft. Then, retired from active service, he turned to the writing of the books on politics and war which have given him his reputation. Can anyone really doubt that he was guided by his political experience in his choice of those illustrations of his doctrine which, in accordance with the taste of his time and his country, and his own taste, he drew from classical history? Guicciardini, his younger and more fortunate contemporary and friend, may have had Machiavelli in mind when he jeered at those who on every occasion would adduce the example of the Romans.[16] Vittorio Rossi, the great authority on the literature of the Italian *Quattrocento,* has no hesitation in saying that Machiavelli, among others, "could seek in the history of Rome support for the doctrines which his genius had extracted from the observation of contemporary men and events. But in fact battles were fought, negotiations conducted, peaces made—all political life carried on—outside of every actual influence of antique memories."[17] Henri Hauser, of the Sorbonne, has the same idea: "The statue of the State," which Machiavelli chiselled, "looks as if it were copied from antiquity, from the Rome of Titus Livius. Its real models are at Florence, at Milan, in the Romagna."[18] It could not possibly have been otherwise.

It is beyond the purpose of this essay to study the influence of Machiavelli's ideas upon Richelieu, Frederick II of Prussia, Bismarck, Mussolini, and Hitler—all of them practitioners of Machiavellism. It is pertinent, however, to take note of Machiavelli's chief defects. First, he failed to keep in mind that the purpose of the state is not power but the well-being of the private indi-

---

16 *Counsels and Reflections of Francesco Guicciardini,* No. 110.

17 Rossi, *Il Quattrocento,* p. 404.
18 Hauser, *La modernité du XVIe siècle,* p. 61.

viduals who compose it. Secondly, he did not realize the degeneration which the exercise of unlimited power works in its possessor. Finally, lacking confidence in the good will and moral standards of the normal human being, in "the living forces"—to quote from John Morley's great essay on Machiavelli—"by which societies subsist and governments are strong,"[19] he could not imagine the strength of the higher ideals of mankind, which in our time have enabled the free peoples to overwhelm in ruin the diabolic purposes and calculated bestialities of Mussolini and Hitler. It is true that Machiavelli was an Italian patriot; but it is equally true that "patriotism is not enough."

19 *Machiavelli,* the Romanes Lecture.

CHAPTER IV: DANTE, PETRARCH, AND BOCCACCIO

Dante.—The literature pertinent to this investigation starts with the writings of Dante Alighieri (1265–1321), the great Florentine poet.[1] His political experience and ideas have already been examined. In this passage we must consider, first of all, his preparation for his life work. That his exile, on the humiliating charge of graft, drove him into himself and liberated him from political office-holding goes without saying. Before his exile he had won recognition as a lyrical poet, writing in the Florentine dialect, and had joined with other poets in the development of the *dolce stil*

[1] Zingarelli, *Dante;* English translations of Dante's works.

nuovo, the sweet new style of handling the theme of love. In this his chief "instructors" were the two Guidos—Guido Guinizelli of Bologna and his friend, Guido Cavalcanti of Florence. In the new theory, love is "an attribute of the noble heart alone." A noble object excites its response and love springs to life and ennobles its possessor, compelling him to seek only that which is good. "The worshipped lady, without ceasing to be a real woman, becomes a symbol of the heavenly intelligence." Dante's *Vita Nuova* (1292?) handles the theme of his love for Beatrice in the new mode. Here he carried to a nobler conclusion the cult of the lady which the poets of Provence had established.[2] In the *Divine Comedy* he achieved her ultimate apotheosis.

Dante knew Provençal and French, as well as Latin. The lyrics of Provence and the French epics and romances which had spread their fructifying influence over Europe in the twelfth and thirteenth centuries, when French civilization was dominant, were familiar to him. Brunetto Latini had written an encyclopedia of current knowledge, *Le Trésor,* in French. He was an Italian and Dante's friend and counsellor. Dante's knowledge of philosophy and theology was deep. The foundation of this was probably laid in the schools of the Dominicans in Florence, for the Dominican impress—the theology of Thomas Aquinas and the natural science of Albertus Magnus—constantly appears in Dante's writings, especially in his masterpiece.[3] The

2 Wechssler, *Das Kulturproblem des Minnesangs.*

3 Mandonnet, *Dante le théologien.*

superstructure of learning, with Dante as with every
scholar, was his own achievement.

Of Dante's familiarity with classical Latin literature
it will be enough to state that it was equal to that of
John of Salisbury, the secretary of Thomas à Becket,
later bishop of Chartres until his death in 1180. The
medieval scholar, as H. O. Taylor has repeatedly remarked in his *Mediaeval Mind*, drew his chief intellectual sustenance from the patristic tradition and the
classical tradition, from the Church Fathers and the
ancient classics.   Dante was a great medieval scholar.

But Dante would also be a teacher. His *Convivio*,
or *Convito (Banquet)*, was designed to serve as a sort
of encyclopedia for the great majority of literate Italians who could not read Latin.   He would give them
instruction on scholarly matters.   The *Convivio* was
probably written about 1308, at the university city of
Bologna, where reference books were available.   The
plan of the work is a series of commentaries upon
some of Dante's own poems.   It must be said of what
we have of it—for Dante did not finish it—that the
author had a very high opinion of the intellectual capacities of his readers.   The pedagogical motive which
animated Dante was doubtless reinforced by the desire
to demonstrate to his countrymen that the government
of Florence had exiled a virtuous and innocent citizen.
Boethius had performed a similar act of vindication in
writing his *Consolation of Philosophy*.

Contemporaneously with the *Convivio*, it would appear, Dante was also at work on his *De vulgari elo-*

quentia (On Style in the Vernacular), a Latin treatise on the literary value of the vernaculars, the mother tongues, naturally with special attention to the Italian. The two books were to be complementary. The *Convivio* was to educate the non-Latin readers and the *Eloquentia* was to encourage the displacement of Latin by Italian for the discussion of important themes. What Italian? In the *Eloquentia* Dante surveys the many Italian dialects, one by one, and argues for a select Italian, the "illustrious vernacular," to be formed of the best common features of all the dialects. Then he discusses at considerable length the characteristics of great literature in poetry and in prose. His analysis is acute and masterly. George Saintsbury, in his striking chapter on Dante the critic, says, with ironical overtones: "He, groping dimly in the benighted, the shackled Middle Ages, actually attains to a freer and more enlightened kind of criticism than the Greeks, with all their 'play of mind,' all their 'lucidity,' had reached."[4]

The *Eloquentia*, like its companion treatise, the *Convivio*, was never completed. Why? The most reasonable conjecture is that Dante, having conceived of —perhaps having begun—the *Divine Comedy*, realized that all his purposes could best be achieved in it, garmented in high poetry, and consequently turned away from the lesser works.

The *Divine Comedy* is of course Dante's masterpiece. He called it the *Commedia,* but in the opening lines of the twenty-fifth canto of the *Paradise* he speaks of it as "the sacred poem to which both Heaven and earth have put their hands," and it is not surprising that in the Venetian edition of 1555 the editor finally gave the work its present title. "Divine," because it treats of divinity, and in a supremely exalted fashion.[5]

The judgment of six centuries, beginning with Giovanni Villani, has affirmed the greatness of the *Divine Comedy* and has recognized its author as one of the three greatest poets of the world, associating in full equality with Homer and Shakespeare. The writer of the present essay will not attempt to demonstrate its poetic values; that is beyond him. Taking a hint from the *Convivio,* he will quote a statement of that grand old American medievalist, H. O. Taylor, and then add some comments and observations.

"Emotionally as well as intellectually, the final *Summa,* and a supreme expression, of the Middle Ages was the *Divina Commedia.* It was composed in the most stately and potent of the vernaculars. Beautified and vibrant with the quintessence of the gathering religious emotion of the centuries, it also brought to expression much that had hitherto had its exclusive home in Latin. For it reset in *terza rima* the heart of Aquinas' *Summa Theologiae;* it held the natural knowledge of the time, hitherto kept in Latin; and it was intended to carry such fulness of spiritual allegory as Holy Scripture:—symbolism was inwoven in it. On

5 Zingarelli, *Dante,* pp. 443-44.

the other hand, it rendered the very vernacular incidents and hates and loves of Dante's time, of Dante's self; it bore, as in a greater vessel, the matter of Trouvère and Troubadour, already told and sung in French and German and Italian. In fine, it expressed what had grown up in the vernacular, and belonged to the spontaneous thinking and open speech of men, while it also translated and re-expressed the loftier matters of theology and thought, which hitherto had been confined to Latin. Not merely from the fact that the *Commedia* was written in Italian, but from the nature of its translated Latin matter, it represents the turn of the noblest forms of expression from the Latin to the vernacular."[6]

Allegory, long before and long after Dante, was beloved by writers and readers, by preachers and congregations. It was the subtle and superior meaning which underlay the literal meaning of Holy Writ and other real literature. St. Bernard expounded to his monks, in a series of eighty-six sermons, the religious significance of that great epithalamium, the *Song of Songs*. The authors of the *Romance of the Rose,* most popular of medieval poems, personified the virtues and vices. The difficulty with the scheme is that the literal meaning usually loses its power to convince.

The *Divine Comedy* is the allegory of the human being achieving salvation. The human being is Dante, is also every man, is humanity. Virgil is the great

6 H. O. Taylor, *Thought and Expression in the Sixteenth Century,* II: 378–79.

Roman poet; he is also human reason, also the knowledge which reason may achieve. Beatrice is a lady of Florence, and also revelation, divine wisdom. Virgil (earthly knowledge) and Beatrice (revelation) conduct Dante through Hell, Purgatory, and Paradise. And so on. Now, the notable thing about Dante's great poem, in this connection, is that the literal meaning is entirely convincing and complete; it is never allowed to evaporate or weaken. Dante, a real man, in Easter week, 1300, goes through Hell, Purgatory, and Paradise and meets scores of people whom he has known or known about on earth. Each of these people speaks in his own characteristic way. For example, Piero delle Vigne, Frederick II's talented minister, expresses himself in the ornate language for which he had made Frederick's chancery famous. St. Thomas Aquinas and St. Bonaventura talk as, from reading their writings, one would expect them to talk. There is endless talk. Dante does not so much tell what he sees and hears as picture what he sees and report what he hears —the dialogue is most convincing—with the result that the *Divine Comedy* can be read and enjoyed by one who knows or cares nothing about its allegories.

Of course the use of allegory raises many questions. In the poems of the *Vita Nuova,* we have the authentic tremors and ecstasies of the adolescent love of Dante for Beatrice. Was she a real person, Beatrice Portinari by name, or is she an abstraction, a personification of theological lore which Dante loved and abandoned for a time? We cannot be dead sure, since

Dante makes his abstraction so real, his allegory so literal, that we give it willing credence—and then hesitate.[7]

Another feature of the *Vita Nuova* and the *Divine Comedy,* which a reader may ignore or enjoy, is the consummate exhibition of the common medieval belief in the significance of numbers. The *Divine Comedy* is composed of three books, each of which has thirty-three cantos, which, with the introductory extra canto, attached to the first book, give a total of 100 cantos. The verse form, invented by Dante, is *terza rima;* the circles of Hell and its approaches are nine; Dante was nine when he first saw Beatrice, etc., etc.[8]

The secular and religious knowledge which Dante's verse carries with such apparent ease is skillfully distributed. Natural science appears chiefly in Hell, psychology in Purgatory, and metaphysics and theology in Paradise. Dante's theology is mostly Thomist, with due respect shown to the Augustinianism of St. Bonaventura. He is most orthodox and rarely slips. Mandonnet, however, believes—his argument is cogent—that Dante erred, through ignorance, in giving Siger de Brabant, the Averroist, a post of prominence in Paradise.[9]

The "architecture," the organization, of the *Divine*

---

7 Zingarelli, *Dante,* p. 376, says it is impossible to determine whether Beatrice is real or abstract. Father Mandonnet, *Dante le théologien,* is certain that she is an abstraction in both the *Vita Nuova* and the *Divine Comedy.*

8 For the significance of three, seven, ten, thirty, etc., see Mandonnet, *Dante le théologien.*

9 Mandonnet, *Siger de Brabant,* I: 287–309.

Comedy, as that of the *Vita Nuova,* is most symmet-
rical.[10]   There is nothing of the so-called rambling
quality of the average medieval tale about these works.
The variety within their organic structure can be compared only with that of the Gothic cathedral, which
alone rivals the *Divine Comedy* as "the true expression
of the medieval mind."

The Italian which Dante employs so triumphantly
in these vernacular works is the Florentine dialect.   We
hear nothing more about the "illustrious vernacular,"
advocated in the *Eloquentia.*   Dante coins a number
of new Italian words from the Latin; but, generally
speaking, he is able to handle the most abstruse matters with the existing resources of his mother tongue.
His demonstration of its adequacy and beauty undoubtedly had much to do with its general acceptance as the
literary Italian.

The interest in the affairs of this world which is displayed by virtually all the residents of the three realms
beyond the tomb is important to Dante's purpose as a
teacher; but, theology apart, it is a striking recognition
of the central place which man must assign to the life
of man upon the earth, whatever his picture of the
cosmos.   "Copernicus, it is true, gave us liberty and
space," says Lowes Dickinson, "but he bereft us of
security and intimacy.   And I thought of the great
vision of Dante, so terrible and yet so beautiful, so
human through and through,—that vision which, if it

10 Zingarelli, *Dante,* pp. 651 f.

contracts space, expands the fate of man, and relates
him to the sun and the moon and the stars."[11]

One thing remains to be said. Dante preceded the
Revival of Learning. What he did he did within the
limits of the Middle Ages and of their relation to the
ancient classics. To call him a precursor or a herald or
a harbinger of that revival—"the two-faced Dante"—
is to deck the Revival with stolen jewels and to confuse
the issue. The present writer will have none of it.

Petrarch.—[12] The political revolution which exiled
Dante also drove out Petrarch's father. His mother
took refuge for a time in Arezzo, a small town in the
Florentine countryside, and there Francis was born in
1304. His parents moved to another place nearby,
then for a time to Pisa and finally, in 1312, settled in
Avignon. (The papacy had definitely located there in
1309.) The father was a notary, and he planned a
legal career for Francis, his eldest son. The lad's
preparatory education gave him a good grounding in
Latin literature, and his years in Avignon made Provençal easy for him. In due course he was apprenticed
to the law. He spent four years at Montpellier and
then three years at Bologna, the two great centers of
legal studies. He made some good and useful friends
in both places, but his grasp of law may be gauged by
the fact that when his father died the executors of his

11 Dickinson, *Appearances,* p.
173.
12 Volpi, *Il Trecento; Petrarch*

(Robinson and Rolfe, edd.),
English translations of Petrarch's principal works.

estate had no difficulty in making away with it; Francis and his brother Gherardo got nothing.

On his father's death, Francis gave up the pretence of studying law and devoted himself wholeheartedly to Latin literature and the writing of Italian verses. Composition in Latin came a bit later. His livelihood was assured by his friends, the Colonnas, and other Church authorities; he took minor orders and thus was eligible for appointment to benefices which required little or no residence or labor. In effect, the Church was, for him as for other talented youths in the Middle Ages, the patron of the intellectual life. Francis had other resources; his genius for friendship, and his growing reputation as a writer, brought him the support of princes as well as of cardinals and popes. The tyrants felt honored by his presence in their dominions and placed houses and lands at his disposal in their zeal to retain him. The bloody Visconti of Milan, the perpetual foes of Florence, were the most prominent of these princely patrons; but the republic of Venice also exhibited its favor, with a palace.

Petrarch's travels broadened his mental horizon. He went to Gascony, Paris, the Netherlands, the Rhineland, and Bohemia. His lay patrons sent him as a decorative member on various embassies, and the Avignon popes gave him friendship and preferment. He liked travel; but he also liked to retire to quiet places, where he could enjoy seclusion and untarnished nature and write. Near Avignon, at Vaucluse, he had a charming country place, and in later life another at

Arquà, near Padua. He could afford to have servants and copyists.

Some of his biographers have argued that there was something very modern about his love of nature.[13] They forget that the Cistercians, to cite only one instance, always located their monasteries in sightly places. The same biographers usually make quite a to-do over his ascent of Mt. Ventoux (near Vaucluse) and speak of him as the first of the Alpinists. The long account of this expedition, with brother and servants, which Petrarch sent to his confessor, gives little support to their argument; for the old shepherd who showed Petrarch's party the best trail, told them that he had gone up fifty years before (and that the journey was rough). Worse still for the theory of these biographers is Petrarch's statement that the beautiful view of the clouds and the Alps turned his thoughts to his sins and led him to open his little volume of the *Confessions* of St. Augustine at random, and lo! his eyes fell upon the sentence, "And men go about to marvel at the heights of the mountains, and the huge waves of the sea, and the broad reaches of the rivers, and the circuits of the ocean, and the revolutions of the stars, and forsake their own souls." Then, irritated at himself, as he says, for still admiring the things of earth, he turned his thoughts inward and bewailed his past.[14]

One other word may be said about the love of nature.

13 For instance, Holloway-Calthrop, *Petrarch, His Life and Times,* pp. 67–71.

14 *Petrarch* (Robinson and Rolfe, edd.), 307–20. Translation revised.

H. M. Tomlinson quotes what the Indian said to the missionary who had been talking about heaven: "And is it like the land of the Musk-ox in summer, when the mist is on the lakes, and the loon cries very often?"[15]

Petrarch, like most men of his day, was intermittently religious. His orthodoxy is unquestioned. In his confessions, which he calls his *Secret,* he expresses the very medieval and even monastic view, that the best way to live is to meditate constantly on death. (Montaigne was to assert the contrary.) Likewise medieval is his opinion that sexual desire, without which the human race would cease to be, is evil. Marriage, too, is to be avoided. He never married; but he had two illegitimate children. The mistress of his poetical affections, Laura, was another man's wife.

Petrarch's denunciations of the avarice and luxury of the papal court at Avignon—Babylon, he called it— were quite in the medieval vein. They lack, however, the indignation of Dante's invectives in the *Divine Comedy*. Petrarch's attacks did not disturb the Avignon popes, who continued to favor him; nor did he consider it necessary, for the sake of consistency, to refuse the popes' favors.

Petrarch loved Italy. His poem, *Italia mia,* is still admired, and justly so. His love was not localized, as was Dante's, for he had never lived in Florence, the home of his ancestors, and he viewed Italy as a whole from Avignon. All Italy was embraced in his affec-

15 *The Sea and the Jungle,* p. 73.

tions, and Rome overwhelmed him with its memorials of ancient glory. He adjured the popes at Avignon to return to Rome; he urged the emperor, Charles IV, to go thither as to his proper seat; in published epistles, he encouraged Cola di Rienzo, the self-appointed tribune of the Roman people, to destroy the barons who misgoverned the city and to restore the glories of the empire. (The barons included the great Colonna family, which had first befriended him in Avignon.) The proper relations of pope and emperor, which Dante had tried to work out, to say nothing of their possible relations with a successful Cola di Rienzo, did not bother Petrarch. What he felt acutely was that Rome ought again to be the capital of the civilized world. But the gift of ancient Roman coins, which Petrarch brought to Charles IV, did not persuade that canny monarch to abandon his beloved Prague, nor did the popes at Avignon yield to his urging and leave the banks of the Rhone for those of the Tiber; and Cola failed. Politics obviously were not Petrarch's forte. His strength lay elsewhere.

It was his Italian poems, written in the Florentine dialect of his parents and of the Florentine colony in Avignon, that first drew favorable attention to Petrarch in Avignon. Avignon was located in Provence, the original home of Provençal poetry. Its influence is discernible in Petrarch's lyrics, as is also the influence of Dante and of other Florentine poets. The greater part of Petrarch's Italian verse revolves around his love for Laura, a married lady of Avignon. On the flyleaf of his Virgil there is still to be seen a note, in his own handwriting, which reads, in part, as follows: "Laura, who was distinguished by her own virtues and widely celebrated by my songs, first appeared to my eyes in my early manhood, in the year of our Lord 1327, upon the sixth day of April, at the first hour, in the church of Santa Clara at Avignon; in the same city, in the same month of April, on the same sixth day, at the same first hour, in the year 1348, that light was taken from our day . . . I am persuaded that her soul returned, as Seneca says of Scipio Africanus, to the heaven whence it came . . . ."[16]

There were those, in Petrarch's lifetime, who said that Laura was an abstraction for the laurel crown, which he sought on the basis of his Latin writings. The whole question is interesting, and still undecided. The troubadours sang the praises of married ladies, and Dante's devotion to Beatrice follows their example. Is Petrarch following it because it was an accepted tradition, or did it just happen? Is the similarity of Laura and laurel (in Latin as in English) another coincidence? We cannot be sure.

Petrarch's Italian verses were written chiefly in his early manhood. They were in his eyes "trifles," for he was convinced that literature worthy of the name must be written in Latin. That did not mean that he should not keep copies of them, polish and classify them, and round them out, to show the progress of his

16 Petrarch (Robinson and Rolfe, edd.), p. 88.

love for Laura and its elevating effect upon his character—in accordance with the doctrine of the "sweet new style." What is worth doing is worth doing well. The result was his *Canzoniere (Song Book)*, which contains 366 poems in several verse forms, the great majority of them sonnets.[17] The volume includes the better part of his Italian writings. It is the only one of his books that is still read by others than scholars.

The Laura of the *Canzoniere* is less remote and less ethereal than Dante's Beatrice. Petrarch wanted Laura, married though she was, but he tells us that she forced him to be content to keep their relations on a Platonic basis. (This may, of course, be fiction.)

It is hard to escape the impression that Petrarch was jealous of Dante. He had no copy of the *Divine Comedy* in his library until Boccaccio sent him one, probably in 1359. When Boccaccio wrote him and tactfully intimated that some people were saying he was jealous, Petrarch replied in a long letter of defence. He said, "Without hesitation I yield him [Dante] the palm for skill in use of the vulgar tongue." Yet he does seem to protest too much. "Who indeed could excite envy in me, who do not envy even Virgil?—unless perhaps I should be jealous of the hoarse applause which our poet [Dante] enjoys from the tavern-keepers, fullers, butchers, and others of that class, who dishonour those whom they would praise. But, far from desiring such popular recognition, I congratulate my-

17 *The Sonnets of Petrarch,* English verse translation by Joseph Auslander.

self, on the contrary, that, along with Virgil and Homer, I am free from it, inasmuch as I fully recognize how little the plaudits of the unschooled multitude weigh with scholars."[18] That is not very handsomely said.

It serves, however, to show that Petrarch regarded the judgment of scholars upon his work as the real test of its quality. (This must be kept in mind.) That is, his appeal was to the students of classical Latin literature. His Latin writings, which were chiefly in prose, enjoyed a wide and increasing circulation among the learned; for Latin was still their universal language, and Avignon, under the popes, was the cosmopolitan city of the West, from which copies of his published works were easily spread over the educated world of Latin Christendom. Their wide circulation shows that the ground was well prepared for them.

The matter of the laurel crown which he received on the Capitol at Rome from "the representatives of the Roman people" is a good illustration. Petrarch ardently desired this recognition. Indeed, he sought it most actively from Rome and from the University of Paris, where the chancellor was an Italian friend. There is no reference to this solicitation, of course, in Petrarch's letters announcing the astounding receipt of invitations from both Rome and Paris on the selfsame day.[19] He

18 *Petrarch* (Robinson and Rolfe, edd.), pp. 184, 187. A comparison of the introduction to this edition (1914) with that of the first edition (1898) shows a significant change in Robinson's views.

19 Denifle and Châtelain, *Chartularium Universitatis Parisiensis,* II: 501–2.

accepted the Roman one, which came through the good
offices of the Colonnas, aided probably by his sovereign
lord, Robert, Count of Provence and King of Naples.
Petrarch went down to Naples and was examined by
the king for three days as to his fitness for the honor.
The king was a competent examiner. He maintained a
group of Latin scholars at his court and was himself
well versed in ancient lore. Two hundred and ninety-
eight of his sermons, which survive (he was a layman,
but also a king loyal to the papacy, which was established in his city of Avignon), are replete with apposite
arguments and quotations from the Latin classics in
support of the teachings of Christianity, although the
sermons are scholastic in temper and form.[20] The actual coronation with the laurel took place in 1341, in
Rome, and Petrarch could and did speak of himself as
Poet Laureate.

Scholasticism, which Petrarch and most of the other
Humanists abhorred, undoubtedly helped to prepare
the soil for the Revival of Learning. Thomas Aquinas,
in reshaping theology with the aid of Latin translations
of Aristotle's writings and *vice versa,* had unquestion-
ably enhanced the repute of classical antiquity. The
revival of interest in the Roman law, codified by Justinian, which is associated with the name of Irnerius (*ca.*
1100), and which contributed greatly to the development of the canon law, had a similar influence. (That
Thomism and civil and canon law, for their part, were

20 Goetz, *König Robert von Ne-*
    apel (1309–1343), *seine Per-*   *sönlichkeit und sein Verhält-*
    nis zum Humanismus.

indebted to the growth of interest in the affairs of this world is also well established.)

Petrarch's Latin writings are voluminous. They are well classified and illustrated, with English translations, by Robinson and Rolfe. His *Letters* do much to reveal the man that he was and his thoughts on all sorts of subjects. They are rich in quotations from the Latin classics and in allusion to antiquity. Knowing that his correspondents circulated his letters, Petrarch took pains to give them literary form. Many of them are substantial essays. He kept copies of them, classified them, revised and polished them, and published them. He desired to be, and he was in this matter of letter-writing, the Cicero of his times.

Petrarch's Latin style was achieved by practice rather than by philological analysis. Cicero and Seneca were his chief models. He had a keen ear for the music of language, and the extant revisions of his writings are almost always improvements. Later scholars have since found him less classical in style than he thought he was; but his own age believed that he had recovered ancient eloquence and was easily the peer of Cicero and Virgil.

In the field of history Petrarch is represented principally by his *De viris illustribus,* biographical sketches of twenty-four illustrious ancients. The group includes Romulus, Alexander, Hannibal, Scipio Africanus, Julius Caesar, and Nero. The book was designed to recall the glories of ancient Rome. His principal source is Livy. His critical powers were very slender.[21] His cri-

21 Fueter, *Historiographie,* pp. 1-5.

terion of choice among his authorities, when he had more than one, was reasonableness. As his sources were exclusively classical, he was saved from the common medieval vice of "explaining" events by supernatural interventions.

That is not to say that Petrarch was free from superstition. He was a fatalist, of a sort; he was sure that he would not die until his time had come; precautions were useless. The note on the coincidences of his first glimpse of Laura and her death, quoted above, shows that he felt that there was some occult bond between her and himself—unless, perchance, he is thinking of the significance of numbers—twenty-one is seven times three. His belief in the so-called Virgilian Lots is illustrated by his excitement over the passage from Augustine's *Confessions* which his eyes lit upon on the summit of Mt. Ventoux. On the other hand, when Boccaccio was terrified by the vision of a dying holy man, foretelling Boccaccio's approaching death and admonishing him to give over his classical studies, Petrarch, in a long letter, discounted the report: "I do not belittle the authority of prophecy . . . . But I venture to question whether Christ was the author of this particular prophecy, whether it may not be, as often happens, a fabrication attributed to Him in order to insure its acceptance." He advised Boccaccio to go on with his classical labors, saying, "Neither exhortations to virtue nor the argument of approaching death should divert us from literature; for in a good mind it excites the love of virtue, and dissipates, or at least diminishes, the

fear of death."[22] This is good counsel, almost worthy
to stand beside—indeed, it may have been inspired by
—John of Salisbury's quotation from Seneca, "Leisure
without literature is death and the burial of the living
man," and John's own words, "All things yield fruit to
a wise man, and whatever [things] are said or done
furnish [him] with matter for exercise of virtue."[23]

Petrarch's most ambitious work was his *Africa,* a
Latin epic, in hexameters, of the second Punic war and
the final triumph of the great Scipio over Carthage, the
enemy of Roman greatness. The materials for the
poem he drew from Livy and Florus. It is possible
that its secondary purpose was to awaken the pride of
the Italians and encourage them to deeds worthy of
their ancestors. Petrarch dedicated it to King Robert
of Naples. He had read some of it to the king in
demonstrating his fitness for the laurel crown (1341).
The poem has a number of effective passages, and,
when the author treats of love and the degeneracy of
Scipio's times, his skill and interest in handling such
themes are again made manifest. But, as a whole, the
Africa was not a success. Petrarch's talent was not
epical but lyrical; sustained heroic verse was beyond
him. He suspected the truth and refused to publish
the *Africa,* although it was finished about 1342, and he
continued to work it over. It was not printed until
1501. Petrarch's contemporaries, who knew parts of
it, and the ensuing generations of Humanists, who

22 *Petrarch* (Robinson and Rolfe,
   edd.), pp. 389, 391.

23 *Policraticus,* I: 17, 65. John
   died in 1180.

knew all of it, acclaimed it as a masterpiece that ranked with the *Aeneid* and declared that it would, in the words of Coluccio Salutati, give its author "an eternal name."

Petrarch's moral and religious status is best revealed by his *Secretum*.[24] It is a volume of confessions, resembling in some ways Augustine's *Confessions,* and with some echoes of Boethius's *Consolation*. The form is that of a dialogue between Augustine and Petrarch, lasting three days and carried on in the presence of Truth, a comely virgin who, after the exchange of a few words with Petrarch, requests Augustine to give him counsel. (Compare Beatrice's selection of Virgil to guide Dante.) Truth remains with them, but holds her peace. In this book Petrarch puts into the mouth of Augustine, a sinner who had reformed, the expression of most of his own ascetic impulses, while he himself defends himself as well as he can. Augustine gets the best of him, but in the end does not succeed in persuading him to abandon his classical studies, although Petrarch admits that it would be much safer for him to attend only to the care of his soul.[25]

The *Secret,* Petrarch tells us, was written only for his own use, to remind him of his weaknesses and help keep him in the paths of righteousness; but it may be safely assumed that the artistic impulse operated in its creation, smoothing here and there the rough texture of reality. It was written about 1342, that is, when Pe-

24 *Petrarch's Secret,* translated   25 *Ibid.,* p. 192.
by Draper.

trarch was about thirty-eight years of age. No doubt, as the years passed, Petrarch retouched it, as was his wont.

Petrarch defends at length his love for Laura as an ennobling element in his life. He praises her chastity, which had withstood his entreaties, and says that she has taught him "what should be the honour and duty of a man."[26] He reflects, however (through Augustine), "that that fair form, worn by sicknesses and the bearing of many children, has already lost much of its first strength";[27] concludes that she had "mocked, despised, scorned" him, all "with an air of haughty disdain"; and opines: "For few be there that have once tasted this seductive pleasure and can retain enough manliness, not to say courage, to rate at its true value that poor form of woman of which I speak."[28] Alas for Petrarch's chivalry! The monastic depreciation of woman has won.

Petrarch might have done well, in the interest of a full confession, to discuss with Augustine the birth of his illegitimate son, Giovanni, in 1337, and, in retouching his book, the birth of his illegitimate daughter some six years later. But, not a word does he utter on this topic.

There's a considerable amount of talk about Petrarch's love of fame or glory. Since the kings of Nineveh and Egypt had sought to perpetuate the mem-

---

26 *Ibid.*, p. 130.
27 *Ibid.*, p. 116.

28 *Ibid.*, pp. 163, 164. None of this sort of thing in the *Canzoniere!*

ory of their deeds in granite, and as every normal man
has always desired success, it seems unnecessary to regard Petrarch's ambition for fame or glory as anything
out of the ordinary. The same holds true of his confession of intermittent melancholy. On both matters
Petrarch was deceiving himself or posing.

The use of allegory gets some attention in the *Secret.*
It will be recalled that in his oft-cited letter to his
brother Gherardo, a monk at Montreux, Petrarch explains at some length—and rather condescendingly—why
"allegory is the very warp and woof of all poetry."²⁹
In the *Secret* Petrarch remarks, in a purely medieval
way, that "by that fury of winds that Virgil describes
hidden in deep caves," ruled by "his King Œolus sitting
above," Virgil "may have meant to denote anger and
the other passions of the soul . . . which, unless controlled by the curb of reason, would in their furious
haste . . . drag us in their train and sweep us over sea
and land and the very sky itself." Then Petrarch reflects (through Augustine) that Virgil may not have
"had this in mind when writing," and may have "only
meant to depict a storm at sea and nothing else."³⁰
This is a good conjecture; and certainly the *Canzoniere*
has long been praised for its freedom from allegory.

The most significant feature of the *Secret,* however,
is Augustine's support of ascetic doctrines with substantially nothing but quotations from the ancient classics. He cites from Petrarch's writings ten or eleven

---

29 *Petrarch* (Robinson and Rolfe,   30 *Petrarch's Secret,* pp. 101-2.
    edd.), p. 262.

times; but the Bible (except for one phrase from the Psalms and one from the Book of Wisdom) and the Fathers are completely ignored.   John of Salisbury and King Robert of Naples, to mention only two familiar examples, use classical quotations as ancillary to the teachings of the Bible and the Fathers, and in a later age Erasmus did the same.   But Petrarch goes far beyond them in demonstrating how the classics may be employed to support the strictest morality.   The significance of this would be enhanced if Petrarch's followers, the Humanists of the Revival of Learning, had also stressed the importance of the *matter* of the classics in addition to the *form;* but this they did not do.

Petrarch's respect for the ancient classics was intense and exclusive.   Of all the intellectual interests of the Middle Ages the classics alone enjoyed his affection.   Law, after seven years of study at his father's expense, he abhorred; medicine, he jeered at; theology, he lacked all interest in; and scholastic philosophy and Averroism, he scorned.   Apparently following Cicero, he held Aristotle inferior to Plato, although he knew little about the former and of the latter nothing beyond what the Middle Ages knew. Petrarch was the first specialist in the classics, and as such he was the inaugurator of the Revival of (classical) Learning. This is indubitable, even when one recalls that he knew no Greek and held that the Latin literature was superior to the Greek.   Of course, he had predecessors and contemporaries who also loved the ancient classics ardently, but his narrow and intense devotion, communicated in his letters and Latin works, kindled a flame which swept over the learned circles of Europe. True, he was wrong—stupidly wrong—in thinking that the vernacular was no fit vehicle for high literature; true, too, that in greatness of soul and in poetical achievement he ranks far below Dante. The fact remains that for better and for worse Petrarch inaugurated the Revival of Learning.

Michelet's and Renan's characterization of Petrarch as the "first modern man" has rightly fallen into desuetude. Robinson and Rolfe's "first modern scholar and man of letters," the sub-title of their 1914 edition, still claims too much. Sismondi's "first man of his time" pleases Guglielmo Volpi.[31] The present writer prefers "first man of letters of his day." That avoids impossible comparisons, and the facts fully support it—and nothing stronger.

Boccaccio.—In Italy the second man of letters of Petrarch's day was his intimate friend and confidante, Giovanni Boccaccio.[32] Boccaccio (1313–1375) was the illegitimate son of a travelling agent of the banking and commercial house of Bardi in Florence and of a Frenchwoman of Paris, whose identity is unknown. The father soon returned to Italy, married another girl, and

31 *Il Trecento,* pp. 161–65. Here Volpi traverses the whole matter of Petrarch's alleged modernity.

32 Volpi, *Il Trecento;* Hauvette, *Boccace, étude biographique* *et littéraire:* Hutton, *Giovanni Boccaccio, a Biographical Study; The Filostrato of Giovanni Boccaccio,* a prose translation with parallel text by Griffin and Myrick.

sent for the child, who spent his early years in his
father's home and birthplace, in Certaldo, not far from
Florence. The father wanted his bookish son to have
a gainful occupation, and when the boy was fifteen or
so his father took him from school and sent him to
learn business at a branch of the banking house in
Naples. Giovanni's father was known and respected
by King Robert, the monarch who was to examine Petrarch for the laurel, and the lad easily made good ac-
quaintances. He found Naples with its beautiful setting and its stirring and luxurious life much to his taste.
After six years of the young man's inattention to business the father decided that he should become a lawyer,
and instructed him to study canon law at the University
of Naples. The change of purpose did not take the
youth away from the life of the city and of the royal
court, and for another six years he desultorily attended
lectures in arts as well as in canon law at the University.
He made no progress in his legal studies, but he was
not exactly idle. He studied astronomy with the king's
"astrologer" and classical mythology with the king's
librarian, and read voraciously in the Latin classics,
presumably in the large royal library. He also became
acquainted with French romances and Provençal lyrics,
for Robert's dynasty was French and contact with Provence, of which Robert was count, was close.

Young Boccaccio was also amorous. His early loves
in Naples are alluded to in his writings; but the lady
who definitely won his heart, if we may trust his books,
was the high-born Maria d'Aquino, illegitimate daugh-

ter of King Robert and the wife of a nobleman of the royal court. Maria yielded to Boccaccio's wooing and his verses, and about 1336 became his mistress. But, after a couple of years, she transferred her affections to another paramour—we are still relying on the interpretation of Boccaccio's writings—and for about a dozen years, in verse and prose, he vainly strove to win her back. In 1340 business reverses compelled his father to bring him home, and the Neapolitan period of his life was over. Maria died of the Black Death in 1348 or 1349. Boccaccio's father died a short while later, leaving to Giovanni a small property in Certaldo. With this as a backlog and with occasional employment by the government of Florence, Boccaccio maintained himself. His means were slight, but after an unfortunate experience or two with high-placed patrons, he decided to reject the proffered support of princes and their ministers and clung to his independence.

Most of Boccaccio's vernacular writings, in both prose and verse, revolved around his real or alleged passion for Maria d'Aquino. Most of them suffer from the injection of much classical lore and, of course, from the intervention of the gods, which impede the development of the story he is telling. The *Filostrato* is based upon a French and a Latin version of the romance of Troilus and Briseida (or Criseida). It is in octave rime, a popular verse form which Boccaccio here brings to its full dignity and power. The *Filostrato* is regarded as the most successful of his vernacular tales and is unusually free from classical débris. In the *Ameto*

Boccaccio adopts the form of Dante's *Vita Nuova* for a version of the romance of the young hunter and the seven nymphs (representing the four cardinal and the three theological virtues), who tell him the stories of their intimate amours. In the *Amorosa Visione* Boccaccio uses as his model the *Divine Comedy*. Now, however, it is an allegory of earthly love—the only sort that Boccaccio understood—and its lesson is that learning and natural love give beatitude. These three works of Boccaccio give an adequate indication of the character of the half-dozen devoted to Maria d'Aquino. She appears under a variety of names, preferably as Fiammetta.

The greatest of Boccaccio's vernacular writings is, of course, the *Decameron*. It is the only one which is still read by non-specialists; it is for Boccaccio's popular fame what the *Canzoniere* is for Petrarch's. Seven young women and three young men retire from the horrors of the Black Death in Florence to the greater safety of a country villa and then of a country palace. They spend two weeks, with plenty of servants to do the work, in diverting themselves with banquets, dancing, and story-telling. Friday is regarded as a holy day and Saturday as a day for bathing and the like, so that the stories are told only on the first five days of the week. For each story day a theme is set and each of the ten tells a story. The result is one hundred short stories, composing Boccaccio's "Human Comedy."

The stories, collected by Boccaccio from hither and yon, though witty and full of surprise, are in the main scandalous. The worst of them are told on the clergy. Fidelity to the marriage vow is exceptional. In legal language, "virtue is derided and vice is made attractive." In the "Conclusion" of the *Decameron,* Boccaccio undertook to defend himself from the charge of licentiousness. "Some of you may say," he remarks, "that in writing these tales I have taken too much licence, by making ladies sometimes say and often listen to matters which are not proper to be said or heard by virtuous ladies. This I deny, for there is nothing so unchaste but may be said chastely if modest words are used; and this I think I have done."[33] This specious doctrine obtains a qualified approval from Hauvette. Boccaccio, he avers, is "perhaps the first among the moderns to relish the satisfaction of the Artist" in "knowing how to paint scenes of little decency without using indecorous words."[34] What a gulf between this sort of thing and John of Salisbury's noble words, quoted above: "All things yield fruit to a wise man, and whatever [things] are said or done furnish [him] with matter for the exercise of virtue"!

The *Decameron,* it is agreed, is Boccaccio's masterpiece. In it he has discarded the classical trappings which encumber most of his vernacular writings and has mirrored directly the seamy side of the life of his time as he had observed it in Naples and Florence. The rising interest in the realistic portrayal of life here below, depicting the actual or the possible, explains in

33 *Decameron* (Aldington's translation), II: 339.

34 *Boccace,* p. 271.

large part the success of this book. Some critics used to
think that Boccaccio had painted a new society and a
new culture then springing into being under the influence of the nascent Revival of Learning. The great De
Sanctis lends some support to this opinion.[35] The facts
do not warrant any such view. The specialized study
of Latin literature was just beginning, and much time
would be needed for the ripening of its fruits. Moreover, the pleasure-loving folk, who enjoyed witty and
dissolute stories (and behavior), were not the creation
of Boccaccio's times; they were already in existence
long before Dante himself, and his *Inferno* is filled with
their kind. The world of the *Decameron* is a partial
one, a selection made in accordance with the tastes of
its author. As wise old Henry Osborn Taylor remarks,
Boccaccio's "cheerful and facile and abundantly carnal
nature did not rise to those spiritual heights which may
be just as veritable as the streets and gutters of human
life."[36]

Juan Ruiz.—If further evidence is desired in support of the view that the Revival of Learning had nothing essential to do with the reappearance of secular-
minded literature and with the realistic treatment of
life, it can be found in abundance in the rowdy and
ribald *Libro de buen amor*,[37] written in Spain by Juan

35 De Sanctis, *History of Italian
    Literature,* Vol. I, Chap. IX.
36 *Sixteenth Century,* I:23.
37 *The Book of Good Love,*
    translated into English verse
by Kane. See also Fitzmaurice-Kelly, *A New History of
Spanish Literature* pp. 46–47.
and his *Chapters on Spanish
Literature,* pp. 25–54.

Ruiz, archpriest of Hita, virtually at the time of the composition of the *Decameron*. Ruiz knew nothing of the Revival of Learning; yet he was a master of realism, and a worthy progenitor of the picaresque novel.

Boccaccio (continued).—The publication of the complete *Decameron* in 1354 represents a turning point in the career of Boccaccio which separates his writings in the vernacular from those in Latin, his creative works from his works of acquisitive scholarship. The influence of Petrarch is discernible in the new orientation. Petrarch's fame as a Latinist had reached Boccaccio while he was still in Naples, although the two did not meet until 1350, when Petrarch, on the way to the Jubilee in Rome, stopped over in Florence. Soon afterward, Boccaccio carried to Petrarch the invitation of the government of Florence to accept a professorship in the University, an invitation baited with the offer to restore him the property of his father, which had been confiscated in 1302. (Petrarch declined the invitation, and the government confirmed the confiscation.) Other meetings of Petrarch and Boccaccio and frequent letters followed. Boccaccio revered Petrarch as his master. Nor did the pupil lack success in familiarizing himself with all the extant Latin classics, although he never was able to write as good Latin as his master. If Petrarch was the first Latin scholar of his century, Boccaccio held the second place.

The switch from the vernacular to Latin was momentarily interrupted by Boccaccio's decision to defend

himself before the people of Florence. The occasion
was his unsuccessful wooing of a rich and comely Florentine widow—we seem to be on solid ground here.
He had become excessively stout, and she made fun of
him and his advances before her friends. Boccaccio
felt humiliated and enraged. In revenge he wrote and
published the savage *Corbaccio*. In this book he dreams
that he is in an odd, desert place—apparently the kingdom of love—where a strange being, clothed in scarlet,
appears before him. It is the shade of the former husband of the widow, sent to him from purgatory by the
Virgin, to free him from woman's wiles and the bonds
of vanity, and to persuade him to devote his attention
to works of erudition. Is he not a man of advanced
age? (He was forty-one.) The specter then tells him
of all the disreputable tricks of his wife, of her greed
and ugliness, of her deceptions and concupiscence, and
warns him to flee from the labyrinth of love, for all
women are domineering, vicious, and snares. There
are many echoes of the *Divine Comedy*—in reverse—
in this vulgar, little book, which draws heavily on
Juvenal.[38]

Boccaccio's principal Latin work is the *De genealogia
deorum gentilium,* which he began to write some little
time before 1350 and rounded out and revised down to
1373. It is essentially a dictionary of classical mythology, in which the author strove to establish the parent-
age of the gods of the Gentiles, that is, of classical

[38] For a good summary of the
diatribes see Chubb, *Life of*
Giovanni Boccaccio, pp. 184–
91.

antiquity. The task was a formidable one, since some of the gods appeared under different names and some different gods bore the same name. Boccaccio did his best, with inadequate sources and incomplete success, and endeavored to explain the origins of the myths by means of the good old device of allegory. The last two of the fifteen books into which the *Genealogy* is divided are given over to a defence of "poetry" and of the author against the detractions of lawyers, "hypocritical theologians," and other classes of critics. These prolix chapters knock down many men of straw and seem to overlook the fact that poetry and the study of the classics no longer needed defence.[39] Nevertheless, with all its faults, the *Genealogy* became a convenient handbook for the Humanists who followed Boccaccio and desired to employ mythological machinery in their writings.

Another work of mere erudition, and a much shorter one, is Boccaccio's dictionary of geographical names, the *De montibus, silvis, fontibus,* etc. Under each topic of the lengthy title, the place names are given alphabetically, with the modern equivalents; and the author chats about the places on the basis of tradition and of his own visits. This book also, although swarming with errors, was a handy reference work for the Humanists.

The drudgery involved in these two dictionaries re-

39 The *Decretum* of Gratian (12th century), a great and current source book of canon law, defends the classics adequately. For an English translation of the last two books of the *Genealogy,* with a good commentary, see Osgood, *Boccaccio on Poetry.*

flects great credit on Boccaccio's stamina.   More to his taste was the *De claris mulieribus (Lives of Illustrious Women)*, which was designed to do something to balance the attention that noted men had received. The book lists 104 ladies, beginning with Eve and coming down to Constance of Sicily and Joanna of Naples. Saints are explicitly excluded, and the ancients, including some goddesses, receive the major part of the space. A few rather dubious anecdotes remind the reader of the author of the *Decameron,* but the moral observations which accompany the sketches are generally of the commonplace, ascetic type. Thus, ladies should always follow their husbands even in exile and poverty, and widows should never remarry but find refuge in Christ. After all, women are weak, imperfect, and inferior in general to men.

A companion and somewhat superior work, suggested by one of Petrarch's books, is the *De casibus virorum illustrium,* which was begun about 1356, dropped, and finished in 1374. Here the shades of the illustrious dead appear to Boccaccio and recount the miseries of their days on earth. Adam and Eve lead off, followed by the others, including Paul the Deacon and Gregory of Tours, down to such famous contemporaries as Walter of Brienne. The alleged purpose of the book is edification, to show the fragility and emptiness of human grandeur; the moralizing is of the usual medieval sort. The detailed description of the physical charms of Samson's deceiver, Delilah,[40] suggests that

40 Translated in Chubb, *Life of Giovanni Boccaccio,* pp. 199-200.

Boccaccio's old interests had not completely changed.

Boccaccio also promoted the study of classical Greek. Petrarch, although he believed in the superiority of Latin literature, was eager to learn the language of Homer. He made a brief and unsuccessful effort to do so in 1342 with the aid of a Calabrian monk named Barlaam. Greek was still spoken in parts of southern Italy, and it would seem that classical Greek was cultivated there.[41] Years later Boccaccio undertook to satisfy Petrarch's desire to know the *Iliad* and the *Odyssey* in Latin. He took into his house another Calabrian, Leonzio Pilato, in 1360, and in the course of nearly three years wrote out and worked over a Latin translation of these works which he extracted from his guest. A clean copy of the translation went on to Petrarch by 1367. In the course of the work of translation Boccaccio acquired an elementary knowledge of the language, and he was entitled to boast that he was the first to bring back the books of Homer to Tuscany. Unfortunately Boccaccio's plan to have Pilato teach Greek in the University did not work out, for the restless Calabrian left Florence for Greece, and the teaching of Greek lapsed. (It was, however, resumed in the closing years of the century.)

In his "Latin period," Boccaccio twice reverted to the vernacular, and properly, for both times he dealt with Dante. Boccaccio had never concealed his admiration for Dante's writings, his superior endowments, and his character. In his *Vita di Dante,* which was appar-

41 Siciliano, *Medio Evo e Rinascimento,* pp. 60-61.

ently written between 1357 and 1362, he drew upon the great poet's writings and upon living tradition. He could not handle Dante the politician successfully, but he did his best to characterize the poet and the man. He gives some little space to Beatrice and to Dante's marriage to Gemma Donati, and incidentally animadverts on the infelicities of matrimony. (Boccaccio's constant diatribes against matrimony should not cause the reader to forget that he had five illegitimate children.) The *Vita di Dante* is overly declamatory, but it has some historical value and is significant as the first biography of an artist. The other vernacular work is a commentary on the *Divine Comedy,* apparently based on notes for the public lectures which, at the request of the government, Boccaccio began to give in 1373. Ill health compelled him to abandon the course when he had reached the seventeenth canto of the *Inferno.* The commentary deals with the literal and the allegorical meanings; it ranges from explanations of obvious expressions to displays of erudition and moral preachings.

In his later years, after the fright which the message of the dying saint gave him in 1362, Boccaccio wore a monastic robe, followed the practices of religion, and spoke regretfully of the lascivious writings of his first period. Petrarch, as the reader knows, persuaded him to continue with his classical studies, and also excused the tales of the *Decameron,* on the ground of the writer's youth. Boccaccio was still interested, perhaps only in a curious literary way, in Fiammetta. He knew from the *Divine Comedy* that Beatrice was in paradise; he also knew that Petrarch, in his *Canzoniere,* had celebrated Laura's presence there. What of amorous Fiammetta, long since departed from this life? Among his sonnets, there is one in which he begs Dante to intercede for him, that he might join Fiammetta in the third heaven; and in another, written in the next to the last year of his life, he salutes Petrarch as having the happiness to behold his beloved "Lauretta" seated by the side of Fiammetta in the presence of God.[42] The reader is invited to supply his own comment.

Boccaccio's services to Italian literature and to the Revival of Learning may be briefly assessed.[43] His Italian, although "more rich in sound than dense in ideas," added consistency to Italian syntax and harmony to Italian prose, and it made the final contribution to the establishment of the Florentine dialect as the literary language of Italy. He was a happy innovator in the forms of Italian literature, for from Latin literature he derived the pastoral *(Ameto),* he dignified the short story *(Decameron),* and he perfected the octave stanza *(Filostrato).* Of equal importance was his demonstration that the reading public preferred the realistic portrayal of life on earth to allegory and symbolism *(Decameron).* As a scholar Boccaccio helped to promote, for good and ill, the Revival of Learning. To be sure, unlike Dante, who studied Virgil so that he

42 Torraca, *Per la biografia di Giovanni Boccaccio,* pp. 81–83, quotes from these sonnets.

43 This paragraph leans heavily on Volpi, *Il Trecento,* pp. 232–35.

might learn how to develop his own style, Boccaccio studied the great Roman writers in order to write as they did. In this he was only too faithfully followed by the succeeding generations of Humanists, who, broadly speaking, thought that great style implied great content. One recalls William Allen White's cognate observation: "The great error of Americans is thinking that an orator is a statesman." Finally it seems likely that the political-diplomatic values attributed later to a good classical style were beginning, with Boccaccio, to gain recognition; for while Petrarch was used by his princely patrons primarily as a decorative member of embassies, Boccaccio was employed by the government of Florence personally to conduct some difficult negotiations.

CHAPTER V: THE VICTORY OF THE VERNACULAR

Chaucer.—Geoffrey Chaucer (1340–1400)[1] was a busy public servant of the English government. He was a soldier, a diplomat with important missions to France, the Netherlands, and Italy, a top official of the export customs staff in the port of London, and at different times superintendent of buildings, of forests, and of highways for the government. Lowes needs more than

[1] *The Poetical Works of Chaucer,* edited by Robinson; Lowes, *Geoffrey Chaucer and the Development of His Genius* and "The Art of Geoffrey Chaucer" in *Essays in Appreciation,* pp. 77–118; Manly in *Proceedings of the British Academy,* XII: 95–113; Saintsbury in *Cambridge History of English Literature,* II: 179–224; Chute, *Geoffrey Chaucer of England.*

a page and a half to list his many jobs.[2] These brought him into contact not only with the royal court, but with nearly all classes of the English people, as well as with many foreigners at home and abroad. If he had never written a line of poetry no one could accuse him of slothfulness, yet he found time to compose works which have established him as the greatest English poet prior to Shakespeare. And he lived the rounded life of the normal man, being both husband and father.

Chaucer learned not only from people but also from books. The eagle, in his "House of Fame," reproaches him for his much reading:

> For when thy labour doon al ys,
> And hast mad alle thy rekenynges,
> In stede of reste and newe thynges,
> Thou goost hom to thy hous anoon;
> And, also domb as any stoon,
> Thou sittest at another book
> Tyl fully daswed [dazzled] ys thy look,
> And lyvest thus as an heremyte,
> Although thyn abstynence ys lyte.[3]

His knowledge of the Latin classics was that of the medieval scholar who was interested in literature; it probably was not quite so extensive as that of Petrarch and Boccaccio. He knew also medieval Latin literature, theological works excepted. Above all he knew inti-

THE VICTORY OF THE VERNACULAR

mately French vernacular literature, for French was
still the usual literary language of the English court,
although it was giving ground before English; and
French literature, at least in Chaucer's early manhood,
still held the first place in European estimation. We
cannot be sure when he learned Italian; but his diplomatic journeys to Italy introduced him to the published
works of Dante, Petrarch, and Boccaccio, although the
critics are inclined to believe that he did not know the
Decameron. He may even have met Petrarch.[4] Finally,
Chaucer knew English literature and the fondness of
the North and the Northwest of England for alliterative verse.

Chaucer's own writings are in English, the Middle
English of London. If there ever had been any question as to the dialect which was to become the literary
language of England, that question was resolved by
Chaucer's works. And if the rivalry over poetic form,
between the iambic measure and rhyme on the one
hand and the old and popular alliterative measure on
the other (used by Chaucer's contemporary, "William
Langland"), was still keen in Chaucer's youth, that too
was ended by Chaucer's choice of the former.[5] Chaucer's writings are in English, not in Latin. Obviously,
he was not a Humanist.

Three stages are discernible in Chaucer's creative
progress: the French, the Italian, and the English. In

4 Jusserand, *The School for Am-*
bassadors, pp. 325–41, can-
vasses the evidence pro and
con.

5 Monroe and Henderson, edd.,
The New Poetry, pp. viii–ix.

the first, the main foreign influence (in addition to
Latin) was that of French literature; in the second,
the writings of Dante, Petrarch, and Boccaccio opened
fresh horizons—"they stimulated his powers of reflection by forms and ideals of art different from those
with which he was familiar"; in the third, the English
life of his day, together with his emancipation from
the rhetorical prescriptions of the professional rhetoricians,[6] enabled him to offer the reader "God's plenty."

"The Book of the Duchess,"[7] which was written in
1369 or 1370, is a good illustration of his French period.
It is of the conventional dream type, similar to many of
the works of Machaut, Froissart, and Deschamps, his
French contemporaries, and celebrates the virtues of
the beautiful Duchess of Lancaster, the first wife of his
patron, John of Gaunt. She had died all too soon. It
is replete with allegory and with the nobility of the
heroines of antiquity; yet, conventional though it is, it
"expresses real feeling," and can be read even today
with pleasure.

"The House of Fame"[8] is the first large-scale work
of Chaucer's Italian period. It is another dream poem,
and is more sprightly than "The Book of the Duchess."
Geoffrey is borne aloft to the airy and shining House
of Fame, where earthly reputations resound (after the
fashion of the widening circles of water into which a
stone is cast), and whence, by the decision of Fortune,

6 Manly in *Proceedings of the*   7 *Poetical Works,* pp. 315–29.
  British Academy, XII: 95–113.   8 *Ibid.,* pp. 330–53.

they return to earth, usually in a perverse and distorted form. The influence of Dante is to be seen in the idea of the journey into the upper spaces, and also in the appearance of the eagle "that shon with fethres as of gold," which carried the poet safely in its claws, although, as he says, he was no Enoch or Elijah or Ganymede. The poem abounds in crisp, classical reminiscences of the medieval type. "It is rich in fancy, thought, and humor—the humor of situation and bright retort. It presents at least one comic character, the eagle, whose conversational powers are not unworthy of comparison with those of Chaunticleer."

"The Parliament of Fowls" was written about the same time as "The House of Fame." It is difficult to determine the relative shares of Latin, French, and Italian reminiscences in "The Parliament," although it seems as if the second part of the *Roman de la Rose* was preponderant. Again in a dream, the poet is taken by Scipio—the Scipio of "The Dream"—to a hillside, where all the birds are gathered before the goddess of Nature on St. Valentine's Day, as is their wont, to choose their mates. The principal dispute is between three royal eagles or falcons, all competitors for the beautiful formel or lady eagle, perched on the wrist of the goddess. The protestations of the rivals echo the chivalrous cult of love. Nature finally decides that the formel shall choose for herself, and she announces, as a wise lady would, that she will take a year to make up her mind. The humbler birds—worm-fowl, water-fowl, and seed-fowl—are mostly commentators on the debate

of the eagles. One suspects (and the influence of the
Romance of the Rose would support the conjecture)
that there is more than a touch of allegory here, and
that the more lordly birds represent the aristocracy,
and the humbler ones the lower classes, who seem to
have Chaucer's sympathy.

"*Troilus and Criseyde* is not only the first great
poem in English; it is also, independently of period and
language, one of the very great and beautiful poems of
the world." With these words Lowes opens his impressive chapter on Chaucer's "Mastered Art."[9] Chaucer's
apprenticeship is completed; in this poem, finished
shortly before 1385, he has passed from his Italian to
his English period and has filled it not with "French
life nor Italian life, but English." Professor Manly
makes clear how this came about. "Chaucer's greatness
arose from his growing recognition that for him at
least the right way to amplify a story was not to ex-
pand it by rhetorical devices, but to conceive it in terms
of the life which he had observed so closely, to imagine
how each of the characters thought and felt, and to
report how in this imaginative vision they looked and
acted."[10]

Chaucer found the framework and some of the content, a minor part, of his "Troilus and Criseyde" in
Boccaccio's *Filostrato*. Boccaccio's great poem was
derived, we know, though only in part, from a French
romance and a Latin version of it. The threads of all

9 *Geoffrey Chaucer,* Chap. v.   10 *Proceedings of the British
                                          Academy,* XII: 110.

these accounts lead back and back to Homer's *Iliad*. Chaucer also drew on the sources which Boccaccio had employed. Saintsbury's characterization of Chaucer's use of the *Filostrato* is apt: Chaucer, "though still playing the part of the hermit-crab . . . has quite transformed the house which he borrowed and peopled it with quite different inhabitants."[11]

There are also in "Troilus and Criseyde" many reminiscences of the classics, of Boethius's *Consolation,* of the chivalrous romances, and of Dante. Chaucer's wide reading of books enriched his reading of life. He knew that this was so, and he expresses it neatly in the early part of "The Parliament of Fowls":

> For out of olde feldes, as men seyth,
> Cometh al this newe corn from yer to yere,
> And out of olde bokes, in good feyth,
> Cometh al this newe science that men lere.

The plot of "Troilus and Criseyde" is that of the passing of the lady from one chivalrous lover to another. Chaucer's psychological insight into the complicated feeling of his Criseyde far surpasses Boccaccio's insight into the simple feelings of Troilo, the main character in the *Filostrato.* The significance of the change from Boccaccio's wanton Neapolitan lady of pleasure to Chaucer's reluctant Englishwoman is explained by Lowes:[12] "For it is precisely Chaucer's transformation of Criseyde from the typical figure of the woman quick-

---

11 *Cambridge History of English Literature,* II: 197–98.

12 *Geoffrey Chaucer,* p. 178.

ly won to the complex, bafflingly subtle, lovely and hesitant creature he has made which sets the two central books of his poem among the masterpieces." At the end of his poem Chaucer, always sympathetic with women, takes tender and pitiful leave of his errant heroine.

Passing over the "Legend of Good Women"—stories of celebrated ladies of antiquity who were faithful to their men—which Chaucer abandoned in favor of a direct treatment of the variegated life he knew, we reach his masterpiece, the "Canterbury Tales." In these, "instead of any longer filling empty forms or reconstructing full ones, he drew straight from life a framework of his own" and "opens the door of the Tabard Inn to Harry Bailly and the Wife of Bath and the Miller and the Pardoner and their goodly fellowship."[13]

The delightfully informative chapter that Lowes devotes to the "Canterbury Tales"[14] makes extensive comment here quite unnecessary. The General Prologue presents us, so to speak, with static pictures of the nine and twenty pilgrims who met together with one Geoffrey—hardly Chaucer himself—at the Tabard Inn of landlord Harry Bailly, in London, to make the pilgrimage to the shrine of Becket at Canterbury. They ride, and on the journey they while away the time with their stories, gathered by Chaucer from the lips of the motley assortment of people he had met both at home and abroad or in books. The stories, which illustrate and

13 Lowes, *Essays in Appreciation*, pp. 117-18.

14 *Geoffrey Chaucer*, pp. 198-246.

occasionally parody the chief types of medieval literature—the *fabliaux,* romances, *exempla,* animal tales,
etc.—are mostly in verse, with only two in prose. In the
telling, the tales encounter interruption, comment, and
quarrel among the listeners; they round out the charac-
terizations of the General Prologue and of the pro-
logues which introduce each tale, and they reveal the
unmistakable characteristics of each individual pilgrim.
It is the simple truth that the stories, suited to the
callings of the tellers, are "drenched in life."

In comparison with Chaucer's pilgrims, the story-
tellers of the *Decameron* are wooden figures; the
stories told by any one of them might have been
ascribed to any other without the least damage to the
book. Not so the Canterbury pilgrims; their stories fit
them and define them. Five tell tales that to us are
frankly and coarsely indecent; but they are Rabelaisian
in their coarseness and not, as nearly all of Boccaccio's,
lascivious.

Most readers agree that the Wife of Bath, frank
though she is, abounds in earthborn wisdom and lusti-
hood of life. Her defence of matrimony and her attack
on the monastic depreciation of women are a welcome
change from the denigration which her sex receives
from the pens of the aging Petrarch and Boccaccio.
Recall one of the Wife's sallies:

> For trusteth wel, it is an impossible
> That any clerk wol speke good of wyves,
>   .   .   .   .

By God! if wommen hadde writen stories,
As clerkes han withinne hire oratories,
They wolde han writen of men
        moore wikkednesse
Than al the mark of Adam [the men]
        may redresse.[15]

And who can forget the witty advice that the hen, "fair
madame Pertelote," gives to her flustered "lord,"
Chauntecleer, who has had a terrifying dream?   The
remedies she prescribes, even to the worms, were those
of the therapeutics of Chaucer's day:

A day or two ye shall have digestyves
Of worms, er ye take your laxatyves.

What has become of the medieval dogma of the infe-
riority of women?

Chaucer is "the first of modern poets to give a large,
complete, and humorous representation of human action."[16] His humor, "mixed and streaked with serious-
ness and tenderness," is characteristically English. On
the technical side, he perfected the five-accent or decasyllabic line.   "The couplets of *The Prologue*," Saintsbury declares, "are the most accomplished, various,
thoroughly mastered verse that we find in Chaucer himself or in any English writer up to his time, while they
are not exceeded by any foreign model unless it be the
terza rima of Dante." He eulogizes Chaucer's inven-

15 *Poetical Works*, p. 99.   16 Ker, *Essays on Medieval Lit-
                                        erature*, p. 100.

tion or perfecting of "the great stanza called rime royal
—that is to say, the seven-lined decasyllabic stanza
rimed ababbcc, which held the premier position for serious verse in English poetry till the Spenserian de-
throned it."[17]

At the end of "The Parson's Tale," a prose sermon
on the seven deadly sins, there is appended in most
manuscripts the so-called "Retractation" of Chaucer,
in which he revokes his writings of "worldy vanitees"
and "many a song and many a leccherous lay," and lists
for condemnation, among others, the innocent "Parliament of Fowls." "I hope," John Masefield remarks,
"that this paragraph is a forged interpolation . . . . We
all know man's weakness, we all suffer from it. But the
great man's strength is the important thing."[18]

Villon.—This chapter, designed to furnish a basis
for a comparison of the achievements of the greater
non-Humanist and the greater Humanist writers from
Dante onward, now reaches Villon, the only first-rate
poet of the otherwise dull fifteenth century.[19]

François Villon was born late in 1431 or in the early
part of 1432, and as an exile departing from Paris
passed into oblivion in January, 1463. He was born

---

17 *Cambridge History of English
Literature,* II: 205, 195. *Cf.*
Robinson's remarks in Chau-
cer, *Poetical Works,* p. 613.

18 Masefield, *Chaucer,* pp. 29–30.

19 François Villon, *Oeuvres,* edited by Longnon, revised by
Foulet; *Oeuvres,* edited by
Thuasne; Lewis, *François
Villon;* Foulet in *Histoire de
la littérature française illustrée* (Bédier and Hazard,
edd.), I: 110–17; *The Complete Works of François Villon,* English verse translation
by Nicolson.

in Paris of poor parents and, when he was about six, was taken into the home and the affections of a worthy cleric, William de Villon, Master of Arts and Bachelor of Canon Law of the University of Paris, chaplain, and sometime reader in law in the University. He taught François the rudiments of Latin—the language of university instruction—, sent him to the University, and allowed him, as a young man, to take his well-respected name. The boy was bright and secured his M.A. in the old-fashioned, scholastic Faculty of Arts when he was twenty or twenty-one. He may have enrolled in the Faculty of Canon Law, but if so he soon dropped out.

William de Villon had social connections with the higher clergy and the royal officials, and François was able to enter the same circles. In these as well as in the University he was early recognized as a budding and rollicking versifier. Other circles also knew him— the tavern, the brothel, and the riotous, rapscallious youth of town and gown. The manners and morals of Paris and the rest of the country had not yet recovered from the demoralization wrought by the English occupation and the Hundred Years' War, and in spite of the fatherly care of his benefactor, François slipped easily into evil ways and became the welcome companion of thieves and harlots. The young man was not inherently vicious, but he was easily led; and as he had no business or profession to steady him, he travelled rapidly down the primrose path.

In 1455, apparently because of rivalry in love, he was attacked by a priest with a knife; Villon killed him

in self-defence. He received a pardon for this homi-
cide, but he was on the books of the police. On the
eve of Christmas, 1456, he was one of a small gang of
hoodlums who robbed the Collège of Navarre of 500
gold crowns. Prudence counselled departure; and partly
because he was a poet and partly because an alibi might
be useful, he wrote his *Lais* (usually called the "Small
Testament"). In this he bemoans the deceitfulness of
the girl of his heart, and in view of his approaching
absence, "caused by her faithlessness," he distributes
his "property" among sundry folk of his acquaintance.
The *Lais* is crammed with wit and irony, with jollity,
confidence, and bravado. The scheme of the work, a
mock will, is old; and the verse forms are also the customary ones. The performance, however, is masterly.

Villon's flight after the robbery of the Collège took
him over a good part of central France and as far south
as Roussillon. He was a vagabond for some five years.
Surviving court records and the avowals of the *(Great)
Testament* and his other poems give a striking although very fragmentary picture of the ups and downs
of his wandering. He visited Charles d'Orléans, the
royal poet, at Blois, and distinguished himself in one of
the prince's poetical tournaments; he became acquainted
with and probably joined the *Cagoulards,* the organized
gang of thieves operating on the highways of France
(similar, it would seem, to the *Apaches* of recent
days); and he was in a dungeon of the bishop of Orléans in 1461, fed on bread and water, subjected to the
torture, and momentarily expecting execution. The

"joyous entry" of Louis XI in 1461 liberated him and
the other prisoners in Orléans. He returned, in hiding,
to the neighborhood of Paris, and there awaited, not in
vain, the success of the efforts of his friends—including
of course his benefactor—to secure for him another
royal pardon. His participation in the robbery of the
Collège of Navarre had been known to the police since
July, 1458.

François seems now (toward the end of 1461) to
have realized that he was done for. An honorable
career was no longer possible, and his health was ruined
by his excesses, privations, and the hardships of his incarceration in Orléans. His youth had suddenly taken
wings, and he felt that he was ambushed by death.[20]
He was only thirty years of age.

In these straits Villon's better self took charge. He
resolved to give to the world his mature thought on life
and death, and he wrote it out in his *(Great) Testament*. "The surprising thing is to see in this feeble
body, emaciated by privations and miseries of every
sort, a spirit so strong, so serene and still capable—of
'laughing through tears.' "[21] The *Testament,* in spite
of its apparently mosaic nature, is a perfectly organized masterpiece.[22] Its ruling themes are disappoint-
ments in love—not the high-falutin love of the troubadours—and horror of sickness, poverty, old age, and

20 *Complete Works* (Nicolson
translation), Verses XXII and
XXIII. Longnon's numbering
varies somewhat from Nicolson's; but the original texts

are easy to find.
21 *Oeuvres* (Thuasne edition),
I: 50–51.
22 For the evidence, see *ibid.,*
pp. 86–92.

death, as well as of the dungeon. Lighter notes are struck by the insertion at suitable points of three *rondeaux* and sixteen ballades, half of them probably composed in the happier days of his gay and careless youth. The most rollicking of these is the "Ballade and Prayer" for the soul of thirsty John Cotard; the most beautiful, and the one which sounds the keynote of the whole composition, it is agreed, is the "Ballade of Dead Ladies," with its haunting refrain (Rossetti's translation) :[23]

But where are the snows of yester-year?

The most devout is the "Ballade to Our Lady," which he wrote for his mother, beginning, in Rossetti's translation:

Lady of Heaven and earth, and therewithal,
Crowned Empress of the nether clefts of hell,
I, thy poor Christian, on thy name do call,
Commending me to thee, with thee to dwell,
Albeit in nought I be commendable.

This moving poem, which it must have comforted her son to write, is surpassed only by his "Ballade of the Hanged." The circumstances under which this poem was written explain its poignancy. After Villon

---

23 The best English translations of the ballads referred to in this section, from John Cotard's on, are conveniently collected in Section IV, "The Cream of the Testaments," of Lewis's *François Villon*.

had finished the *Testament,* and his last royal pardon
or "remission" had been duly enrolled, he felt free to
return to his benefactor's house, but not many weeks
later he was picked up by the police for some theft or
other, though on unclear evidence, and was about to be
released when the theologians of the Collège of Navarre heard of his arrest. They had long since known
of his part in the theft of the 500 gold crowns. The
king's pardon, formally registered, had freed him from
criminal prosecution but not from civil prosecution, *i.e.,*
for debt. François and his sureties—one may guess
that William de Villon was the important one—had to
agree to pay to the Collège a hundred and twenty gold
crowns in installments for the one hundred he had received as his share of the loot before the Collège consented to his release.

In less than a month, however, he was again in the
hands of the police. The facts are well established.
After dining with three cronies at their favorite tavern,
he was present when they, heartened by drink, picked a
quarrel with some scriveners which ended with a dag-
ger thrust at the proprietor of the scriptorium. François
had run home when the fracas began to look serious,
but he had been recognized. He was seized, as were
the real culprits. The Chatelet, patience exhausted,
sentenced him to be "hanged and strangled."

Hanging in those days was the customary conclusion
to the sort of life he had led. Several of the comrades
of his early days had already swung at the end of the
rope. The subject had often engaged his attention. It

was in grim contemplation of this imminent fate that he wrote his powerful "Ballade of the Hanged." The central stanza of the poem, in Swinburne's translation, reads:

> The rain has washed and laundered us all five,
> And the sun dried and blackened; yea, perdie,
> Ravens and pies with beaks that rend and rive
> Have dug our eyes out, and plucked off for fee
> Our beards and eyebrows; never are we free,
> Not once, to rest; but here and there still sped,
> Drive at its wild will by the wind's change led,
> More pecked of birds than fruits on garden-wall:
> Men, for God's love, let no gibe here be said,
> But pray to God that He forgive us all.

But François had not lived with his lawyer benefactor altogether in vain. He appealed to the Parlement of Paris (the supreme court) against the unjust sentence. His appeal was successful and the sentence was quashed, but "in view of the evil life of the said Villon," he was banished from Paris for ten years. He departed and vanished without an authentic trace.

Villon's poetry is of the fifteenth century, but like all great poetry it is of all time—universal. He "bursts into a dying twilit world full of half-poets mumbling their wornout formulae, and creates the first modern poetry in Europe." That is the judgment of his best English biographer.[24] "He is our first modern poet,

24 Reprinted from page 336 of *François Villon* by D. B. Wyndham Lewis. Copyright, 1928, by Coward-McCann,

one of our great poets," declares Foulet.[25] "An intense and suggestive palpitation," says Siciliano, "the vague and magical palpitation of the infinite, vibrates in the lyricism of a poor wretch, the greatest lyrical poet of France."[26]

What was the secret of Villon's greatness, in addition to his poetic genius? It was experience, bitter experience or, if you will, reality. He tells us so in the twelfth stanza of his *Testament*:

> Trouble has ground my wits to bring
> Some points to bear on bawd and bottle,
> And taught me more than any thing
> In Ibn Rushd on Aristotle.[27]

"Miserable people," it has been said, "make the most exciting music." It is a hard truth that a prosperous Villon would not have had the profundity of understanding, the grasp on the poignancy of life, which "the great rascally thief and runner after women" garnered from sorrow and misery. A weak man? Yes; but deadly sincere in his confessions ("Who dies ought

Inc., and used by permission of the publisher.

25 Bédier and Hazard, edd., *Littérature française,* I: 117.

26 Siciliano, *François Villon,* p. 524. Siciliano's belief that Villon merely gave the Middle Ages "a splendid funeral" (*ibid.,* p. xiii) need not detain us here. His idea of the creative power of the Revival

of Learning, which has been set forth in the first chapter of this book, is surely an elaborate *post hoc ergo propter hoc.* But more of this later.

27 *Complete Works* (Nicolson translation), p. 23. Ibn Rushd, or Averroës, was the great commentator on Aristotle, whose many treatises were the chief study of the arts students.

everything to tell")[28]—witness the dreadful Hogarth-
ian "Ballade of Fat Margot"——, grateful to his friends,
loyal to his country ("Ballade against the Slanderers of
France"),[29] and trustful in the everlasting mercy.

As a poet Villon was not a technical innovator. He
employed the literary forms of his day and the language
of his beloved Paris, but what marvelous harmonies
he secured! And the life that he crammed into his
verses in the half-lifetime which was his lot! Compared with him, Petrarch, in his celebrated *Canzoniere,*
seems engrossed in pretty make-believe.

"The Return to the Italian."—The pause in the production of significant Italian literature, which set in
with the death of Boccaccio and lasted almost a century,
seems to have been largely due to the growing repute
of Latin as the only fit vehicle for artistic writings.
Cesare Foligno, a high authority, puts it thus: "As the
most gifted minds of the time were drawn into this
movement [the Revival of Learning], the vernacular
literature was impoverished, and the literature of the
country [being written in Latin] became in great part
independent of the people and incomprehensible to
them."[30] "The professional writers," observes Philippe
Monnier, "have gone over to the enemy; . . . instead of
taking up and transforming the old national *genres,*
they have taken to writing in Latin, betraying the
cause of 'that Italic tongue in which Dante wrote, which

28 *Ibid.,* p. 49.
29 *Ibid.,* pp. 127–28.

30 Foligno, *Epochs of Italian Literature,* p. 17.

is more authentic and worthy of praise than all their Greek and their Latin.' "[31] In their ivory towers, detached from the life of the people, the Humanists strove valiantly to write in the style of the great classical Latin authors. That was their goal and their achievement. Unfortunately, as a rule, they had nothing very important to say, nothing that today interests anyone except the specialists.

Meanwhile, the great majority of the Italian people, knowing only Italian, had to depend for their literary food on what had been written in the past and what the amateurs of their own time could compose. The so-called lower classes, the peasants and the artisans, had their popular songs, old and new, written by Dante and those who came after him, down to "the latest rustic" —sonnets and ballads of all sorts and origins. They had hymns, or "lauds," and simple dramatizations of biblical stories, also the tales recited or chanted by the itinerant story-tellers, the *cantastorii,* who earned their pence by entertaining the crowds, large or small, that were wont to gather in the market places and town squares to listen to them and to the revivalists and to observe the feats of jugglers and dancing bears.

The *cantastorii* had large repertoires of rimed tales, each divided into "chants" or cantos, and broke off at exciting points for the passing of the hat. The tales were of all sorts and all origins, were composed in the standard octave stanza, and lent themselves to occasional improvisations by a talented *cantastorie*. Among these tales a favored place was held by Italian re-vampings of French *chansons de geste,* of which the most celebrated was the "Song of Roland," and of French chivalrous romances revolving around King Arthur and the Knights of the Round Table. These tales had originated in France in the twelfth century and had been imported into all the neighboring lands in the days when French literature led the European procession. In Italy they were at first recited in French, then in partly Italianized French, and, finally, in the various dialects of the north and center of the peninsula. The tales were freely modified by the Italian versifiers, and the heroes were often given Italian origins. The peasantry and the artisans preferred the fight-making of the *chansons* to the love-making of the romances. The upper middle class, aspiring to the rank of gentlemen, and the nobility, who at times invited into their palaces the best of the *cantastorii,* favored the chivalrous romances. But the two genres were not kept distinct by their "vendors"; love and magic crept into the Italian versions of the *chansons,* in which religion and war with the infidel had originally excluded all but a trace of the love element.

Something must also be said about the use of Italian by writers of the middle class. They kept alive the written use of their mother tongue—only a few of them had Latin—in their diaries, memory books, and brief chronicles. They even versified after the fashion of Dante, Petrarch, Boccaccio, and other vernacular poets;

but the vigor of their writings did not equal that of the fourteenth century. No doubt partly because of the "treason" of the intellectuals, Italian now tended to fall "to the rank of an a-literary language, good for commerce and the street, but no longer supporting good usage, and no longer consecrated by any masterpiece."

It tended to fall; Italian literature had sailed into the doldrums. But the winds cannot permanently be stilled. The Humanists might have recalled the vain efforts of Roman writers, at the dawn of the Christian era, to establish the dogma that literature worthy of the name must be written in Greek. The vernaculars, in which men and women make love and express the joys and sorrows of life, in which mothers soothe their children to sleep, are the only true vehicles for literature.

The re-establishment of Italian as the literary language of Italy was hastened by the recantation of leading Humanists in Florence. The earliest of these to see the light was Leon Battista Alberti (1404–1472). He was not only a scholar but a man of affairs—architect, and painter also. In his youth he had written in Latin; subsequently he had employed the mother tongue. Why? The answer is simple; he wanted to be understood by all his fellow citizens. "Prudent men," he said, "will perhaps praise me if, in writing in such a fashion that all can understand me, I prefer to help many than to please a few; for it is known how few the lettered [readers of Latin] are in this day." Other prominent Humanists echoed his thought. Christoforo Landino, best known as a teacher of Lorenzo the Magnificent and as the author of the *Disputationes Camaldulenses,* declared that if Italian lagged somewhat behind Latin, "the only reason is the dearth of excellent writers." Here he was copying Lorenzo the Magnificent.

The decisive blow for the literary employment of Italian had really been struck by Lorenzo, the uncrowned master, the *arbiter elegantiarum,* of Florence. He composed his sprightly verses in the mother tongue and argued for its use: "It is rather that the men who employ the vernacular have been unequal to it than that the vernacular has been unequal to the men and to subject matter." The opposition of the old-line Humanists collapsed in Florence—Florence, which had led in the Revival of Learning; and the rest of Italy followed. The revolution can be dated. In 1481 the government of Florence revoked the decree of exile of the author of the *Divine Comedy* and honors were heaped on his memory.

H. A. L. Fisher has recently and succinctly stated the reason for the change: "The humanism of the Renaissance, unlike those mediaeval types of piety or heroism which are embodied in the Gothic cathedrals or the *Chansons de Geste,* was not popular but aristocratic. The message of the humanist was to the elect. The soul of a people will never be greatly stirred by the religion of the artist or the savant."[32]

32 *A History of Europe,* II: 464.

The re-establishment of Italian as the literary language of Italy was marked by the appearance of three long poetical works, masterpieces respectively of Pulci, Boiardo, and Ariosto.[33]

Luigi Pulci (1432–1484) was an impecunious client and favored dinner companion of Lorenzo the Magnificent and his court. He was not a Humanist, but he was a witty Florentine with a gift for racy speech, anecdote, and verse. Lorenzo's mother asked Luigi to write for her a poem of adventures after the fashion of the Italian *cantastorii* or minstrels. The poem *Morgante Maggiore* was the result. It was finished in 1483 and was read to the court in the course of its composition. It is based on two fifteenth-century Italian recastings of tales of Roland and his peers, that is, upon two "chant-histories" concocted by *cantastorii*. Pulci introduces marvels of his own, but the pleasure his poem gave the court consisted chiefly in his literary treatment of the vivacious materials of his untrained predecessors, a treatment which allowed his listeners to recognize, beneath his more polished lines and along with his jests, the invocations, transitions, and other clichés of his itinerant predecessors. After all, the court of the Medici was a bourgeois court, and the manners

---

33 Foligno, *Epochs of Italian Literature;* Gardner, *The Arthurian Legend in Italian Literature;* Ford, ed., *Romances of Chivalry in Italian Verse;* Edwards, *The Orlando Furioso and its Predecessor;* Ariosto, *Orlando Furioso,* translated by Rose; Gardner, *King of Court Poets . . . Ariosto;* Hauvette, *Littérature italienne;* De Sanctis, *History of Italian Literature;* Monnier, *Le Quattrocento,* Vol. II; Saintsbury, *A History of Criticism,* Vol. I, Bk. III.

of chivalry were to the courtiers something to enjoy
rather than to share.

Matteo Boiardo, Count of Scandiano (1441–1494),
viewed chivalry rather differently. He was an official
of the Este, dukes of Ferrara (Reggio and Modena),
who regarded themselves as the embodiment of the
chivalrous virtues, staged jousts and tournaments,
maintained a considerable armed force for defence
against their powerful neighbors, and had a library
of French *chansons* and romances. Count Matteo was
a poet and a Humanist, although he disclaimed a real
knowledge of Greek. He did not need to "return to
the vernacular," for Ferrara had never abandoned the
literary employment of Italian, and it was in that language that he wrote his shorter poems and comedies
as well as the chivalrous romance which he called *Orlando Innamorato (The Enamored Orlando)*. The
first two books of the *Innamorato* were published in
1486, and thereafter a few cantos were leisurely added.
The work was left broken off (when the French in-
vaded Italy in 1494) with Charlemagne besieged in
Paris by the Saracen host.

The title which Boiardo chose for his masterpiece
was apt. The *Orlando* suggested that the *chansons
de geste* furnished the broad framework for the clash
of great armies, a framework which the episodic nature
of the Arthurian romances could not supply; and the
Innamorato of the title signified the introduction of the
love theme and magic of the romances. This fusion
or marriage of *chanson* and romance, already practiced

by the *cantastorii,* was carried out systematically, with
the romantic element dominating.

The chief figures of the *Innamorato* include those
that tradition demanded, that listeners were accustomed to, and that Pulci presented in his *Morgante*:
Roland, Rinaldo, Astolfo, Oliver, Turpin, and Charlemagne. Yet Pulci and Boiardo are believed to have
worked independently, neither knowing what the other
was doing. The characters in Boiardo's poem act as
gentlemen and ladies, as was fitting for the entertain-
ment of a court that thought of itself as chivalrous. The
magical waters inspiring love and repulsion, the magical
weapons rendering their owners invisible, the disap-
pearances and pursuits, the giants and enchantments,
the doughty contests of rival knights, and the rescues of
beautiful damsels conform to the best traditions of the
Arthurian romances.

The *Orlando Innamorato,* as already indicated, left
the struggle between Charlemagne and the Saracens in
suspense, ready for further developments. These were
furnished in abundance by Ariosto.

Lodovico Ariosto (1474–1533), son of another official of the ducal house of Este, was born in the castle
of Reggio. His father had apprenticed him to the law,
but finally allowed him, when he was twenty, to devote
himself to literature. For livelihood he served the
ducal family in various capacities, commander of the
citadel of Canossa, secretary of Cardinal Ippolito
d'Este, and governor of the mountain fortress of Gar-
fagnana. His bookish education was solidly Humanist;

but he was also widely read in the romantic literature of France, Italy, and Spain. He wrote Latin verse so well that the great Bembo urged him to confine himself to Latin composition. He chose, however, to write his masterpiece, as well as his satires and comedies, in the language which the court and the nobility of the duchy understood.

The *Orlando Furioso* of Ariosto is in a sense a free continuation of Boiardo's romance. In another sense it is an independent work, although referring to events described by Boiardo much as Boiardo had drawn upon the common store of traditional material in the chant-histories. It should not be forgotten that there is no inevitable sequence or culmination to the adventures and love-makings of this type of tale.

The central theme, promised by the title of the work, should have been the madness of Orlando, fitting punishment of the traditional Christian champion for his infatuation with the Saracen Angelica. Actually, however, the center of the stage is more largely concerned with the story of the Christian Roger and the Saracen warrior-princess, Bradamante, whose happy marriage forms the legendary foundation of the ducal house of Este. (The flattery of the Este is none too subtle.) To this central thread is attached a multitude of episodes, begun, intermitted, resumed, and interwoven. There is, we have remarked, no inevitable end to these; they resemble, in their variety and unity, the comic strip which continues for years and years.

The complete *Furioso*, in forty-six revised and polished cantos, was published in 1532. In the English translation of W. S. Rose it runs to almost a thousand pages. The sources of the great work are medieval, classical, and contemporary, all neatly knit together. The external form dear to the *cantastorii* is preserved; but the "invocational space" at the opening of each canto is used by Ariosto for comment and prophecy, which permits him to compliment the Este and other contemporaries and to comment on the great events of the recent past.

The classical element is more potent in Ariosto than in Boiardo. "The true culminating point in the history of the Italian romance of chivalry," says Pio Rajna, the Italian authority, "is represented by the first [the *Innamorato*] rather than by the second *Orlando* [the *Furioso*]. With the poem of the Count of Scandiano ends the natural and spontaneous development of the genus. With the *Furioso,* born of an Italian father, but of a Latin mother, there begins in the stem another branch, which, if it still recognizes the *Chanson de Roland* and the *Roman de Tristan* among its ancestors, nevertheless derives a good part of its blood from the *Aeneid,* from the *Metamorphoses,* and from the *Thebeiad.*"[34]

It was the Latin classics too which are given credit for the disciplining and refining of Ariosto's Italian style. Carducci, a high authority, sums up the argument as follows: "The study and practice of Latin

34 Rajna, *Le fonti dell'Orlando Furioso: ricerche e studi,* p. 39; quoted in Gardner, *King of Court Poets,* p. 266.

poetry disciplined and trained Ariosto (redundantly prosaic and rugged in his first attempt in Italian verse) to that gracious harmony in its easy flow, that elegance in its abundance, which is lacking in other even great Italian poets and is his most special quality. Terence and his acquaintance with the Latin drama have aided Ariosto considerably in the places where his great poem discourses familiarly; Catullus and Horace have polished the most musical of his octaves, and cleared them from those superfluities and excrescences which impede and sometimes suffocate the poetry, for instance, of Boiardo, who, nevertheless, had so much imagination and so much power of representation."[35]

The *Furioso,* then, is a very successful poem. The author has humor and gentle irony; he is only rarely coarse; he smiles indulgently at the extravagances of his chivalrous characters and falls only infrequently into something approaching caricature, as in his handling of the terrestrial paradise and the lunar sphere; and his scenes are depicted with the clarity and beauty of High Renaissance paintings. Yet we are not satisfied. What is lacking? The question may be broadened to include the *Morgante* and the *Innamorato.*

It is a circumstance of some note that Pulci, Boiardo, and Ariosto, whose masterpieces mark "the return to the Italian," chose the chivalrous material of the high Middle Ages in which every class of the Italian people found pleasure, especially the peasants and artisans.

35 Quoted in Gardner, *King of Court Poets,* p. 292.

That fact does signify a rapprochement of a sort between poets and people. The poems entertained the people; but their hearts were not touched. "Most of Raphael's paintings," Cesare Foligno remarks, "have religious subjects, and yet religion had certainly not a primary place in his mind. His saints and madonnas are to him just what chevaleresque knights and adventurers are to Ariosto, the means of giving expression to the beautiful. Both are unsurpassable artists, but both are artists of a period in which art, while it influenced life, did not have its roots in it."[36] Hauvette, speaking of the *Furioso,* expresses a similar thought: "The feebleness of the work, especially when one thinks of the *Divine Comedy,* is the absence of all philosophic thought."[37]

The criticisms apply to all three masterpieces. These works of art do not cast light upon the perennial problems of human destiny or touch the deeper springs of human emotion. The brevity of life, devotion to one's native land, the joys and sorrows of love and friendship, the mystery that envelops human life, the hopes and fears of immortality, the efforts of religion to pierce the veil, the struggles for freedom and justice, the simple courage of the ordinary man, and all the other situations, issues, and enigmas that comfort or confront mankind, "the permanent possibilities of human nature as distinct from the acts of the individual" —few if any of these engage to any appreciable extent

36 Foligno, *Epochs of Italian Literature,* p. 23.

37 Hauvette, *Littérature italienne,* p. 245.

the heart and mind of Pulci, Boiardo, or Ariosto. As a consequence, their masterpieces lack universality, and time has withered them.

True, they have beauty. Vittorio Rossi, the authority on the Italian *Quattrocento*, believes that this came from the Revival of Learning, which, he says, gave to the Italians "the sense of formal beauty" and the skill to express it, even though it tended "to make content vacuous and to accentuate rhetoric and classical ornamentation."[38] Perhaps this is sound; but the main assertion looks dangerously like a *post hoc ergo propter hoc*. To most students of the subject, the sense of beauty, if not of "formal beauty," seems a natural endowment of the Italians. Furthermore, Rossi's opinion is based on a comparison which ignores the decadence which vernacular literature had suffered at the hands of the scornful Humanists. Guglielmo Volpi sees this clearly. "No one," he says, "can say what Italian literature might have become if Humanism had not occurred; but it is permissible to think that the latter hurt more than it helped. If it did nothing else, it arrested the progress of the vernacular."[39]

The argument of this extended chapter may now be drawn together. It is the life-giving or life-enhancing element in any literature that gives it enduring worth. Whence did the great writers we have studied derive it? Surely it was from the life that encompassed them, not from classical works. Consider, briefly, for corroboration, two later literary giants, Cervantes, the author of *Don Quixote,* the world's greatest novel, and Shakespeare, the sublime author of the thirty-six plays. They were contemporaries, and they died within ten days of each other, in April, 1616. Neither of them was a Humanist—a devotee of Latin and Greek literature—, a finished scholar, or a university man.

Shakespeare (1564–1616), "so far from turning aside," says Macneile Dixon, "to essay a new departure, to write plays as scholars, like Sir Philip Sidney, urged they should be written, after classical models, was content to be a man of the people, to remain an Englishman and make the best of it.   In everything—form, method, choice of subjects—he displayed a willingness to follow rather than to lead, and took his country's way. Treading closely . . . in the steps of his predecessors, he was borne aloft on a rising wave of national effort and enthusiasm . . . . Doubtless what others had done he did better, yet it was his country's wealth he gathered in . . . . Where is it to be supposed he found the models from which he studied human nature but in the London streets and Warwickshire villages? . . . And not the human face alone, but that of the countryside, the Cotswold wheat-fields and Stratford meadows, the trees and flowers, the birds and beasts of our English Midlands."[40] "Who in the world is like Shakespeare?" asks E. E. Stoll; and he answers, "Why, Chaucer, and Fielding, and Scott, and the English people."[41]

40 Dixon, *The Englishman,* pp. 199–201.

41 Stoll, *Shakespeare and Other Masters,* pp. 306–7.

The situation with Cervantes (1547–1616) is much the same. Ormsby, who made the only satisfactory English translation of *Don Quixote* (first published in 1901), characterizes the novel as "a mine of shrewd observation on mankind and human nature. Among modern novels there may be, here and there, more elaborate studies of character, but there is no book richer in individualized character. What Coleridge said of Shakespeare *in minimis* is true of Cervantes; he never, even for the most temporary purpose, puts forward a lay figure. There is life and individuality in all his characters . . . ."[42] Anyone who recalls the varied contacts of Cervantes with all classes of the Spanish people will be inclined to agree with Madariaga that "that which gives the work [*Don Quixote*] its immortal value, is the creative spirit of the race, as manifest in Cervantes' predecessors . . . ."[43] The development of Madariaga's argument is even more enlightening.

"The Spanish Golden Century—like its English counterpart, the Elizabethan Age—," Madariaga explains, "was in effect an epoch in which a splendid outburst of spontaneous and creative vitality coincided with an exceptional interest in and knowledge of classical and Italian models. The two events were so evenly timed together that . . . we imagine them as two different aspects of the same fact, namely, the blossoming out of a brilliant artistic era . . . . Yet it is, I believe, helpful . . . to realize that we are in the presence of two

---

42 Cervantes, *Don Quixote*, translated by John Ormsby, I:lxxi.

43 Madariaga, *Don Quixote*, p. 46.

different phenomena, two different currents of spirit which happened to manifest themselves in the same men. The one is a purely vital and creative movement, which reveals the national soul seeking expression in spontaneous forms of art harmonious with her own genius. It is rooted in the genuine national forms, the most popular. It hails from the *Cantar de Myo Cid* and the *Mester de Juglaría*. It is linked with the Great Century by . . . the great Archpriest of Hita, the Archpriest of Talavera, La Celestina and the oral tradition of the ballads. It is romantic in inspiration, free and purely aesthetic in its outlook, and though tainted here and there with erudition in its actual creations, it owes nothing in its essence to Greece or Rome, still less to Italy or France."[44]

The conclusions of this chapter could not be more effectively stated.

44 *Ibid.,* pp. 42–43.

CHAPTER VI: THE GREEK RENAISSANCE

In the preceding chapter an effort was made to determine what influence the Revival of Learning, mainly a
Latinistic one, had upon the production of significant
literature, especially that in the Italian vernacular.
There is another and adverse claim to be examined before we are done with literature, namely this: that it was
the renewed study of classical Greek literature which
was the seminal force. Every so often one encounters
obiter dicta like the following, which appeared the
other day in the *Saturday Review of Literature:* "Renaissance culture was the marriage of Christendom

with the intellectual curiosity and restlessness of ancient Greece."[1]

The volume entitled *The Legacy of Greece*[2] elaborates this very claim. Arnold Toynbee, for example, says, "The Renaissance was a study and assimilation not only of Ancient Greek literature and art, but of architecture, natural science, mathematics, philosophy, political ideas, and all the other higher expressions of a great society. The absorption of this vast current of life largely accounts for the wonderful impetus which has revealed itself in Western civilization during the last four centuries."[3] Percy Gardner remarks that in the Renaissance, "the pessimism of the Middle Ages . . . gave way before the revival of Greek literature and art. The world seemed suddenly to have renewed its youth."[4]

Professor Livingstone, the editor, is almost equally sure: "At the Renaissance as in the eighteenth century, Greece found the world in chains, and broke them and threw them down the prison walls. The fetters of the two epochs were different, but freedom was brought, at the Renaissance partly, and in the age of Winckelmann entirely, by the vision of beauty which Greece exhibited."[5] Manifestly this claim of the Renaissance for Greece must be scrutinized.

Few scholars of European history are in ignorance of the long-range pedagogical role of Greece in the

1 Issue of 7 September 1946.
2 Edited by Livingstone.
3 Livingstone, ed., *The Legacy*
of Greece, p. 294.
4 *Ibid.*, p. 383.
5 *Ibid.*, p. 285.

development of European civilization, beginning with that of conquering Rome. Rostovtzeff's statement will not be seriously gainsaid: "The infectious character of Greek civilization had also a powerful influence on the creation of Western European civilization, chiefly in Italy and, to some extent, in Gaul and Spain. The Latin culture of Italy and the West is one branch of the Greek culture of the third and later centuries— not a slavish copy, nor an imitation, but an independent national development of Greek ideas, Greek art, and Greek literature in the Latin West . . . ."[6] And in the closing paragraph of the penultimate chapter of his second volume, Rostovtzeff takes leave of the ancient world with these (and other) moving words: "Though that world grew old, it never died and never disappeared: it lives on in us, as the groundwork of our thought, our attitude toward religion, our art, our social and political institutions, and even our material civilization." A large number of supporting statements could be cited. Alfred North Whitehead, for instance, has said, "Latin literature is the translation of Hellenic culture into the mediaeval modes of thought, extending that period to end with the French Revolution. Throughout that whole period culture was backward looking."[7] Here we have frank assertion of our debt to Greece, but not a whisper about the Renaissance or the revival of the study of classical Greek in Italy or in

6 Rostovtzeff, *A History of the*   7 *Adventures of Ideas*, p. 67.
  Ancient World, I: 382.

Europe.   Let us retrace our steps and examine the
revivals of Greek literature.

In the early years of the sixth century Boethius (*ca.*
480–524), conscious of the progressive decline in the
study of Greek in the West, formed the ambitious de-
sign of translating all important Greek works into
Latin.   He had not got very far with it when King
Theodoric clipped the thread of his life. The next important effort to get closer to the Greek sources came
in the twelfth and thirteenth centuries, when Greek
works in philosophy, mathematics, medicine, natural
science, and theology were translated into Latin via the
Arabic and directly.[8] The outstanding feature of this
development was the restatement of Christian theology
by Thomas Aquinas on the basis of Aristotelian science.
It is to be noted that classical Greek works in literature and history were virtually ignored.   The age was
very "practical."

The third wave of effort to make Greek thought
more accessible to the West owed its inspiration to
Petrarch and Boccaccio and its effective commencement
to Manuel Chrysoloras, who was brought from Constantinople to Florence in 1397 to teach Greek in the
University.   He remained for only three years, but he
was followed by other talented Greeks, of whom the
most impressive was Georgios Gemistus Pletho, who
came West with the Greek emperor and his theologians

8 Haskins, *The Renaissance of
the Twelfth Century*—especially Chaps. IX and X — and
*Studies in the History of Med-
iaeval Science*—especially
Chap. VIII; Loomis, *Medieval
Hellenism.*

to attend the Council of Ferrara-Florence (1438–
1439). The growing Italian interest in Greek also led
Italians to study in Constantinople and brought about
the importation into Italy of hundreds of manuscripts
of the classical Greek authors. Nicholas V (pope, 1447–
1455), resuming the programme of Boethius, selected
a group of translators—Italians and also Greeks—to
turn into Latin a considerable number of important
Greek books. Indeed, the translation of a Greek work
into Latin became an almost obligatory chore for each
Italian Humanist in the second half of the fifteenth
century, and the invention of printing enabled them to
spread their translations before the lettered public.[9]

The list of Latin translations of Greek writings
printed by 1492 is long; but as Firmin-Didot notes,[10]
they consist principally of works on philosophy, morals,
and history—that is, of a limited portion of Hellenic
literature. "The great dramatic authors, Aeschylus,
Sophocles, Euripides, Aristophanes, remained unknown,
and it is these principally which bear witness to the
incomparable sublimity of the Greek genius." Down
to 1492 only four profane Greek authors were printed
in the original Greek: Aesop, Theocritus, Homer, and
Isocrates.[11]

It was not until 1498–1515 that this defect was sub-

9 Voigt, *Die Wiederbelebung des classischen Alterthums;* Sandys, *A Short History of Classical Scholarship;* Livingstone, ed., *The Legacy of Greece;* Monnier, *Le Quattrocento,* Vol. II.

10 Firmin-Didot, *Alde Manuce et l'Hellénisme à Venice,* pp. xliii–xlv; Monnier, *Le Quattrocento,* Vol. II, Chap. v.

11 Firmin-Didot, *Alde Manuce,* pp. xlv, xliii.

stantially corrected with the publication, in beautiful editions, of Greek masterpieces by Aldo Manuzio (1450–1515) and his learned collaborators of the distinguished Aldine Press in Venice. As a consequence of this late appearance of the greater Greek works—at the very time, it is important to note, when Italian zeal for Greek scholarship had cooled[12]—it is obvious that they cannot account for the culture of the Italian *Quattrocento*. It is further obvious that it is to the Latin translations from the Greek that we must turn to discover the significance of the Greek revival in fifteenth-century Italy and to test the value of the assertions of the contributors to *The Legacy of Greece*. The results are well summarized in three quotations.

Samuel Lee Wolff, in his searching review of J. P. Mahaffy's Lowell Lectures of 1908–1909, which were entitled *What Have the Greeks Done for Modern Civilization,* reaches this conclusion: "The literature of the Renaissance, both in and out of Italy, is four-fifths of it Latinistic—Virgilian, Ciceronian, Senecan, occasionally Horatian, very heavily Ovidian. It springs not immediately, often not mediately, from Homer, Demosthenes, Pindar, Aeschylus, Sophocles, or even Euripides. The other fifth, which does draw nourishment from Greek literature, draws it from the Greek literature not of the golden but of the silver and the pinchbeck ages." "It seems well within the truth to say that when Renaissance literature is Greek at all, it is almost

12 Monnier, *Le Quattrocento,* II: 138 f.

certain to be in the Alexandrianized, Romanized, By-
zantinized, and Orientalized vein that we call Greek
only because we have no better name for it."[13]

Philippe Monnier, a very friendly critic, explains the
matter thus: "The innumerable translations [from the
Greek], which constitute one of the principal branches
of the activity of the Humanists, were severely judged
by the vigorous criticism of the sixteenth century and by
contemporary German philology: people no longer
[bother to] count the errors, point out the mistakes,
underline the blunders; the individual physiognomy of
the writer is not respected; a continuous flood of uniform magniloquence submerges and drowns it. But
that which the modern age blames Italian humanism
for, Italian humanism counted as a merit, persuaded as
it was that Greek, the teacher of Latin, was only in
some sort a superior Latin . . . ."[14]

Louise Loomis substantially agrees: "But there was
no serious effort to determine the Greek point of view,
which was supposed as a matter of course to have been
the same as the Roman . . . . Such writing as was produced in Italy, comparable at all in straightforward
originality and acumen to the Greek, *was prompted by
the stress and stir of contemporary life* and except in
surface embellishments shows little effect of the Greek
Renaissance."[15]

It appears, therefore, that the claim of the Italian

13 *The Nation* (U.S.A.), 7 April
   1910.
14 Monnier, *Le Quattrocento,*
   II: 134.

15 Loomis in *American Historical Review,* XIII: 257-58.
   Italics mine.

Renaissance for Greece will not stand up. Further evidence to that effect, probably even more cogent, will be found in an examination of the work of Ficino, the leader of the Platonic Academy of Florence, the most celebrated of the Italian foundations concerned with Greek thought. This will be presented, against a background of Thomist and Ockhamist thought, in Chapter VIII.

CHAPTER VII: HISTORY

The best brief treatise on medieval historiography was written a few years ago by Charles Homer Haskins. It forms the eighth chapter of his *Renaissance of the Twelfth Century* and is entitled "Historical Writing." The last paragraph of the chapter will form a good introduction to this section: "By 1200 vernacular history had come to stay, and this fact is one of more than linguistic or literary significance, since it involved ultimately the secularization and popularization of history. So long as history was confined to Latin, it perforce remained primarily an affair of the clergy and reflected their preoccupations and view of the world. When it came to be written for laymen, it must make its appeal to them, first at the courts which gave its writers their support, later in the towns whose chronicles meet us in the later period of the Middle Ages . . . ."[1] Molinier declares that "the historical literature in the French tongue is no less abundant in the thirteenth century than that in Latin and includes several works of the first rank."[2]

The most interesting of the vernacular chronicles of the thirteenth century are those of Villehardouin and Robert of Clari, which report on the Fourth Crusade, and of Joinville, which deals with the crusading of King Louis IX. All three are the work of laymen who participated in the events they narrate, and all have been translated from the original French into English.[3] How the form of these writings was developed out of the vernacular prose tale or story and in some measure out of the vernacular epics and romances of the preceding century—with which they were designed to compete—is set forth in the introductions of the translators.

When history came to be written for the laity, Haskins has said, it had to be written in the vernacular. Also, it had to deal, more and more, with the affairs of

1 Haskins, *The Renaissance of the Twelfth Century,* p. 275.

2 Molinier, ed., *Les sources de l'histoire de France,* Vol. V, p. cix.

3 Marzials, trans., *Memoirs of the Crusades by Villehardouin and De Joinville;* Robert of Clari, *The Conquest of Constantinople,* translated by McNeal.

this world, with which laymen had to wrestle. That is, as time passed, the secular element grew, and the other-worldly element—in Croce's phrase, the "medieval transcendency"—shrank and fell into the background and ultimately out of the historical picture. That does not mean that the clerical historical writers had not rendered immense service to medieval and modern historiography. In the first place, under the influence of Christianity, they broke with the antique idea of the perpetual return of human affairs to their starting point, the cyclical theory, in favor of progress toward and under the guidance of God. In the second place, they viewed this progress as involving all humanity, and consequently they regarded history as properly universal. The clerical writers were not always faithful to this view, "but the new idea of history as the spiritual drama of humanity remains."[4] Remains? It is now central in the hopes of mankind for a peaceful world.

Froissart.—The fourteenth century is notable for the number and quality of the writers in the vernacular. Among the historians, the outstanding figure is Froissart. Sir John Froissart (*ca.* 1337–*ca.* 1404) was born in Valenciennes, then in the Netherlands, of bourgeois parents. (His "Sir" is that of a priest, not of a knight.) While still in his teens, he attached himself to Philippa of Hainault (also born in Valenciennes), queen of Edward III of England, and went to England

4 Croce, *The Theory and History of Historiography,* pp. 205 ff.

as a poet-courtier. There he spent five years, associating with the royal court, the captive King John of
France, and the scores of French noblemen who were
with him awaiting ransom. The dominant subject of
this, his first stay in England, was naturally the war
which we know today as the Hundred Years' War, and
Froissart ultimately decided to spend his life in de-
scribing it. The result was his justly celebrated *Chronicles,*[5] which he wrote in French. He continued to compose amatory verse; indeed, he thought more of it
than of his histories, but posterity has judged otherwise.

Froissart was a priest, and his noble patrons gave
him Church livings as well as direct financial aid. He
never lacked a patron. This happy situation was due in
part to the desire of every great noble to have his
prowess figure in the historian's book, and in part to
Froissart's personal charm. "As regards his personal
character, Froissart depicts it himself for us. Such as
he was in youth, he tells us, so he remained in more
advanced life; rejoicing mightily in dances and carols,
in hearing ministrels and poems; inclined to love all
those who love dogs and hawks; pricking up his ears
at the uncorking of bottles . . . ; pleased with good
cheer, gorgeous apparel and joyous society, but no commonplace reveller or greedy voluptuary,—everything in
Froissart was ruled by the good manners which he set

5 Best English translation by
Lord Berners (first published
in 1523), edited by Ker;
Everyman's Library version
condensed from the Johnes
translation); Shears, *Froissart,*
Chronicler and Poet; Coulton,
The Chronicler of European
Chivalry; Molinier, ed., *Les*
sources de l'histoire de France,
Vols. IV, V.

before all else; and always eager to listen to tales of war and battle."[6]

Froissart's *Chronicles* cover the period 1325–1400. For 1325–55, the span prior to the battle of Poitiers (1356), Froissart depends on the excellent chronicle of his fellow countryman, the worthy John of Liége— priest, father of children, and warrior. Some of Froissart's best pages come from his predecessor, but Froissart supplemented and corrected him with additional information secured from participants, and honorably gave John credit for the borrowed material. From Poitiers onward Froissart made his own narrative, collecting his facts from the men, on both sides of the wars, who had taken part in them. As the central conflict, between France and England, drew in the neighboring countries, he broadened his canvas to include them. As a result we see, as in a series of dramatic pictures, the striking happenings of three-quarters of a century in France, England, Scotland, Ireland, and Flanders. Many details touch the affairs of the rival popes of Rome and Avignon and the affairs of Spain, Portugal, Italy, and more distant lands. The theme of it all is the life of the nobility—their wars, battles, stratagems, ravages, tournaments, and festivals. The names of the contestants are usually given. That interested them and interests us. Froissart was, in Coulton's phrase, "the chronicler of European chivalry."

Froissart's sources, it has already been indicated,

6 Besant, on Froissart in *Ency-clopaedia Britannica,* 11th ed.

were mainly the oral accounts of participants. He was tireless in securing such firsthand information. He spent months in Scotland, royally entertained; he went to Gascony with the Black Prince and to Milan with the duke of Clarence; he crossed France from Valenciennes to the court of Gaston de Foix at Orthez, in the Pyrenees, to get the southwestern point of view; he revisited England. Wherever preparations for great military or naval movements were on foot, there he was to be found. Never was any priest less sedentary. As his sources were chiefly oral, so too, in a sense, is his narrative, for he undertakes, whenever feasible, to give us the very words of the doers. The result is a dramatic pageant. The choicest bits are doubtless the description of the Battle of Poitiers, Edward III's anger at the burghers of Calais (from John of Liége) and his courting of the Countess of Salisbury, the revolt of Wat Tyler and his death, and the oatmeal of the Scottish raiders (from John of Liége). The latter two are stock pieces in English history.

A significant feature of the *Chronicles* of Froissart is the author's attitude toward causation. It must be granted that he is more concerned with the event than with its cause or significance, but he does from time to time touch upon causation. When he does, he seeks a rational explanation. His predecessors and most of his contemporary chroniclers were wont to surmount the difficulty of investigating complicated origins by alleging the intervention of God. Thus, according to a contemporary, the defeat of the French at Crécy was due to God's anger at the indecorous dress of the French nobility.[7] Was it the growth of realism that led Froissart to avoid such reasoning or rather lack of reasoning? He does not examine the problem of the relation of so-called "secondary causes" to God's purposes, but he seems to have realized that the ascription of events to God's will is no explanation; that it is rather an evasion of the historian's task.

Froissart's method of collecting his material involved him in errors of fact. What does it really matter? He shows us with color and vivacity the life of the chivalry of western Europe during three quarters of a century of agitated action. Sir Walter Scott's judgment still stands up: "In Froissart we hear the gallant knights, of whom he wrote, arrange the terms of combat and the manner of the onset; we hear their soldiers cry their war-cries; we see them strike their horses with the spur; and the liveliness of the narration hurries us along with them into the whirlwind of battle. We have no hesitation to say, that a skirmish before a petty fortress, thus told, interests us more than the general information that twenty thousand Frenchmen bled on the field of Cressy. This must ever be the case, while we prefer a knowledge of mankind to a mere acquaintance with their actions; and so long also must we account Froissart the most entertaining, and perhaps the most valuable historian of the middle ages."[8]

---

7 Shears, *Froissart*, pp. 108–9; Coulton, *The Chronicler of European Chivalry*, for contemporary illustrations.

8 Froissart, *Chronicles* (Everyman's Library edition), pp. vii–viii.

Commines.—"The only good histories," Montaigne has said, "are those that are written by such as commanded or were themselves employed in weighty affairs, or were participants in conducting them, or at least have had the fortune to conduct other affairs of the same sort."[9] In this select group Montaigne places Commines. The dictum would seem to exclude Froissart, were it not for Montaigne's readiness to contradict himself, and for the praise which he gives "the good Froissart" in the same chapter for his honesty and his representation of the different reports which were made to him "so that each reader may profit in proportion to his understanding." The dictum can only be accepted as proof that Montaigne attached great importance to the reports of participants in "weighty affairs." Such a participant Commines pre-eminently was.

Philippe de Commines (1445 ?–1511 ?)[10] was another Netherlander. He was a member of the higher nobility of Flanders; in his boyhood he became squire to the future Charles the Bold, Duke of Burgundy; and when the latter succeeded to the duchy in 1467, the young man became his chamberlain and most intimate counsellor. As squire he had been privy to his master's efforts, in alliance with other turbulent French princes

9 *Essays,* Bk. II, Chap. x.

10 *Mémoires de Philippe de Commynes,* edited with a valuable introduction by Mandrot; *The History of Commines* (an English translation of the *Mémoires* made by Thomas Dannett in 1596) ; Molinier, ed., *Les sources de l'histoire de France,* Vol. V; Fueter, *Geschichte der neueren Historiographie;* Henry O. Taylor, *Thought and Expression in the Sixtenth Century,* Vol. I, Chap. x.

of the blood, to increase the lands of the Burgundian duchy at the expense of the French king, Louis XI (1461–1483), and had participated in the Battle of Montlhéry, which was confusedly won by the allied princes. It was, says Sainte-Beuve, a sort of parody of the battle of Poitiers, for chivalry was now in full decay. He was present at the meeting of Charles the Bold and Louis XI at Péronne in 1467, the celebrated "episode of Péronne." There the wily king, confident of his skill in cajolery, put himself in the power of the duke, forgetting that his own emissaries, at the very time of the meeting, were successfully persuading the citizens of Liége to rebel against the duke, thus violating the terms of the safe-conduct which the king had received from the duke. This meeting gave the youthful Commines an insight into the characters of the rivals, revealed at a moment of highest tension, which he never forgot. Commines and the other advisers of the incensed duke finally succeeded in persuading him to honor the safe-conduct and content himself with great territorial and other concessions from the king.

In 1472 Commines left the camp of the duke in Normandy—the associated princes were again in revolt—and slipped away to enter the service of Louis XI, thus deserting the vassal for the overlord. He had concluded that the patient, calculating, astute, treaty-making, and treaty-circumventing king would be a better and more successful master than the headstrong and violent duke. The king was certainly a better paymaster, for he heaped riches on his new counselor.

(Had the king secretly demonstrated his generosity at Péronne? We do not know. But we do know that in his *Mémoires* Commines commends the policy of giving pensions to the advisers of rivals.) Thus, at the age of twenty-seven or thereabouts Commines became the intimate counsellor of Louis XI, sharing his secrets and serving him in all of his affairs. Their fundamental political views were harmonious: the king was to centralize the state; the insubordinate and pleasure-loving nobility were to be brought to heel; and the middle class was to be cultivated as the firmest support of the monarchy. Both men were astute and resourceful and studied the opponents of the monarchy at home and abroad. Commines was sent on many missions and learned the strong and weak sides of the other rulers at first hand or through their ministers. Commines and his master had sharpened each other for nearly twelve years when the king died in 1483.

Under Louis's immediate successors, Charles VIII (1483–1498) and Louis XII (1498–1514), Commines lost his position of chief adviser to the king. This loss was due, for a time, to a very unusual misreading of the political barometer by Commines. He had supported the intrigues of the Duke of Orléans (the future Louis XII) against Anne of Beaujeu, the talented daughter of Louis XI, who was serving as regent for her young brother, Charles VIII, during his minority. Commines paid for his blunder by spending several months as a prisoner in one of the iron cages which Louis XI had built to display captive nobles in. He

was not embittered or despondent; in fact, he learned
his lesson and again was admitted to the service of the
crown. But he was not able to dissuade Charles VIII
from his wrong-headed invasion of Italy in 1494, and
he had to be content with helping to extricate that
feeble and romantic monarch from the Italian trap into
which he had marched. Under Louis XII, Commines's
rôle was increasingly minor.

It was doubtless the loss of his influence and the
errors of the government of Charles VIII which led
Commines to write his *Mémoires,* which were designed
to teach the future rulers of France the lessons which
he had learned while serving Charles the Bold and
Louis XI. The bulk of the *Mémoires*—the first six
books, which cover the period 1464–83—was written
in 1490–91. The last two books, an appendix of a
sort, dealt with the invasion of 1494 and were drafted
and revised in 1495–98. They are written in the colloquial French of the time. Commines has expressed
regret that his education, which was slender and "chivalrous," did not include Latin and Greek; but Sainte-
Beuve, in his *Causeries,* says Commines was lucky, for
it was easier for him to throw off the "pedantic rhetoric" of the age. "He had not had any more education than La Rochefoucauld, only that of men and affairs; for well-constituted minds that is the best education and it suffices."

The *Mémoires* are a sort of history of the times of
Commines, with emphasis on the conduct of the main
actors, stress on causes and results, and wise comment

on lessons to be learned. "My selfe for my part," Commines writes, "have seene some experience in the world, having beene by the space of eighteene yeares and better, emploied continually in Princes services, and privie all that while to the waightiest and secretest affaires that have passed in this realme, or the countries bordering upon it, and sure in mine opinion the best way to learne wisedome is to read ancient histories, which will teach us by example of our auncestors, wisely to behave our selves, safely to defend our selves, and advisedly to attempt any enterprise. For our life is so short that experience cannot sufficiently instruct us . . . ."[11] Commines appears as a modest participant reporter. Vanity is not his weakness nor panegyric of Louis XI his purpose. He has studied in the school of the shrewdest of kings and will tell what he has learned. Louis XI teaches how a successful monarch should behave; Charles the Bold and Charles VIII show the errors that a statesman should avoid. The book of Commines is a French classic, and it has been translated into many languages.

Commines, it need hardly be said, lacks the color and vivacity of Froissart. The warlike ardors of the nobility interest him not. Their conduct at the Battle of Montlhéry opened his eyes and, with the history of the Hundred Years' War before him, he conceived a great distaste for war, the curse of the Middle Ages. Knightly honor, forsooth! "He who has the profit has

11 Bk. II, Chap. VI (Dannett translation).

the honor," Commines declares. The diplomats, he was sure, did a better job than the generals. Trickery—or as he would say, ruse—and moderation were altogether preferable to war.

Unlike Machiavelli, Commines sketches no political system, but in his praise of the English government it is easy to discern the lineaments of the form of government which he believed in. Taxes should be voted by the representatives of the people; they should not be imposed (as they were in France) by the king. The Estates should meet regularly. The discussions in parliament strengthened the government and saved the country from the influence of sycophantic whisperers in the royal ear, prating of the boundless authority of the king and urging him on to mistaken courses. Somehow the English managed affairs better. In the War of the Roses it was the nobility and not the poor people who paid with their blood. There were too many ruins in France. It is clear that Commines favored what came to be known as a limited monarchy.

Commines had no doubts about the truths of Christianity. He believed in the divine government of the world. He points out that Providence has provided a check on the overambitious state by surrounding it with rivals. "Look closely," remarks Foulet, "and you will see that Providence is necessary to his system of interpreting the facts . . . . He appreciates cleverness, foresight, wisdom so strongly, he is so persuaded that the world is governed by these virtues, that whenever carelessness, ignorance, fickleness register a success, he is tempted to cry out that that is not playing the game, and he has to confirm his confidence in his skill by invoking the impenetrable designs of Providence. And the more so because Providence seems to lean toward the side of the kingdom of France."[12]

The *Mémoires,* we have said, lack the color and vivacity of Froissart. They are, however, extraordinarily interesting. The preposterous features of the Battle of Montlhéry, the tension of the episode of Péronne, the craftiness of Louis XI, who "made greater war upon Charles the Bold by letting him go his own way and in secret creating enemies for him than if he had openly declared against him," the joy of the king at the news of the death of the duke, which was so great as to be thought indecent, the suspiciousness and bizarre efforts of the dying king to circumvent approaching death—these are only high spots in an engrossing story.

Commines has of course been compared with Machiavelli. The Italian is more theoretical, more pessimistic, more brilliant, and less wise. The "Machiavellism" which can be found in Commines is of the native, home-grown, French variety, uninfluenced by Machiavelli or Italian Humanism. In fact, both Machiavelli and Guicciardini were indebted for some of their ideas to the French statesman, who preceded them in time and publication.[13] This is a matter of some importance, as will

---

12 Foulet in *Littérature française* (Bédier and Hazard, edd.), I : 120.

13 See Fueter, *Historiographie,* pp. 150 f.

appear after we have studied the histories of Machiavelli and Guicciardini; but before doing so we must consider the earlier medieval historical writings of Italy.

Dino Compagni.—Medieval historical activities in
Italy, as in the other regions of the West, broadened
into vernacular chronicles in the thirteenth century. For
Italy these have been analyzed by Ugo Balzani.[14] Two
of them, composed in the first half of the fourteenth
century, are of outstanding merit; they were written by
two Florentines, Dino Compagni and Giovanni Villani,
both contemporaries of Dante.

Dino Compagni (*ca.* 1260–1324) was a successful
and public-spirited silk merchant of Florence. He was
a prior several times, and in 1293 was Gonfalonier of
Justice, head of the state, when the Ordinances of Justice were enacted. (These established a democratic,
middle-class control of the government.) Along with
Dante and others he was a prior in the fatal year, 1301,
when, with the connivance of Pope Boniface VIII, the
democratic government of the city was overthrown,
and its leaders exiled, by the magnates—the big merchants. The announcement of the coming of the emperor, Henry VII, into Italy, which took place in 1310,
stirred the exiled Dante to write his *De Monarchia*; it
had a similar effect on Compagni. He resolved to tell
the story of the division of the people of Florence, all
of them technically members of the Guelf Party in

14 Balzani, *Le cronache italiane nel medio evo.* This is a revision of an English version of the same work.

1293, into two factions, the more democratic *Whites* and the predominantly aristocratic *Blacks,* and of the dire results of the division. The subject Compagni selected to write about was well chosen; he had participated in or witnessed nearly all its phases; for, although a *White* and a leader, he had by a lucky technicality escaped exile. Thus he was able to describe the consequences of the overthrow of the *Whites* upon the inner as well as the outer life of the city. He called his book, which he wrote in 1310–12, *The Chronicle of Dino Compagni on the Events of his Times.*[15]

Compagni's *Chronicle* falls naturally into three divisions. In the first part, the author reaches back to 1280, when the Guelf Party was establishing its control of the city, and tells of the subsequent progress of middle-class democracy which culminated in the Ordinances of Justice. In the second part, he discusses the rise of the aristocratic faction, the party of the magnates, the *Blacks,* within the Guelf Party, and their struggle with the middle-class party, the *Whites*, which ended with the overthrow of the latter in 1301. In the final part, he sketches the troubles of the city, within and without, under the ensuing regime of the *Blacks;* and in the very last paragraph, he hurls his maledictions at the iniquitous citizens and predicts, too hopefully, their punishment by the oncoming emperor.

Compagni's book is a well-constructed monograph with an introduction, a middle, and a conclusion. He

15 *La cronica di Dino Compagni delle cose occorrenti ne' tempi suoi,* edited by Lungo; translated as *The Chronicle of Dino Compagni* by Benecke and Howells.

states his purpose at the outset—to write the truth concerning those things of which he was certain, through
having seen and heard them, and for those things which
he did not clearly see, to write according to the most
authentic report—and then he begins with a description
of the land and the people of Florence. The reasoning
is good, the argument persuasive. The book obviously
is not a chronicle as we understand the term, the type
which records important events of all sorts, year by
year. Why, then, does he call it a chronicle? Lungo,
his learned editor, gives the answer: In Compagni's
day *cronica* was a generic name for historical writings
of every sort. Lungo observes that Compagni gives a
factual account of the events which Dante handles
allegorically in his *Divine Comedy*. In short, Compagni,
although passionately committed to a *White* interpretation, is an indispensable source for the history of
his and Dante's times. Yet his book could not serve as
a source for some two centuries. The heat of the passions that burned in Florence in those years made the
outspoken book, naming persons and offences, dangerous; and Compagni and his descendants for generations
prudently kept it hidden.

Giovanni Villani.—No such danger was attached to
Giovanni Villani's chronicle, which was written from a
Black, a moderate *Black*, point of view. It is the second
great source for Dante's times.[16]

16 The relevant parts, chosen to
serve as an aid to the study
of Dante, are translated into
English by Selfe and Wick-

Giovanni Villani (*ca.* 1276–1348) was another merchant of Florence. He was a member of the influential Calimala guild and thrice occupied the high office of prior. The papal jubilee of 1300 attracted him to Rome, and the monuments of its past and fading glories inspired him to write the story of his own flourishing and resplendent city, which all Florentines regarded as the great daughter and heir of Rome. He would write not only of Florence, but of all the world with which the merchants of Florence traded. He seems to have felt competent to write in Latin, for he says in his first paragraph that he decided to use "the plain vernacular"—that of Florence—in order that "the laity as well as the lettered" might derive "fruit and delight" from his book. He himself was somewhat of a traveller, ranging from Naples to Flanders; his fellow merchants brought him news from the commercial centers of Europe and the Levant; the city intrusted many important tasks to him; but his spare time, from 1300 to the day of his death, was given over to the collection of material for and the actual writing of his book. It is the most important of all the Italian chronicles, perhaps of all the European chronicles, of the Middle Ages.[17]

The chronicle starts out with the Tower of Babel

steed under the title, *Villani's Chronicle, Being Selections.* . . . See also Lungo, ed., *Le più belle pagine di Dino Compagni e di Giovanni Villani.*
17 *Cronica di Giovanni Villani,* edited by Gherardi Dragomanni. *Cf.* Schevill, *History of Florence:* "Introduction on Florentine Historiography" and Chap. xv, "Seeing Florence with Giovanni Villani."

and comes down, through Troy, Aeneas and Dido, Rome, Fiesole, Florence, Charlemagne, Barbarossa, and others to the Countess Matilda of Tuscany. This "antique" section is of course traditional and fanciful. The ground becomes less treacherous when the author reaches the countess, and it is surprisingly firm for his own times, that is, from about 1280 to his death in the Great Pestilence, 1348. (His brother and his brother's son in turn continued the chronicle down to 1364; but their contribution must be passed over.) The events discussed by Compagni receive due attention from Giovanni, but from the *Black* point of view. The two accounts supplement each other admirably. Villani, however, is concerned with all sorts of happenings, at home and abroad. "His immense achievement," Ferdinand Schevill well says, "is the accurate description of the town under his eyes, his story of its trade, its industry, its social classes, its religious customs, its relation to its neighbors, its ceaseless and passionate domestic conflicts."[18]

Villani describes at length the adornment of the city with new churches and public buildings, the rebuilding of the great bridge over the Arno, the rent the city collected from its shops, and the construction of the third circuit of walls for the protection of the expanding suburbs. Dante's death in 1321 is duly noted, with a keen evaluation of his writings and personality: He was "not easy in his converse with laymen; but because of the lofty virtues and knowledge and worth of so

18 *Ibid.*

great a citizen, it seems fitting to confer lasting memory upon him in this our chronicle, although, indeed, his noble works, left to us in writing, are the true testimony to him, and are an honorable report to our city."[19] The attention which Villani devotes to financial matters shows the merchant-banker's appreciation of the economic foundations of city life. He records the normal and abnormal price of grain, the cost to the city of holding down the price of food for the citizens in time of famine, the expenditures for the walls, the income and outgo of the city government, that is, its budget, and so on. He is the first chronicler to make note of such matters.

Villani shared the religious and superstitious ideas of his time. Famine and pestilence were God's punishment for sin; peace and well-being were God's reward for virtuous behavior; and yet "when it came to business and politics, in which he felt securely at home, he did not hesitate to use his personal judgment and to buttress it with rational analysis. In these related fields he has all the essential earmarks of one who has left the medieval outlook behind him."[20] This pregnant remark of Ferdinand Schevill's should be pondered by anyone who is seeking clues to the nature of the Renaissance.

The Humanist Historians.—The orderly develop-

---

19 *Villani's Chronicle* (Selfe and Wicksteed translation), pp. 448–50.

20 Schevill, *History of Florence,* p. 227.

ment of historical writing in Italy, so well illustrated by Dino Compagni and Giovanni Villani, was interrupted for a time by the intrusion of the Humanistic type of historical work. This was the offspring of the Revival of Learning, which regarded a classical Latin style as all-important for works of merit. That this type of history, once it was launched in republican Florence by Bruni and Poggio, quickly won over the rulers of the other Italian states, and had a considerable success in foreign countries, is an interesting proof of the prestige of the neo-Latin writers. They for their part repaid their employers with a defence of their characters and policies.

The Latin which the Humanist historians employed was no longer the living and growing medieval Latin, the Latin of the Church, but the more formal and polished Latin of Cicero, so far as they could achieve it. Unfortunately it lacked, inevitably, the useful technical terms for new tools, weapons, political parties, etc., which medieval Latin had steadily coined as the need for them developed. The writing of chronicles, diaries, and what not in the vernacular of course continued, but there was a falling off from the level of Giovanni Villani. One explanation of this retrogression is that the talent which might have gone into it was diverted into Humanistic scholarship and writings. It is more probable that businessmen of the type of Compagni and Villani felt that their sort of history was now hopelessly unfashionable.

The rise of Humanistic historical writing is to be

credited to Coluccio Salutati (1330–1406), chancellor of Florence, a learned Humanist who first employed classical Latin in the diplomatic correspondence of the republic. The innovation was regarded as lending increased dignity, and therefore weight, to state communications. His sucessors as chancellor, Leonardo Bruni and Poggio Bracciolini, followed his practice and also produced the first and the typical historical works of Humanist authorship.

Bruni and Poggio.—Leonardo Bruni (1369–1444) wrote a *Florentine History,* which he brought down to 1404 before death stilled his hand. His successor in the chancellorship, Poggio Bracciolini (1380–1459), followed with his *History of the People of Florence, 1352-1455.* Both these men strove to imitate Livy, the Roman historian. Bruni was not altogether lacking in critical power; he excluded fables and supernatural explanations of events. He also excluded industry and commerce, which had made Florence great, and the Revival of Learning, which had made his career possible. His purpose was to write political and military history eloquently, from what it is not inaccurate to call the dramatic point of view. The great event, in his practice, was invariably the result of the oratory of the individual leader who harangued his army or the multitude and bent them to his will. In Bruni's hands, the Ordinances of Justice, so carefully explained by Dino Compagni and Giovanni Villani, become the consequence of Giano della Bella's inflammatory, demagogic oratory on the assembled citizens of the city state.

The annalistic form, taken over from Livy, prevented the Humanist historians from handling successfully any protracted and complicated movement. Poggio's history, which dealt mainly with the warfare between Florence and the dukes of Milan, naturally found the annalistic form less embarrassing. But his explanation of the Tumult of the Ciompi—that complicated economic-political insurrection among the downtrodden artisans of Florence in 1378—as the result, according to some, of divine displeasure and, according to others, as just one of those things that happen from time to time in the intervals of peace, indicates sufficiently his caliber as a historian. That the Humanists of their day rated Poggio, the better stylist, above Bruni, the better historian, is only another proof of the weakness of their historical insight.

Ferdinand Schevill's judgment on Bruni and Poggio, that, "except to pin on them their historiographical tag, there is no reason to drag them from the limbo to which they consigned themselves by their own deliberate vacuity,"[21] is perhaps too severe. In mitigation it is fair to recall that their obsession with style had a useful side. In organizing the materials that appealed to them effectively from the standpoint of rhetoric, they made it more likely that some day the essential facts would be organized on the basis of their logical connec-

21 *History of Florence,* p. xvii. Ullman (in *Medievalia et Humanistica,* IV: 45–61) ar- gues that Bruni was "the first modern historian."

tions. Moreover, their scepticism and the scepticism of their hard-boiled, realistic patrons inclined them to avoid miraculous explanations.

Biondo.—Flavio Biondo (1388–1463),[22] born in Forli, was a notary and then an apostolic secretary at the papal court. He wrote in Latin; but he was not a stylist, as most of his fellow secretaries strove to be. Nor was he a blind admirer of things classical, as were the typical Humanists, nor interested, as were they, in Roman wars and Roman civic virtues. In short, if he was in any real sense a Humanist, he was a most unorthodox one. As a consequence, he was poorly paid and lightly esteemed by his papal masters, yet he produced a number of historical works that outclassed the writings of his Humanist rivals. They were interested in form, in style; he was interested in facts, in content. Three of his books deal with Roman and Italian antiquities; the fourth, and the most important, is a history of the Middle Ages, in which Italy occupies most of the stage—*Decades of History from the Decline of the Roman Empire* (A.D. 412–1440).

All Biondo's works are essentially collections of extracts, duly cited from the sources, which he assembled from various countries with the aid of influential correspondents; they are compilations with only a slender amount of connective tissue and an occasional, fabricated, and rather sober speech. His critical powers

22 Fueter, *Historiographie, pas-sim;* Monnier, *Le Quattro-*   *cento,* I: 266 ff.

were rudimentary; an old source was for him a good source. Still, he excluded the miraculous, the preposterous, and later traditions not corroborated by the sources. It did not occur to him or to any of his contemporaries that the oldest source was not necessarily a reliable one, yet Biondo helped to rescue history from the Humanist rhetoricians and to base it upon "objective facts." "He was the real inaugurator of historical criticism." The scientific historians of the seventeenth century were in his tradition. His immediate successors, Humanist or not, paid tribute to his worth by taking over whole pages from his books, usually without acknowledgment of their indebtedness. Among these borrowers was Machiavelli.

Guicciardini and Machiavelli.—Guicciardini and Machiavelli were the best historians of the sixteenth century.[23] Their superiority over the Humanist historians and the great chroniclers seems unquestionable today. Hauser goes so far as to say that Guicciardini is "truly the first historian of his times and one of the creators of modern history."[24] How explain the emergence of these most talented men at the very time when the independence of Florence and the freedom of the Italian states from external coercion were being destroyed?

23 Villari, *Life and Times of Niccolò Machiavelli;* Luciani, *Francesco Guicciardini and his European Reputation;* Fueter, *Historiographie* and "Guicciardini als Historiker" in *Historische Zeitschrift,* C: 486–540. My debt to Fueter will be obvious to those who know.

24 *Les sources de l'histoire de France, 1494—1610,* I: 61–68.

Does the crisis always produce the man? The greatness of Elizabethan literature has been accounted for as the consequence of England's advance; the Golden Age of Spanish literature arrived when Spain was obviously in decline. The answer to these questions will have to wait.

The reader of Chapter III is already acquainted with Machiavelli's career and with his writings on government. Francesco Guicciardini (1483–1540) was fourteen years younger than his friend Machiavelli. His scholastic preparation was narrowly legal. He took a doctorate in civil law at the age of twenty-two. His wife's connections brought him good clients and a good income, and in litigation he learned to pierce to the heart of the issue. In 1511, after seven years of a growing practice, he was sent by the government of Florence on an embassy to the court of Ferdinand of Spain, to help find out what that wily monarch was planning for Italy. The experience was valuable. After the re-establishment of the Medici in Florence, the Guicciardini family went over to their side; and soon Francesco entered the service of the Medici popes (Leo X, 1513–1521; Clement VII, 1523–1534) as governor of the papal provinces (1516–1524), president of the Romagna (1524–1525), and a papal lieutenant-general in the War of the League of Cognac (1526–1527). After the death of Clement VII, Guicciardini became adviser to Alessandro de' Medici, master of Florence, and, after his murder, to his young successor, Cosimo de' Medici, later Grand Duke of Tuscany. The constitution which Guicciardini helped to draw up—he believed in government by the aristocracy, who "knew how to rule"—left considerable authority to a senate, and Cosimo, who was resolved to be absolute ruler, dismissed its authors from his service. The blow fell in 1537, and during the three remaining years of his life Guicciardini devoted himself to the writing of his *History of Italy*. Machiavelli's experience had been similar.

Guicciardini was one of those men who clarify their thoughts by reducing them to writing. His reflections and maxims, four hundred and three in number, were not written for publication; they illustrate his personality, temper, and ideas.[25] More significant and more to the purpose of this chapter is his *Florentine History, 1378-1509*,[26] which he wrote between 1509 and 1512, almost before he had any political experience. This substantial book of more than three hundred pages was quite unknown in his lifetime and was kept secret by his descendants until the nineteenth century. Not being designed for the use of anyone but himself, this youthful work in all likelihood reveals many of his real sentiments.

The book opens with a brief survey of the events which took place between the Ciompi revolt and the death of Cosimo de' Medici, from 1378 to 1464. Then follows a careful study of the government of Lorenzo the Magnificent (1469–1492), which serves as a back-

25 *Counsels and Reflections of Francesco Guicciardini*, translated into English by Thomson.

26 *Storie Fiorentine dal 1378 al 1509*, edited by Palmorocchi.

ground for the troubles which ensued upon his death:
the invasion of 1494, the rule of Savonarola, the administration of Soderini, the subsequent invasion, and
the various efforts to establish a satisfactory constitution for Florence, while Italy was in turmoil. Clearly
the author is trying to understand the consequences for
his native city of the intrusion of France, and the possible remedies. Thus his interest in his city and his native
bent have led him into the field of political theory. His
own preference is clear, a government by the best, by an
aristocracy of merit, and not by the populace. The book
breaks off with 1509, while the siege of Pisa is continuing.

The youth is father to the man. The youth revealed
in this early work suspects that selfish motives under-
lie patriotism and that religious self-sacrifice is mostly
a front. Savonarola was a great prophet or a most
talented dissimulator. Intrigue and calculation determine all political actions. The best thing for a man to
do is to shape political relations, within the limits set
by honor, [27] in such a way as to advance the interests of
one's self and one's family, and if possible of one's
party. That is the way of the world he knows. The
pessimism of his later years is only faintly in evidence.

The form of Guicciardini's *Florentine History* is
significant. He breaks completely with the pattern of
the Humanist historians. He writes in Italian, occasionally in colloquial Italian. He is not concerned with

27 Luciani, *Francesco Guicciardini,* pp. 400 f. *et passim.*

the "dignity of history," or with a dramatic presenta-
tion; his goal is the highest objectivity. He does not
write artistic introductions for his separate chapters; he
does not bother to have separate chapters or "books,"
and when he reports arguments pro and con he does so
in indirect discourse and not in the form of speeches.

The *Florentine History* is the first great analytical
history which goes behind the events and studies their
causes, which weighs their influence and is concerned
altogether with content. The *Mémoires* of Commines,
though not a history strictly speaking, exhibit the same
qualities. The style of both authors is direct, fitting,
and unadorned.

The next important work, strangely similar in import to Guicciardini's first book, is Machiavelli's *History of Florence,* which comes down only to the death
of Lorenzo de' Medici in 1492. Machiavelli was commissioned to write it by the future Clement VII, the
cardinal ruling Florence in 1520. Machiavelli began it
toward the close of that year and finished it in 1525.[28]
In his preface, he criticizes Bruni and Poggio for their
failure to realize the bearing of "civil discords and in-
ternal enmities" upon the foreign relations of the government, and this grave defect Machiavelli proposes
to remedy.

The cardinal naturally expected the book to glorify

28 *The Historical, Political, and
    Diplomatic Writings of Nic-
    colò Machiavelli,* translated
    by Detmold; Fueter, *Histori-*
    ographie; Villari, *The Life
    and Times of Niccolò Machi-
    avelli.*

the Medici; the Humanist historians had always sung the praises of their employers. Machiavelli skillfully evaded the implied obligation. His first "book," based chiefly on Biondo, sketches the history of Italy from the decline of the Roman empire to the advent of Cosimo (1434). The second book relates briefly the history of Florence, drawn principally from Villani's chronicle, from the traditional beginning to the time of the Black Death. The third "book" focuses its attention on the Ciompi revolt and its liquidation, and the fourth "book" ends with the recall of Cosimo de' Medici from exile in 1434. In the second half of the volume, which covers the years 1434–92, Machiavelli forgets the promise he made in the preface and devotes his attention primarily to foreign affairs, with stress on the defects of the condottieri system (which he had discussed at length in his *Art of War,* published in 1521), instead of on the influence of party conflicts. This strategic alteration of plan enabled him to avoid a critical consideration of, or a panegyric upon, the growth of the Medicean despotism. The book ends on an ominous note: No one is left in Italy to bridle the ambition of Lodovico Sforza.

Machiavelli's *History of Florence* has many defects. The speeches (the speech system of the Humanists is retained) are used, in the main, not to cast light upon the problems under discussion, but rather to expound the doctrines already set forth in *The Prince* and the *Discourses.* At times it is manifest that the author is led to dwell upon events, and even to select events for treatment, not because they have intrinsic historical importance, but because they enable him to commend his own panaceas of a savior prince and a citizen army.

At the same time, Machiavelli's book has outstanding virtues. The survey of the earlier history of Florence in the second and third "books" shows a vivacity and a power of co-ordination and generalization—an ability to reveal the bearing of individual events upon the general development—which set him off from all his predecessors (except Guicciardini). "Living men replace the rhetorical phantoms" of the Humanists. In externals Machiavelli makes a few concessions to the Humanistic pattern. He uses speeches, and he retains "books"; but his "books" are genuine chapters, and in his Italian he avoids hollow rhetoric.

The most impressive historical work of the period is Guicciardini's *History of Italy,* 1492–1534.[29] It was written, so far as we know, in the last three years of his life, after his enforced retirement from political activity, and it reflects his broad experience as an administrator and his passionate study of the international scene. He was too close to the epoch he wrote about to have the temporal detachment which historians recommend; but his service in Spain and with the international papacy, the definitive mastery of the peninsula by Charles V, and his own seclusion from active political life gave him a fair equivalent. Italy was done for, and so was he. No wonder that he chose to strip away

---

29 *Storia d'Italia,* edited by Panigada.

all the pretences and to describe in all their nakedness the egoistic actions of the governments, at home and abroad, which had brought about the ruin of Italy. He was writing not to flatter a patron prince but to inform men of wisdom.

The years he covered, from 1492 to 1534, embraced the entire critical epoch. It extends from the death of the great Lorenzo, credited with maintaining the peace of Italy through a balance of power, to the end of the second Medicean papacy, that of Clement VII. It witnessed the invasion of Italy by France in 1494, the intervention of Spain, the sack of Rome, the submission of Clement VII to Charles V, and the overthrow of the aristocratic republican government of Florence by the Spanish troops. Machiavelli's criticism of Bruni and Poggio was sound; Guicciardini, for one, does not fail, on his larger canvas, to make clear the relations between Italian domestic rivalries and foreign affairs.

Guicciardini seeks not to entertain but to instruct. Decorative anecdotes are absent, and the politically decisive events are explained. The *History of Italy* is detailed; it runs to more than eighteen hundred well-packed pages in the Bari edition. The sentence structures are very frequently complex, with their subordinate clauses and parentheses, reflecting the shadings of the complicated transactions they portray; but the meaning is never in doubt. And what a picture does the author present! It forms the basis of all scholarly accounts of the period. "Not only is the *Storia d'Italia* the first realistic history of modern times," says Ferdinand Schevill, "but it has the further merit of being the first clear exposition of the European political system as it emerged in Guicciardini's time and has continued without a break to the present day."[30]

The relation or lack of relation of the histories of Guicciardini and Machiavelli to those of their Humanist predecessors, who imitated Livy, is of importance for the purposes of this book. These two abandoned the employment of Latin for the vernacular. They did it, primarily, because they were not trained Humanists and would have found it difficult or impossible to write acceptable classical Latin. Moreover, the clarity, the sharp contours of their exposition, would have suffered from the employment of the inadequate ancient Latin equivalents for the newer and specific medieval words. This is neatly illustrated by the Latin translation of Guicciardini's masterpiece which Curione published in 1566. He excused himself, in his foreword, for not being able to employ "Humanistic" Latin and for having to use medieval technical expressions. Secondarily, it is probable that Guicciardini and Machiavelli realized that the vernacular was coming into favor again for serious purposes, as we have had occasion to notice in Chapter IV. They wrote a distinguished Italian; George Saintsbury gives them high praise as "joint revivers of that accomplishment of Italian prose which Boccaccio had splendidly originated, but which his successors had let slip."[31]

30 *History of Florence*, p. 503. Schevill wrote in 1936.

31 Saintsbury, *The Earlier Renaissance*, p. 155.

Nevertheless, a comparison of Guicciardini's early *Florence* with his later *Italy* shows that in the latter, which was written for publication, he was consciously attempting to conciliate the Humanistic taste of his age. He employs speeches in direct discourse; he describes battles; his work is divided into twenty "books"; he avoids colloquial expressions. In mitigation, it is to be observed that the speeches in the *Italy* have only the rhetoric common to the formal addresses of the times; they lack the high-falutin of the Humanist historians. They are employed to clarify the problems under discussion, not to determine decision or action by oratory. The description of battles is not effective; it is almost as foreign to Guicciardini's temper as it was to that of Commines. The "books" are genuine divisions and not slices of events. In short, Guicciardini, like Machiavelli, took from the Humanists only the bare externals of form. The personal styles of these two are their own. Whose style, if he has one, is not his own?

The restriction of attention to political (and military) history in the historical masterpieces of Guicciardini and Machiavelli has been interpreted in some quarters as a proof of subservience to the practice of the Humanists and the ancient historians. The answer to this argument is simple. Florence, and finally all Italy, had been overthrown by the political and military power of France and Spain. That was the poignant fact that inspired the books of the two great Florentines and that made them necessarily political. At least Guicciardini was conscious that history was more than past politics. In his *Florence,* he dealt at considerable length with matters of taxation. In his "maxim" Number 143, he writes: "All historians, without, as it seems to me, a single exception, are at fault in omitting to relate many things known in their times, as being matters of universal notoriety . . . . But had they reflected that in the course of time cities disappear and the memory of things is lost, and that histories are written for no other reason than that these may be perpetuated, they would have been more careful to write in such a way that men born in a distant age should have every event as much before their eyes as those in whose presence they happened; for this is the true object of history."[32] Granted that the histories of the two great Florentines are narrowly political; their very narrowness led them to explore the problems of statecraft in so penetrating a fashion that their writings were fertile for the future and leave in deep shade both the chroniclers and the Humanist historians.

The histories of Guicciardini and Machiavelli do not measure up to the methodological standards of today or even of the seventeenth century. They are at times plagiarists; "What he thought he might require, he went and took." But plagiarism was legitimate in their day. Their use of literary sources was not always accompanied by adequate criticism, although in this Machiavelli was inferior to Guicciardini, who did check them, when possible, with the diplomatic documents in

32 *Counsels and Reflections,* pp. 63–64.

the archives of Florence.[33] They give no references, no footnotes. These necessary guides to the thoughtful reader came into use by historians in the seventeenth century, under the influence of the sharper conception of evidence engendered by the investigations of the natural scientists.[34] The historians borrowed the device from the medieval theologians and lawyers, who reinforced their arguments with the exact citation of their authorities.[35]

The historians who followed in the footsteps of Guicciardini need not be considered here. Fueter treats them adequately in his *Historiographie*. For the purpose of this book, it is sufficient to have discovered that the superiority of the two great Florentines to the Humanist historians is rooted in their realistic study of events, in their greatly superior objectivity. Commines, in his more restricted sphere, and independently, exhibits the same strength, and for the same reason.

33 Luciani, *Francesco Guicciardini,* pp. 380–95 *et passim.*

34 Fueter, *Historiographie,* pp. 307 ff.

35 Rabelais burlesques the citations of the lawyers in his celebrated tale of the trial of Judge Bridlegoose.

CHAPTER VIII: PHILOSOPHY

St. Thomas Aquinas.—The greatest intellectual revolution of the Middle Ages is associated with the name of St. Thomas (*ca.* 1225–1274), who triumphantly established the principle that physical nature is a legitimate subject for independent human investigation.[1] His achievement, there can be no doubt, was a supreme recognition of the growing interest in natural phenomena which marked his century, an interest which was stimulated and demonstrated by the development of

[1] Gilson, *Le Thomisme, Études de philosophie médiévale, La philosophie au moyen âge, Reason and Revelation in the Middle Ages;* Bréhier, *Histoire de la philosophie,* Vol. I; Mandonnet, *Siger de Brabant,* Halphen in *Revue Historique,* CLXVII: 1–15.

industry and commerce and by the appearance of realistic vernacular literature, as well as by the prolonged
philosophical battle over universals. This interest in nature was rendered virtually irresistible by the circulation, in Latin translations, of the encyclopedic writings
of Aristotle, which gave "an integral explanation of the
phenomena of nature" and furnished "a coherent system
of thought."

It is indubitable that St. Thomas, aided by his older
colleague, Albertus Magnus, tackled the huge problem
of the relationship of reason and revelation because of
the invincible attraction of Aristotle's works for the
inquiring minds of the century, especially numerous at
Paris. For Aristotle was a pagan, and some of his conclusions clashed with some of the fundamental tenets of
the Christian faith—for instance, the divine creation
of the world, the immortality of the soul, and God's
providential care for the individual. St. Thomas saw
that the momentum of Aristotle's scientific notions was
giving dangerous currency to his anti-Christian opinions, and the Catholic doctor and his colleague girded
themselves for the battle. It was indeed a difficult battle,
in which they undertook to defend the natural science
of Aristotle, who knew, St. Thomas said, more about
nature than all the theologians, and at the same time to
confute those Aristotelian conclusions which ran counter
to Christian theology.

It was not enough to correct Aristotle on those points
on which his conclusions clashed with Christian dogma.
It was also necessary, as will be seen, to correct the

dominant Augustinian theory of knowledge, or epistemology, which made the acquisition of knowledge of
anything except the bare data of things outside the
mind depend on the specific, mysterious, divine illumin-
ination of the object with light from the throne of God.
This made the fullness of knowledge possible only to
the devout Christian—*"credo ut intelligam."* Nevertheless, the all-knowing Aristotle was a pagan.

St. Thomas tactfully transformed the Augustinian
epistemology by his argument that knowledge of the
phenomena of nature, scientific knowledge, is acquired
by man's natural reason, given him by God, operating
on what he learns through his five senses and through
the introspection of his own inner states. The field of
nature, then, is open to human reason—of course without depriving the theologian of his right to view nature
symbolically. But there was still another difficulty for
St. Thomas to overcome: Augustinian epistemology did
not distinguish sharply between the acquisition of the
knowledge of nature and the knowledge of divine truths
disclosed by revelation. This difficulty St. Thomas sur-
mounted by his argument that divine revelation gives
to men the truths necessary for salvation, truths that
transcend or are inaccessible to human reason, but which
human reason equally is unable to controvert. In short,
science (*scientia*) is the product of human reason and
faith (*fides*) is the product of revelation. In other
words, rational truths are the domain of philosophy,
and revealed truths are the domain of theology. These
two sorts of truths cannot, in the teaching of St. Thomas,

clash; for God is the author of human reason as well as of revelation, and He will not contradict Himself. Seeming contradictions will doubtless arise; but they will be due to inadequate understanding and will be dissipated by fuller investigation.

The reader who reflects on the Church's claim of infallibility in matters of dogma will not be surprised to be told that, in event of apparent conflict between the two sorts of truths, it will usually be found that it is the scientific conclusion that is at fault. The essential accuracy of the witticism, that St. Thomas Aquinas "officiated at the marriage of Christian Faith and Hellenic Reason, a union in which it was Reason that had to promise to love, honor, and obey," cannot well be gainsaid.

The acceptance by the Church of the relationship of science and faith, as St. Thomas expounded them, took time. He was opposed, in his lifetime and after, by some Christian philosophers and by some Augustinian theologians. He was opposed also by the Averroists, philosophers at the University of Paris and elsewhere who were sure that Averroës (1126–1198), the great Arabic commentator of Aristotle, interpreted him correctly and that all of Aristotle's opinions were philosophically sound. One school of Averroists held that Aristotle's heretical views were incontrovertible philosophically—that is, they were in accord with human reasoning, although not true in the higher light of revelation; and another school went the whole way into unbelief and heresy. And there were other opponents, but in the long run (and it was truly long, although the Dominican order officially accepted the teaching of its greatest doctor in 1278), the view of St. Thomas on the relations of faith and reason became the official view of the Roman Catholic Church. Pope Leo XIII's encyclical letter of 4 August 1879 "to all the prelates of the universe in communion with the Holy See," instructing them "to restore the wisdom of St. Thomas," finally ended all argument.

St. Thomas's demarcation of the separate domains of faith and reason left room for some co-operation between them. Faith can give hints to reason; and reason, or philosophy, can cast some light of understanding, inadequate though it must inevitably be, upon the revelations of God. For example, St. Thomas was convinced that the physics of Aristotle furnished convincing evidence of the existence of God. The first of his celebrated five proofs (based on reason) that God exists turns on Aristotle's argument that movement, which we perceive in the universe through our senses, implies and indeed requires an ultimate motor or mover which nothing moves, and this mover, St. Thomas declares, is God.

St. Thomas knew Aristotle, he knew Averroës and the other great Arabians, and he also knew Maimonides (1135–1204), the Jewish philosopher whose attempt to do for Judaism what St. Thomas was doing for Christianity proved very helpful to Aquinas (and contributed one of his five proofs). St. Thomas, however, was not personally interested in the study of the phenomena of nature; and although the revolution he was working was designed to give a charter of freedom to scientific investigations, he was content, with most of his scientific contemporaries, to accept Aristotle as a reliable and adequate expositor of nature and nature's laws.

Roger Bacon.—Roger Bacon (*ca.* 1214–1292), although not the most effective, is certainly the most famous opponent of the complacent acceptance of Aristotle as the final word in the natural sciences.[2] He was an Englishman and a Franciscan friar. He studied at Oxford under Grosseteste (1175–1253), and imbibed from him the conviction that scientific investigation had barely begun. Like Grosseteste and some others (including Plato), Bacon emphasized the importance of mathematics as a scientific tool; he asserted that it was necessary even for theology. He was certain that dialectical conclusions regarding the things of this world require the confirmation of actual observation before they can be accepted with full confidence—"without experience nothing can be sufficiently known." He was an Augustinian of an extreme sort in his epistemology and was not theologically trained. His ideas on the relations of revelation and natural science were very strange. God, he was convinced, has revealed to men,

2 Sarton, *Introduction to the History of Science,* Vol. II, Part II, pp. 952–67; Charles, *Roger Bacon;* Little, ed., *Roger Bacon Essays;* Thorndike, *History of Magic and Experimental Science,* Vol. II; H. O. Taylor, *Mediaeval Mind,* Vol. II, Chap. XLII.

in the Scriptures, the broad principles of all possible knowledge, and it is the business of scientists to work out the details and the applications. Similarly, "the interior experience of spiritual things" would disclose spiritual secrets without which no one could hope to possess the fullness of knowledge of the natural sciences. Reliance upon authority—for example, upon Aristotle —was one of the four chief impediments to the advancement of knowledge. Experiment—hardly our modern objective assay of hypotheses by controlled tests, but apparently something divinatory, astrological, or alchemical—would lay bare the occult forces of nature and thus enable a great pope and a great king to renovate the world. It would give mankind fundamental inventions, including the possibility of circumnavigating the earth, driving boats by mechanical power, flying, utilizing the explosive potency of powder and the heat of the sun, and improving eyesight with lenses.[3]

Bacon was censorious and irritating. At the University of Paris, to which he went in the days of Albertus Magnus and St. Thomas, and where he lectured for a time in the arts faculty, he again and again expressed his extreme dissatisfaction with the existing state of knowledge. In one of his many writings, he denounced the ignorance of all the authorities from the pope down. His attacks on Albertus Magnus were particularly bitter and were deeply resented. The antagonisms

3 Sarton, *Introduction to the History of Science,* Vol. II, Part II, p. 953. *Cf.* Singer in *Mediaeval* *Contributions to Modern Civilisation* (Hearnshaw, ed.), pp. 142–43.

he provoked and his defence of judicial astrology (the study of the influence of the stars upon human conduct), in the face of its condemnation as heretical by the powerful bishop of Paris in 1277, got him into the most serious difficulties. The heads of the two great orders of friars, the Dominicans and the Franciscans, had agreed to put an end to the mutual recriminations of their members, and Bacon was violating the treaty. The outcome was the incarceration of the turbulent Franciscan by the minister-general of his order. He remained in its prison from 1278 to 1292.

Like his famous namesake, Francis, Roger Bacon was the prophet rather than the practitioner of science. "What we clearly discern in [Roger] Bacon," says Reade, "when we get behind his peevishness, his superstitions, and his arrogance, is a profound discontent with the existing state of knowledge, a conviction that no further advance is possible except by a kind of intellectual return to Nature. In this . . . rather than in actual achievement, lies his title to fame."[4]

William of Ockham.—More important, although less famous than Roger Bacon, was William of Ockham (1280?–1349?), another English Franciscan, who also had studied at the Oxford of Grosseteste. He too went to Paris, the chief university of the age. He had before him the results achieved or promised by several immediate predecessors, notably Duns Scotus (1266?–1308)

4 Reade in *Cambridge Medieval History,* V: 826.

and Bacon. Ockham's philosophical and theological conclusions—for he was a well-grounded theologian—may
be viewed as directed to the dissolution of the Thomist
marriage of Faith and Reason.

Ockham rejected the common medieval belief that
reasoning from an accepted principle will necessarily
lead to reality. Where is the proof? Solid proof of a
proposition consists in showing that the proposition is
immediately evident to the senses or a necessary deduc-
tion from what is evident to the senses—that is, that
it can be verified factually by direct observation or experiment (similarly with our inner experiences). The
individual singular (or thing) alone is real, genuinely
real. One can, of course, make an abstraction from
individual things of the same sort; but these abstractions or conceptions will result in real science only if
the words represent individual things or their qualities.
Furthermore, one cannot reason from effect to cause
and obtain a scientific result; reasoning must proceed
from cause to effect, for then the cause can be isolated
and the existence of the effect verified. For example, one
cannot prove that because the world exists God caused
(or created) it. Indeed, there are no scientific, *i.e.,* rational, proofs of the existence of God; in short, nothing in nature can lead us to God or to His truths. The
harmony between reason and faith which St. Thomas
had established is now declared fallacious, and the
limited freedom of scientific investigation of nature
which he had recognized becomes for Ockham, in effect,
full and untrammeled freedom.

The Christian revelation nevertheless remains un-
shaken. It is to be accepted—dogma and the Church
are to be accepted—because such is God's will. So too
the moral law, not because it accords with right reason,
but because it is God's will. Human reason is incapable
of any valid approval or disapproval. Such is the view
of Ockham. Ockhamist theology rests on the absolute-
ness of God. It was a lively competitor of Thomist
theology for at least a century and a half. Martin
Luther, before his revolt, was an Ockhamist. Even
after his breach with the mother church, his attitude
toward reason in relation to revelation ("You must
wring the neck of the beast [reason]") is good Ockham. It requires no great argument to explain why Ockhamist theology gave a great stimulus to the mystical
approach to God, but that does not concern us here.

Roger Bacon's Augustinianism and his interest in
nature had led him, as we have seen, to advocate scientific investigation primarily for the promotion of
religion. No such purpose animated Ockham. "For
whereas the examination of the nature of knowledge
turned the Augustinians for the most part to the contemplation of God . . . Ockham was turned from the
same problems to the consideration of the principles
and causes of physics and the mechanisms and rules of
logic."[5] It is therefore not surprising, as Gilson points
out, "that the first conquests of positive science appeared . . . in the very midst of the philosophical school

5 McKeon, ed., *Selections from Medieval Philosophers,* II: 356–57.

of which W. of Ockham is the principal representative."[6]

Ockham's insistence on economy of thought, that is, that "one must not multiply beings unnecessarily," is justly celebrated as "Ockham's razor." It was a useful tool. He himself employed it when, in agreement with Duns Scotus, he declared that the celestial bodies and the earth consist of the same materials. Thus did he slice off Aristotle's conception of the sublunary sphere of change and decay in contrast with the incorruptible heavens. Ockham's disciples used the razor too. Jean Buridan (1300?–1368) advanced to the position that the same laws of movement apply throughout the universe. The impetus of a projectile, he argued, would remain unchanged if it were not modified by the resistance of its surroundings (*milieu*) and the action of its weight. (Aristotle taught that it was the agitated air which drives the arrow after it leaves the bow.) "It is not necessary," Buridan explained to his students, "to assume the existence of celestial intelligences which move the celestial bodies in an appropriate way; it is not even necessary [to believe] that God moves them, if it is not under the form of a general influence, that influence by which we say that He co-operates in everything that exists."[7] In this fashion Buridan used the razor of his master to dispose of the celestial intelligences of Aristotle and of St. Thomas.

6 Gilson, *La philosophie au moyen âge*, p. 266. See also Trachtenberg in *Philosophy and Phenomenonological Research*, VI: 212–24.

7 Picard, *La vie et l'oeuvre de Pierre Duhem*, p. 39.

Two other prominent Ockhamist scientists, Albert of Saxony (d. 1390) and the more celebrated Nicholas Oresme (d. 1382) (both of them ultimately high-placed prelates), worked on the associated problem of the acceleration of falling bodies. Oresme arrived at the correct idea, which makes the speed of the fall proportionate to its duration. He was a bishop, a counsellor of Charles V of France, and a monetary expert, but it was his studies in astronomy that led him farthest. He questioned, although he did not actually reject, the Aristotelian teaching that the heavens revolve around the earth, "offering several persuasive reasons to show that the earth revolves daily."[8]

It is regrettable that the Ockhamist scientists and the Augustinian-minded Oxford scientists did not continue their scientific work. Whatever the reasons, and one may reasonably conjecture that the lack of instruments (the telescope had not yet been invented) was the principal one, both groups shifted their attention, before the close of the fourteenth century, to the niceties of logic —to provables and unprovables—and bogged down into the hairsplitting which gives the scholastic philosophy of the closing Middle Ages such a deservedly bad name.

Their scientific work was not stillborn. In the fifteenth century the University of Padua became the center of the physical studies (as well as of barren Averroism), and there the writings of the Ockhamist

8 Gilson, *La philosophie au moyen âge,* p. 293.

scientists were discussed and commented upon. There
these ideas were alive in the days of Leonardo, Copernicus, and Galileo.[9]

The Ockhamist scientists, lacking the telescope and
other instruments of precision, could not demonstrate
that their conclusions were correct; but they were able
to emancipate themselves from the physics of Aristotle
(and of St. Thomas) and to ground science on the
foundation of experience and reason. Indeed, Pierre
Duhem, the great historian of their work,[10] has emphatically declared: "If one wished, by a precise line, to
separate the reign of ancient science from the reign of
modern science, it would have to be drawn, we believe,
at the instant when Jean Buridan conceived this theory
[of celestial mechanics], at the instant when the stars
ceased to be looked upon as moved by divine beings,
when it was admitted that the celestial movements and
the sublunary movements depended on the same me-
chanics."[11]

The significance of Ockhamism must not be missed.
In stressing the importance of experience and the possibility of learning the truth about natural phenomena,
it reinforced the growing realistic temper which insisted
on studying and writing about real things—witness
Pierre Dubois, Marsilius of Padua, Boccaccio, Ruiz,

9 Clagett, *Giovanni Marliani
and Late Medieval Physics;*
Picard, *Pierre Duhem,* p. 39.
10 *Études sur Léonard de Vinci;
Le système du monde, histoire
des doctrines cosmologiques de*

Platon à Copernic; more a-
waiting publication.

11 Duhem, *Études sur Léonard
de Vinci,* III:ix–x; Picard,
Pierre Duhem, p. 39.

and Chaucer—and it indicated the possibility of creating a scientific method of dealing with the real things of earthly life. Merchants more and more were abandoning the theory of the just price in favor of what was later called the "higgling" of the market; peasants and artisans were revolting against injustice. Reality was the thing. Most of the originators of the ideas and movements just alluded to probably never heard of Ockhamism; nevertheless, it furnished an ideological basis for the change in the world view with which this book is largely concerned.[12]

Marsilio Ficino.—The point of view of Marsilio Ficino (1433–1499), the animating spirit of the so-called Platonic Academy of Florence, bears no genetic relation to that of St. Thomas, of Roger Bacon, or of William of Ockham. He is, however, the chief contribution of the Italian Revival of Learning to the side of thought or philosophy, as Monnier explicitly recognizes,[13] and as such his views must be examined with care.

The son of the physician of Cosimo de' Medici, the young Ficino[14] received what may be called the customary Humanistic education, probably including the

---

12 *Cf.* White in *American Historical Review,* LII: 435: "The nominalistic philosophy . . . provided the middle class with a rationale and a program of action for reform of church and state which has been realized in great detail during recent centuries."

13 *Le Quattrocento,* II: 104.

14 Della Torre, *Storia dell' Accademia Platonica di Firenze;* Kristeller, *The Philosophy of Marsilio Ficino;* Pusino in *Zeitschrift für Kirchengeschichte,* XLIV: 504–43.

rudiments of Greek. His study of Cicero, Macrobius, Boethius, and other Latin writers attracted him to Plato, the more naturally when one recalls the aridity which had overtaken the scholastic handling of Aristotle and also Petrarch's praise of the founder of the Academy; and on the basis of his Latin reading Ficino wrote a little treatise in praise of Plato.

It is also possible that the attack on Aristotle and the laudation of Plato in 1439 by Georgios Gemistus Pletho, a member of the Byzantine emperor's suite at the Council of Ferrara-Florence, had something to do with the young Ficino's enthusiasm for Plato, the "underdog" for two centuries in the West. However that may be, the lectures of the Greek Aristotelian, Argyropoulos, appointed to a professorship in Greek at the University of Florence in the year 1457, brought the ancient breach between Aristotle and his teacher, Plato, to the front once more; and Cosimo de' Medici decided that the matter should be settled. In 1459 he persuaded the young Ficino to give up the study of medicine and to devote himself to the translation into Latin of all of Plato's works and to the exposition of his ideas. Ficino should perfect his knowledge of Greek, immerse himself in Plato, and as a private scholar— patronized and supported by the first citizen of Florence—present to the world the Platonic side of the old controversy.

It is in some ways surprising that Ficino regarded Plato as primarily a religious teacher and reached the conclusion that the Neoplatonists, and especially Plotinus, Porphyry, and Proclus, had merely clarified the doctrine of Plato and made it a powerful buttress for Christianity. Did Ficino not know that Greco-Roman paganism had made its last and unsuccessful stand against Christianity, during the short reign of the emperor Julian, under the banners of Neoplatonism? Had Ficino forgotten that St. Augustine, while acknowledging his debt to Neoplatonism for help in overcoming his Manicheistic errors—persuading him that evil was only the absence of good—had noted that it failed to acknowledge that the Word had been made flesh?[15] Did Ficino not know that in his *Retractions* Augustine had expressed regret for having commended Neoplatonism, saying, "The praise which I have given Plato and Platonists [Neoplatonists] displeases me, and not without reason, especially because the Christian doctrine has had to be defended against great errors on their part."[16]

Questions of this sort could be multiplied. Let us rather see how completely Ficino read Neoplatonism into Plato. "The primitive theology of the Gentiles," Ficino declares in his *De christiana religione* (1475), "in which Zoroaster, Mercury, Orpheus, Aglaophemus, and Pythagoras are at one, is to be found entire in the books of our Plato. In his letters[17] Plato prophesies

---

15 *Confessions,* Bk. VII, Chaps. IX–XXI.
16 Quoted in Bréhier, *Histoire de la philosophie,* I: 514. What the Christian Fathers found to approve and to disapprove in Plato is summarized in Shorey, *Platonism Ancient and Modern,* pp. 79–80.

17 Now generally regarded as spurious.

that these mysteries can be made plain to mankind only after many centuries. And that was what happened. For it was first in the time of Philo and Numenius that the thought of the primitive theologians, embodied in Plato's writings, began to be understood. That is to say, it was directly after the preachings of the apostles and of the disciples of the apostles, and their writings. For the Platonists used the divine light of Christians for the interpretation of the divine Plato. This is the reason why Basil the Great and Augustine affirm that the Platonists plagiarized the mysteries of John the Evangelist. I myself have certainly found that the chief mystic doctrines of Numenius, Philo, Plotinus, Iamblichus, and Proclus were borrowed from Paul, Hierotheus, and Dionysius the Areopagite. All the magnificent things they said of the divine mind and the angels and other theological topics, were plainly borrowed thence."[18]

"We need not," Professor Shorey says by way of comment, "take seriously the hypothesis frequently met in Jewish, early Christian, and medieval literature, that Plato was the Attic Moses and learned the philosophy of Moses from Jeremiah in Egypt . . . . Similarly . . . their philosophic and Neo-Platonic adversaries reversed the contention and argued that the coincidences in thought and moral sentiment only proved that the Christians were plagiarizing Plato."[19]

Only a few years before he wrote the *De christiana*

18 Shorey, *Platonism Ancient and*   19 *Ibid.,* p. 73.
      Modern, p. 124.

religione, Ficino, in a letter to Bessarion, read Neoplatonism into Plato much more succinctly: "The doctrine of Plato is as a very rich vein of gold, which only an experienced and lynx eye can discover among the rocks and sand of the rough and involved form. . . . But when Plotinus, Porphyry, and Iamblichus arose, that gold, as if refined in the crucible of the smelter, was freed, through their explicative labors, from all the dross, and shone with the most resplendent light."[20]

The myths of Plato are the chief foundation of Neoplatonism. He seems to many to have gone too far in his teaching that genuine knowledge is knowledge of the supersensible, the transcendental, "objects which lie entirely beyond the range of any possible experience of sense," and that the study of sensible phenomena can yield only an inferior type of knowledge, which he calls opinion. He sees in the physical universe, as A. E. Taylor points out, an irreducible element of evil, precisely because it contains, as the system of pure concepts does not, an irrational and incalculable factor— disorderly material.[21] Plato's purpose, however, in his many myths, which in diverse ways embody his conception of supersensible reality, seems to have been to dam the current of materialism which in his day threatened to extinguish the "sweet hope" of personal immortality after death[22] and to impair the values of ethics and the

20 Della Torre, *Storia dell' Accademia Platonica,* p. 597.
21 A. E. Taylor, *Plato,* p. 60.

22 "Belief in personal immortality had become very feeble among a large number of edu-

social order. Professor Shorey catalogues the myths upon which the Neoplatonists relied, and then declares: "A critical and flexible literary interpretation discovers no trace of concrete superstition in any of these passages. Literary ornament, irony, harmless concessions to popular religion when it is not immoral, and the willingness to use traditional symbols for the faith that there is something more than mechanism in the universe, explains them all."[23]

In his impressive book, *The Myths of Plato*, Professor J. A. Stewart reaches a similar conclusion: "Plato hopes for good from Myth, as from some great Ritual at which thinkers may assist and feel that there are mysteries which the scientific understanding cannot fathom."[24] Chesterton's observation points in the same direction: "Mysticism . . . appeals to realities . . . which have no place in the argument except as postulates."[25]

Plato did not put forward his myths as scientific accounts of actualities, but as probabilities. In the prelude of the dialogue which bears his name, Timaeus says: "If, then, Socrates, in many respects concerning many things—the gods and the generation of the universe—we prove unable to render an account at all points entirely consistent . . . you must not be surprised. If we can furnish accounts no less likely than any other, we must be content . . . and consequently it is fitting

cated and even half-educated people in Athens." Stewart, *The Myths of Plato*, p. 61.
23 *Platonism Ancient and Mod-*ern, pp. 45–47.
24 P. 57.
25 Quoted in Shorey, *Platonism Ancient and Modern*, p. 92.

that we should, in these matters, accept the likely story and look for nothing further."[26] And in the moving conclusion of the *Phaedo*, Socrates remarks: "A man of sense ought not to say, nor will I be very confident, that the description which I have given of the soul and her mansions is exactly true. But . . . something of the kind is true. The venture is a glorious one, and he ought to comfort himself with words like these . . . ."[27]

Plato's comforting myths were, however, treated as allegories by the Neoplatonists—that is, as veiled accounts of dogmatic truths, discoverable by the wise—with consequences which Shorey very aptly characterizes: "All this poetry and symbolism . . . the Neo-Platonists made the theme of obsessed meditation or of hair-splitting refinements of dialectics." "All that the ordinary mind esteems concrete real things, then, the Neo-Platonic mind treats as symbols and suggestions of abstractions which may be half personified in a faint, pale, metaphysical mythology and built up into ingenious systems or strung out in hierarchies stretching from the lowest demon to the supreme and ineffable unknown and unknowable God."[28]

---

26 Translation by Cornford in his *Plato's Cosmology*.
27 Jowett's translation.
28 *Platonism Ancient and Modern*, pp. 46, 43–44. The argument of Professor Stewart in his monograph, *The Myths of Plato*, on the radical difference between myth and allegory is cogent. One statement: "The mark of a true Myth, it must be remembered, is that it sets forth the *a priori* elements in man's experience. An Illustrative Story or Allegory, as such, merely makes easier and more pleasant the task of receiving and recalling *a posteriori* data." (*Ibid.*, p. 221.) "Myth has no *dogmatic* meaning behind its literal sense." (*Ibid.*, p. 244.)

The Neoplatonists, then, "introduced a new first principle into philosophy, viz. the supra-rational, that which lies beyond reason and beyond reality." Neo-platonism, "its sole interest being a religious interest, and its highest object the supra-rational, must be a philosophy of revelation." The later adherents of the school—Porphyry (233—*ca.* 300) and his more immediate successors, Iamblichus (d. *ca.* 330) and Proclus (410–485), who built on the foundation already laid by Plotinus (*ca.* 205–*ca.* 270)— "based their philosophy on revelations of the Deity, and they found these in the religious traditions and rites of all nations. . . . The older any religious tradition or mode of worship is, the more venerable it is, the richer in divine ideas. Hence the ancient religions of the East had a peculiar interest for the Neoplatonist . . . . Neoplatonism contemplated a restoration of all the religions of antiquity . . . making each a vehicle for the religious attitude and the religious truth embraced in Neoplatonism."

The Neoplatonic attempt to reconstitute the ancient religions merely contributed to their destruction. The historical reasons need not be gone into here. But in the sixteenth century Bodin argued that if all religions are only relatively true then there is no true religion. F. H. Bradley's aphorism on "ecclecticism" has made the point even more crisply: "Every truth is so true that any truth must be false." "Why did not Neoplatonism set up an independent religious community? Why did it not provide for its mixed multitude of divinities by founding a universal church, in which all the gods of

all nations might be worshipped along with the one
ineffable Deity? . . . Three essentials of a permanent
religious foundation were wanting in Neoplatonism;
they are admirably indicated in Augustine's *Confessions*
(vii. 18–21). First and chiefly, it lacked a religious
founder; second, it could not tell how the state of inward peace and blessedness could become permanent;
third, it had no means to win those who were not
endowed with the speculative faculty . . . and when
Julian tried to enlist the sympathies of the common
rude man for the doctrines and worship of this school,
he was met with scorn and ridicule."[29]

Nevertheless, it was this selfsame Neoplatonism
which Ficino made the basis of his system. In the early
years of his apprenticeship, after he had accepted the
commission which Cosimo de' Medici had given him,
he was so captivated by it that for a time he lost his
faith in Christianity.[30] But St. Augustine, he tells us,
helped him to recover his faith,[31] and he then settled
down to his life-long task of translating and expound-
ing Plato and harmonizing Neoplatonism and Christianity.

Ficino was a prolific writer; his translation of Plato's
Dialogues, initially begun in 1463, was published, after
much revision, in 1484. His principal work, the *Theo-*

29 The quotations in the preceding two paragraphs, not credited to others, are taken from
   Adolf Harnack's admirable
   article, "Neoplatonism," in the
   eleventh edition of the *Encyclopaedia Britannica.*
30 Della Torre, *Storia dell' Accademia Platonica,* pp. 587 f.
31 *Ibid.,* pp. 592–93.

logia Platonica de immortalitate animorum (composed 1469–74), was revised after he had finished his *De christiana religione* (published in 1475), and was finally printed in 1482. Thereafter, he translated Plotinus, Porphyry, Proclus, and other Neoplatonic sources, ending with Dionysius the Areopagite in 1492. Many smaller treatises rounded out his program.[32]

In the *Theologia Platonica,* he exhibits Plato as essentially Christian; and the *De christiana religione* demonstrates to Ficino's complete satisfaction that Christianity is essentially Platonic. In the introduction to the *Theologia Platonica,* Ficino declares that he has been called by the decree of Providence to make known Plato's philosophical religion (elsewhere he speaks of it as Plato's religious philosophy) for the conversion of those who, being habituated to scientific reasoning, cannot accept any opinion unless it is scientifically proven.[33]

It is manifest that in his attempted reconciliation of Neoplatonism and Christianity it is the former and not the latter that is, in Della Torre's phrase, the formative criterion.[34] Christianity has, so to speak, to compete with the other religions, with philosophy in the judge's stand. Ficino's argument is not difficult to follow. The religious feeling is inborn in all men, and God would not have implanted a deceptive feeling in them. Men have, however, varying shares in God's

32 Kristeller, *The Philosophy of Marsilio Ficino,* pp. 17–18.
33 Della Torre, *Storia dell' Accademia Platonica,* p. 597;

Kristeller, *The Philosophy of Marsilio Ficino,* pp. 321–22.
34 *Storia dell' Accademia Platonica,* p. 596.

gift of reason, and as a consequence the historical religions show various approximations to the truth. In short, religion is a genus, with many species, of which Christianity is one. God approves of these different species; in the *De christiana religione* Ficino tells us that "this variety ordered by God does, perhaps, produce admirable beauty in the universe."[35] But Christianity, he concluded—after the Virgin had cured him of an illness—was the best of the religions, and in 1473 he accepted ordination as a priest. In the *De christiana religione,* on which he set to work after ordination, he went far in his acceptance of the Christian revelation and even said that our inability to understand all the precepts of the Faith was the very proof of their divine origin.[36]

It is obvious, however, that Ficino still relied on reason for the conversion of the intellectuals. The most convincing evidence of this is found in the preface to his translation of Plotinus which he finished some little time prior to 1492.[37] Here he argued that the men of intellect must have a rational religion, that "for this cause God, anxious to recall them to Himself, provided that in Persia with Zoroaster and in Egypt with Mercurius a certain philosophical religion was born which was developed by Orpheus and Aglaophemus, became adult with Pythagoras, was carried to perfect structure by Plato, and was interpreted by Plotinus,

35 Kristeller, *The Philosophy of Marsilio Ficino,* p. 317.

36 Pusino in *Zeitschrift für Kir-* *chengeschichte,* XLIV: 512–13.

37 Kristeller, *The Philosophy of Marsilio Ficino,* p. 18.

Porphyry, and Proclus. The age of miracles being ended, it is necessary to use philosophical reasoning as means of conversion." In short, dogmatic religion is for the unlearned, philosophical religion for men of intellect.[38] Professor Shorey's comment on "the fundamental difference between Christianity and Platonism" is relevant here: "Platonism is intellectual and aristocratic in its appeal . . . . Christianity is emotional and popular . . . . Plato describes conversion as a turning about of the eye of the mind from transitory and material to abiding and ideal objects. For popular Christianity it is a change of heart . . . . 'Come unto me, all ye that are weary and heavy laden,' is the call of Jesus . . . . The Gospel teaches all . . . ."[39]

Ficino modified the Neoplatonic hierarchy of forms (from God to matter) to accord, though haltingly, with the Christian doctrine of creation.[40] He altered the Neoplatonic theory of the mystical ecstasy (which continues to be for him the product of intense mental concentration involving the separation of the soul from the body) from a leap to the One into "the highest peak in the gradual series of contemplation."[41] He changed the six hypostases of Plotinus into five—God, Mind (Angel), rational soul, quality, body, with soul

---

38 Della Torre, *Storia dell' Accademia Platonica*, pp. 595–96; Kristeller, *The Philosophy of Marsilio Ficino*, pp. 322–23.

39 *Platonism Ancient and Modern*, p. 87.

40 Kristeller, *The Philosophy of Marsilio Ficino*, pp. 137, 166–69.

41 *Ibid.*, pp. 216, 228.

constituting the central link.[42] Such patterned conceits interested the theologically-minded Cambridge Platonists, who vainly sought to replace St. Thomas with Ficino, and still interest (and properly) some present-day students of ancient philosophies; but they really have nothing to do with Christianity. Rather do they recall, à rebours, the sturdy declaration of St. Thomas, fighting for the acceptance of Aristotelian science: "An old [Christian] woman knows more about those matters that pertain to the Faith than all the ancient philosophers."[43] Ficino's refinement upon the conception of love developed in the dolce stil nuovo, when he asserts that true love between two persons is by nature a common love of God,[44] is doubtless a pretty fancy for Elizabethan sonneteers to embroider; it is scarcely anything more.

What were the chief defects in Ficino's system which caused it to fail? The answer is definite. He pays only lip-service to the incarnation, the central doctrine of Christianity. He despises the human body as an impediment rather than as a partner of the soul—"the farther behind it [the mind] leaves the body," he says, "the more perfect it is. The mind will therefore be most perfect when it leaves this body entirely."[45] Yet, in deference to Christian doctrine, he recognizes the resurrection of the body—"the pestilence of the body," "this

42 Ibid., p. 395–401.

43 Quoted by Gilson, Études de philosophie médiévale, pp. 118–19.

44 Kristeller, The Philosophy of Marsilio Ficino, pp. 279 f.

45 Ibid., p. 335.

unwholesome body"—explaining it on the strange philosophical ground that every natural appetite will ultimately be satisfied.[46] Actual human life on earth is for
him a species of exile for the soul, instead of "a time
in which God progressively creates out of the man, by
virtue of his grace, that spiritual being to whom is
promised eternal felicity."[47] Despite occasional kind
words along Augustinian lines, Ficino condemns matter and nature as "mere shadows of reality," although
according to the Bible, they were created by God and
He declared them good. Ficino had no interest in
natural science. He knew nothing of the astronomy of
Ockham's school; for him the twelve spheres were still
moved by their souls in circular orbits. The "etheric
soul of man," owing to its immersion in matter, is unable to move "in the same perfect way"—that is, cir-
cularly—"and can return to its appropriate form of
movement only after death."[48] Ernst Cassirer, an ex-
ceptionally competent judge, says that the Christian and
heathen elements which Ficino strove to force together
never fused and that their incompatibility was merely
concealed in the Platonic Academy. He adds: "Die
Einheit, die Ficin und Pico fest gegründet zu haben

46 *Ibid.,* pp. 195, 215, 301.

47 Della Torre, *Storia dell' Accademia Platonica,* p. 433.

48 Kristeller, *The Philosophy of
   Marsilio Ficino,* pp. 239, 387.
   This last fantastic idea is a
   valuable clue to the way in
   which the Neoplatonist builds
   up his airy system. He starts
   with the circle, the perfect
   figure; observe what is made
   to follow. It is entirely possible that the tale told by
   Aristophanes in Plato's *Sym-
   posium* has some share in this
   absurdity.

glaubten, zergeht zuletzt in ein blosses Traum- und Wunschbild."[49] Lord Acton's condemnation of Ficino's system is briefer and fuller: "Neither the knowledge of Plato nor the knowledge of the Gospel profited."[50]

Pico.—The religious views of Giovanni Pico della Mirandola (1463–1494), the only other member of Ficino's circle possessed of original philosophical capacity, are not sufficiently different from those of Ficino to justify close examination in this book.[51] He was a young man of great attainments, with a solid grounding in scholastic philosophy, on which he built the Platonic and Neoplatonic structure so dear to Ficino, and he added thereto Hebrew, Arabic, and Chaldean philosophy and religion. He fondly believed that one of his feudal titles, Count of Concordia, signified that he was destined to be the great reconciler. He was endowed or cursed with a glutinous memory which retained all that he ever read. Ficino had, he believed, rendered accordant Plato and Christianity; he, Pico, would demonstrate the fundamental agreement of Plato and Aristotle, making again what John of Salisbury, back in the

49 Cassirer, *Die Platonische Renaissance in England und die Schule von Cambridge,* p. 7.

50 Acton, *Lectures on Modern History,* p. 80. Ficino's Latin translation of Plato, *contra,* deserves high praise, and gets it from Shorey, *Platonism Ancient and Modern,* p. 121.

51 Della Torre, *Storia dell' Accademia Platonica di Firenze,* *passim;* More's translation of *The Life of Giovanni Pico della Mirandola;* Greswell, *Memoirs of Angelus Politianus . . . ;* Kristeller, *The Philosophy of Marsilio Ficino, passim;* Monnier, *Le Quattrocento,* II: 115–28; Pusino in *Zeitschrift für Kirchengeschichte,* XLIV: 504–43.

twelfth century, had called the "effort to reconcile the dead who never ceased to differ when alive."[52] But a much greater idea captured his imagination: He would prove the basic harmony of all religions and philosophies! His chief tool was the good old allegorical method, and in addition he learned to handle and to prize the techniques of the Hebrew *cabala*,[53] which in his hands established the truth of the divinity of Christ! A good illustration of his lucubrations is his argument that in the opening words of Genesis, "In the beginning," the reason for the creation of the world and all that therein is is clearly set forth.[54] The reader is invited to estimate for himself the values to be found in the highest common factor—to borrow a mathematical term—of all the religions and philosophies. To the present writer they are very close to zero. Further comment would be superfluous.*

---

52 Gilson, *Spirit of Mediaeval Philosophy*, p. 2.
53 Blau, *The Christian Interpretation of the Cabala in the Renaissance*, pp. 14 f.
54 Monnier, *Le Quattrocento*, II: 127.

* It would not help (or hinder) the argument of this chapter to discuss the Platonic Academy, since this informal club, which began to take form in 1462, when Cosimo gave a country place, the villa di Careggi, to Ficino, was hardly more than a sounding board for the ideas of "the new Plato." Under the patronage of Lorenzo the Magnificent the Academy became most fashionable. Over against it was another academy, less well-known today, the *Chorus Achademiae Florentinae*, in which discussions on philosophy and theology, favoring the Aristotelian position, were carried on by the students of the professor of Greek in the University, with the participation of prominent citizens, and under the leadership of the professor himself (Della Torre, *Storia dell' Accademia Platonica*, pp. 380 ff., especially 394–95). There was nothing to choose between the two academies in the matter of freedom of thought.

A word or two may be added on the *Disputationes Camaldulensis* of
Christoforo Landino, usually regarded as giving us a fair sample of the
discussions of Ficino's Academy. Della Torre (pp. 579 ff.) has proved
that the alleged four-day meeting of 1468 never occurred, that Landino
merely spiced his little book with the pretence that it was a genuine
report. Yet it is hardly possible that Landino's account does injustice to
the character of the discussions; it was not objected to by any of the
members as a misrepresentation. The book is not easy to come by; but
the Bibliothèque Nationale has several editions, printed about the turn
of the century, thus indicating that it had its clientele.

On the first day, according to Landino, the topic was the active *vs.*
the contemplative life. According to Ficino's doctrine the contemplative
life should have won; but probably out of deference to the young
Lorenzo, who championed the life of action, the contest was declared
a draw: "Mary and Martha are sisters, dwelling under the same roof."
The second day was given over to the question, "What is the Supreme
Good?" Leon Battista Alberti strung off the names of forty or more
ancient classical writers (quite a display), added the Hebrew teachers,
and ended up with Albertus Magnus, St. Thomas, "Scotus the subtle,"
and Ochan (Ockham). All of these, the participants say, are in substantial agreement that God is *boni bonum*. The last two days were
devoted to the allegorical interpretation of the *Aeneid,* "although every
one knows that there are four sorts of interpretation." Troy is the
concupiscent life which must be destroyed, and Aeneas, after many
wanderings, that is, errors, reaches Italy, that is, the life of Wisdom.
The young Lorenzo (later, the Magnificent), interested as we know in
Venus, opined that the rôles of the two Venuses were not consistent;
but Alberti replied that he is dealing with allegory, not with history;
that the ancients expressed the idea, and the Christians have it too, "for
Paul and his hearer, Dionysius the Areopagite, both recognize the distinction between the things that are grasped by the bodily senses and
those that are not." Mariotto, the steward of the Medici, is represented
by Landino as looking after the meals most debonairly.

The medieval character of the discussions is sufficiently obvious.

CHAPTER IX: PHILOLOGY AND CRITICISM

Lorenzo Valla.—Monnier's dictum, already referred to, that Ficino was the first Humanist *thinker* since Petrarch, has been accepted as convenient rather than convincing, since it passes over Lorenzo Valla (*ca.* 1405–1457)[1] as essentially a grammarian. We shall look into the matter.

Valla, Roman born, with relatives in the papal service, secured a superior Humanistic education in the

1 Monnier, *Le Quattrocento,* I: 280–89; Mancini, *Vita di Lorenzo Valla;* Coleman, *Constantine the great and Christianity* and *The Treatise* of Lorenzo *Valla on the Donation of Constantine* (text and English translation, revised and edited by Coleman).

cloisters of the papal chancery in Rome and, for a time, in Florence. He perfected himself in Greek, as well as Latin, and gained a working knowledge of Hebrew. As a teacher of eloquence at Pavia, he exalted Quintilian, a complete text of whose *Institutes* had been found by Poggio at the Council of Constance, above Cicero. This earned for him the displeasure of the old-line Humanists, to whom Cicero was the master of Latinity. At Pavia, too, he jeered at the unclassical Latin of the great jurist Bartolus and the other medieval civilians. His attack led to riots between the students of law and of arts at the University, and he found it discreet to seek a job elsewhere. Failing in his efforts with the papacy, he entered, in 1435, the service of Alfonso the Magnificent, king of Aragon and of Sicily and claimant to the throne of Naples. With Alfonso he remained, as a prominent member of the royal secretariat, until 1447. In 1448 he realized a long-cherished ambition to get back to Rome and to be admitted to the papal service. Nicholas V, patron of the Humanists, accepted him as a *scriptor* and soon made him one of his apostolic secretaries, and under Calixtus III he continued to enjoy the favors of the papacy. Desiring to be eligible for high Church offices, he never married and, although a layman, received benefices from at least two of the popes and probably also from the Council of Basel.

Most of Valla's many books were written or at least started while he was in the service of King Alfonso. Their range is wide and they have this common char-

acteristic: They were all calculated, if indeed not designed, to disturb the complacency of one entrenched
group or another. For example, in the *De professione
religiosorum,* he asserted that the monks usurp the
name *religious* and evade the ordinary duties of Christians; in the *Disputationes dialecticae,* he condemned
the categories of Aristotle as inadequate and attacked
his physics and his morals; in the *Adnotationes ad
novum testamentum,* he pointed out the grammatical
blunders and mistranslations in the current editions of
St. Jerome's beloved Vulgate (Roger Bacon had attempted the same thing, with much less effectiveness);
in the *Elegantiae linguae Latinae,* he made a scientific
study of the evolution of the Latin language and, as
opposed to Petrarch's aesthetic guesswork, placed the
practice of composition upon a foundation of analysis
and inductive reasoning. (Erasmus published an epitome of this masterly work.) Valla was resolved that
sound Latin should again become the language of Italy,
that it should drive out, for literary purposes, the Italian vernaculars and medieval Latin. Against the dicta
and practice of the die-hard Humanists, he "preached
the necessity of coining new words and phrases apt to
express new ideas, needs, and facts."[2]

Valla's most celebrated book, however, was not the
scholarly *Elegantiae,* but his little treatise on the "Donation of Constantine." Even its title is provocative:
The Falsely Believed and Mendacious Donation of

2 Mancini, *Lorenzo Valla,* p. 328.

Constantine (De falso credita et ementita Constantini donatione declamatio). Valla regarded it as a masterpiece, and in a letter which he sent with a copy of the book to Aurispa, he says it is one of his best *("qua nihil magis oratorium scripsi").*[3] It will be fair, therefore, to use it to test Valla's powers as a critic.

The text of the treatise runs to eighty-two substantial pages. The circumstances surrounding its production are important. It was written in 1440, almost midway in the period of eight years when King Alfonso was making good his claim to the crown of Naples against the bitter opposition of Pope Eugenius IV, who asserted his right to dispose of the realm as a lapsed fief. Alfonso's chief diplomatic weapon was his alliance with the Council of Basel, which had begun its work in 1431. It was at outs with Eugenius and was determined to curtail the economic and political powers of the Holy See. Valla's treatise undertook to prove not only that the "Donation" was spurious, but that the suzerainty which the popes had exercised over Naples and Sicily fell to the ground with it. "I attack," Valla says, "not only the dead but the living." In truth, most of the treatise is given over to bitter diatribes against the political authority and behavior of the popes, including Eugenius IV, outside and inside Italy.

It is altogether likely that Valla formed the idea for his treatise from the somewhat radical program for the work of the Council of Basel which Nicholas of Cusa

3 Quoted in Coleman, *Constantine the Great and Christianity,* p. 197.

(later reconciled with the papacy and created cardinal) presented to the Council in 1433. The program forms a book, entitled *De concordantia catholica,* and in it he devoted some little space to demonstrating the falsity of the "Donation."[4] He was not the first to doubt its authenticity[5]—nor was Dante, who in *De Monarchia* clearly questions its validity—but he was the first who undertook seriously to prove that it was spurious. Since Alfonso's bishops from the South were in attendance at the Council in 1433, having been sent to Basel primarily to look after his interests, it is altogether probable that they sent back to King Alfonso a full report on Cusa's ideas.

Let us pass over the many pages of diatribe in Valla's treatise and summarize his arguments proving that the "Donation" was a forgery.

The *Constitutum Constantini,* or "Donation of Constantine," Valla pointed out (as Cusa had done), had not been included by Gratian (*fl. ca.* 1145) in his *Decretum,* the great source book and treatise on canon law; it had been added later by some unknown person, under the rubric "palea."[6] (There are many such additions.) That proves, he argued, that Gratian believed it to be a forgery. Moreover, Valla asserted, it is utterly improbable that Constantine (emperor, 306–337)

---

4 The Latin text in *ibid.,* pp. 238–42.

5 For the principal forerunners see Döllinger, *Die Papst-Fabeln des Mittelalters,* pp. 61–125.

6 Text from the *Decretum* in Coleman, ed., *The Treatise of Lorenzo Valla.* Digest and discussion of its contents in Coleman, *Constantine the Great and Christianity,* pp. 175–83.

would have given the better part of his empire to the pope; and even if he had wanted to, his sons and the Roman senate would have protested. It is equally improbable that Pope Silvester (314–335) would have accepted the gift, for did not the Lord Jesus declare, "my kingdom is not of this world?" And if Constantine did make the grant, there is no evidence in any history, no commemorative monument or tablet, showing that Silvester accepted it or that Constantine put him or his officials in possession of the countries in question. Further, if it be alleged that Constantine did install Silvester as his successor in the West, who was it that disseized the pope? There is no evidence for this either. On the other hand, there is ample evidence that Constantine and his successors continued to rule over the whole empire. The histories prove it, and so does the gold coinage of Constantine, minted after he became a Christian. No coinage of Silvester's has ever been known.

Furthermore, "almost every history worthy of the name speaks of Constantine as a Christian from boyhood, with his father Constantius, long before the pontificate of Silvester." In support of this erroneous statement Valla cites the *Historia ecclesiastica* of Eusebius of Caesarea (*ca.* 260–*ca.* 340); but the text of this authoritative work does not support the assertion. It is difficult to understand why Valla did not use the *Life of Constantine* of the same Eusebius, which tells the story of Constantine's *conversion* in the campaign against Maxentius, A.D. 312 (*"In hoc signo vinces"*),

nor note the passage in the well-known chronicle of St.
Jerome (*ca.* 340–420), which records the *baptism* of
Constantine in the closing days of his life at the hands
of Bishop Eusebius of Nicomedia (d. 341?). Valla
could have learned the fact of this baptism from Cusa,
if he had read him carefully.[7]

Valla then quotes from a spurious narrative of Pope
Melchiades (310–314), the predecessor of Silvester,
which tells of Constantine's gift of landed estates and
of the Lateran palace to the pope, but makes no mention of the "Donation." Here again Cusa was available to warn Valla that the text ascribed to Melchiades
was fraudulent.[8]

Valla has better fortune in pointing out that Pope
Gelasius, cited in the *palea* as vouching for "The Acts
of the Blessed Silvester" (there were many versions),
does not say that the "Donation" is to be found
therein; and, anyway, the "Acts" are shameless fiction.
Cusa had already made these points.[9]

Valla's most brilliant achievement is his demonstration in detail of the multitude of linguistic anachronisms in the text of the *Constitutum Constantini*. Here
his philological scholarship (he had started work on
the *Elegantiae* in 1435) gave him a tool that enabled
him to show clearly that the "Donation" could not possibly have been composed in the age of the great emperor. The popes, he jeers, are not informed on these

7 Coleman, ed., *Treatise of Lo-*   8 *Ibid.*
   renzo Valla, pp. 71, 73; *Con-*   9 *Ibid.*, p. 240.
   stantine the Great, p. 241.

points; they think that *cephas* means *head,* instead of *rock.* And the "Donation" speaks of Constantinople as a city to be founded and also as already founded.

The argument of the supporters of the pope's temporal power, that many of the emperors subsequent to Charles the Great had confirmed Constantine's "Donation," gets short shrift at Valla's hands. They had to confirm it in order to get crowned. So too with the argument that "the Roman Church is entitled by prescription to what it possesses." No length of years, Valla says—not too convincingly—can destroy a true title; and even if the popes had received such great possessions from Constantine or had a right to them by prescription, either right would have been extinguished by the crimes of the possessors, "for we know that the slaughter and devastation of all Italy and of many of the provinces has flowed from this single source."

Let us postpone a final evaluation of Valla's treatise until after we have considered the handling of the selfsame problem by the English scholastic, Reginald Pecock.

Reginald Pecock.—Reginald Pecock (*ca.* 1395–*ca.* 1460) was a Welshman of humble and unknown birth. He was a distinguished student at Oxford, where he followed the old, scholastic curriculum (there was no other) and on graduation was given a fellowship. Through the favor of the Duke of Gloucester and a papal provision, he was made bishop of St. Asaph, a poverty-stricken see in Wales, and through the favor

of the Duke of Suffolk he was later transferred, again
with a papal provision, to the see of Chichester. His
talents and backing even won him admission to the
royal council.[10]

Pecock was a voluminous writer in Latin and in
English. His surviving English writings are of particular interest because in them he was striving to en-
lighten the laity and especially the Lollard "Bible men,"
who flouted the authority of the Church and relied upon
their own interpretation of the Bible. Their errors
were due, in his opinion, to their lack of instruction in
logic and theology, and this defect he proposed to overcome by graded instruction in the only language most
of them knew. The obligation to instruct them, he
averred, was shared by his clerical brethren, who "shall
be condemned at the last day, if by clear wit they draw
not men into consent of true faith otherwise than by
fire, sword, and hangment." Obviously Pecock did not
sympathize with the statute *De haeretico comburendo*.

Pecock's view of the respective spheres of Faith and
Reason was substantially that of St. Thomas; but as
was his wont, he stated his opinion in bold and provocative language: "It longith not to Holi Scripture,
neither it is his office into which God hath him or-
deyned, neither it is his part forto grounde eny gouer-
naunce or deede or seruice of God, or eny lawe of God,

---

10 Pecock, *The Book of Faith,
The Donet, The Folewer to
the Donet, The Reule of Crysten Religioun, The Repressor
of Over Much Blaming of the*
Clergy; Gairdner, *Lollardy
and the Reformation in England,* I: 202–42; *Dublin Review,* LXXVI: 27–55; Green,
Bishop Reginald Pecock.

or eny trouthe which mannis resoun bi nature may find, leerne, and knowe."[11] Pecock then sweepingly asserts that reason (*i.e.*, the law of nature or "law of kinde") is to govern outside of the sphere of revelation, "that whanne euere and where euere in Holi Scripture or out of Holi Scripture be writen eny point or eny gouernance of the seide law of kinde it is more verrili writen in the book of mannis soule than in the outward book of parchemyn or of velym; and if eny semyng discorde be betwixe the wordis writen in the outward book of Holi Scripture and the doom [judgment] of resoun, write in mannis soule and herte, the wordis so writen withoutforth oughten [to] be expowned and be interpretid and brought forto accorde with the doom of resoun in thilk mater . . . ."[12]

This striking statement of the sphere belonging to reason horrified the Lollard Bible men and frightened the timid orthodox. Actually, it is only a defence of the necessity of theological interpretation, for what is theology but "the subjection of the letter of Scripture to the doom of reason?"[13]

The scholastic slant of Pecock's mind is shown by his high regard for the syllogism. "An argument if he be ful and foormal, which is clepid a sillogisme, is made of two proposiciouns driving out of them and bi strengthe of them the thridde proposicioun." "Wherefore certis if eny man can be sure for eny tyme that

11 *Repressor*, I: 10.   13 *Dublin Review*, LXXVI: 39.
12 *Ibid.*, pp. 25–26.

these two premyssis be trewe, he mai be sure that the conclusioun is trewe; though alle the aungelis in Heaven wolden sei and holde that thilk conclusioun were not trewe."[14]

Pecock's intelligence and learning were massive, but his vanity was great, his sense of humor non-existent, and his appreciation of political realities slight. He was truly rash in his criticisms. The Church Fathers were not always to be trusted, the University doctors of theology erred frequently, and Aristotle was only a researcher after truth who, like the rest of men, failed at many points in natural science and moral philosophy. But Pecock's own writings were reliable.[15] He even laid himself open to the charge that he did not believe in the infallibility of Church Councils.[16] Many of his insights have been vindicated. He knew that the Gospel preceded the New Testament, that John's curse at the end of Revelation applied only to that book, that the Scriptures are to be interpreted historically, that the Apostles' Creed was not composed by the apostles (Valla knew this too), and that the "Donation of Constantine" was spurious.[17]

But Pecock's countrymen were hostile. His great

14 *Repressor,* I:8. Language slightly modernized.

15 *Ibid.,* I: 46, 47, 71, 87, 91; II: 320, 334, *et passim; Folewer,* p. 65; *Book of Faith,* pp. 146 f.

16 *Ibid.,* p. 181 f. Here he was, so to say, arguing with the Lollards, who flouted the authority of the Church. Considering the anti-papal decrees of Constance and Basel, he probably could make a good defence against the broader charge.

17 *Repressor,* I: 60, 64, 292; II: 350–66.

unpopularity is not hard to explain. Biblical Catholics
and Lollards were shocked by his rationalistic handling
of religious topics, old-fashioned Catholics disliked his
opposition to the orthodox method of crushing heresy,
and also objected to his criticism of the Fathers. Far-
sighted prelates were alarmed by his defence of practices it was politic to be quiet about, and the sensitive
patriotism of both Court and Commons was offended
by his condemnation of the failing war with France.[18]
The result of this almost universal reprobation, which
was shown promptly upon the death of his second pro-
tector, the Duke of Suffolk, was his ruin. An illegal
trial before the Archbishop of Canterbury forced the
shocked prelate, under threat of the fire, to confess
heresies he was not guilty of, to recant, to throw into
the flames three folios and eleven quartos that he had
written, and to accept incarceration in a monastic cell,
with paper, pen, and ink forbidden him (1457).[19]

Pecock's longest and most important work, *The
Repressor of Over Much Blaming of the Clergy,* was
completed in 1449 or 1450. It is devoted, as the apt
title indicates, to a defence of the clergy against the
manifold criticisms of the Bible men. It was in rebuttal
of their charge that the possession of landed property
by the clergy was forbidden by the Bible[20] that Pecock

18 Drawn mostly from *Dublin
Review,* LXXVI: 55. But *cf.*
Green, *Bishop Pecock,* Chaps.
IV–V.

xxxvi–lxi; *Dublin Review,*
LXXVI, *passim. Cf.* Burton's
article on Pecock in the *Catholic Encyclopedia.*

19 *Repressor,* Introduction, pp.

20 *Repressor,* I:275 ff.

took up the problem of the "Donation of Constantine" without fanfare of any sort. For the Lollards claimed —one of their many arguments—that when Constantine endowed Silvester with Rome and the western regions the voice of an angel "was herd in the eir," saying that poison was that day infused into the Church.[21]

In reply to this assertion Pecock points out that the earliest teller of this story was Gerald of Wales (*ca.* 1146–1220), who admitted that it was hearsay and, moreover, said that the voice was the voice of a fiend. "Whi and wherto," says Pecock, "schulden we bileeue his seiyng to be trewe . . . sithcn he is a lier and the fader of lesing . . . ?"[22] Be that as it may, Pecock lays down this proposition: If it can be surely proved that Constantine was not baptized by Silvester at Rome or elsewhere, then the tale of the voice in the air cannot be accepted as true.[23] He then proceeds, in fourteen and a half orderly and unimpassioned pages, to prove that the "Donation" was a fraud.

There is no recorded evidence that Pecock knew either Cusa's or Valla's handling of the problem. The chances are quite against his acquaintance with Valla's treatise, which circulated only privately during Pecock's lifetime, but the case would seem to be different with regard to Cusa's argument. English prelates were attending the Council of Basel in 1433, and Pecock, always eager for information on matters touching the Church, resided in London at the time. Still, if Pecock

---

21 *Ibid.,* II:323. *Cf.* Dante's   22 *Repressor,* II: 350–51, 356.
    "Purgatory," xxxii.   23 *Ibid.,* p. 352.

was acquainted with Cusa's work, he enjoyed no advantage over Valla.

Let us then proceed to summarize Pecock's handling of the great theme. The man who knew Constantine most intimately, and who wrote the first part of the *Tripartite History* (covering the years 306–439) and of the *Historia ecclesiastica,* was Eusebius of Caesarea (*ca.* 260–*ca.* 340). He it was who reported "the appering which was mad to Constantyn of the crosse in the eir," and who, in his *Life of Constantine,* related that Constantine was first baptized, in the last days of his life, at Nicomedia, by Bishop Eusebius of that place. This was after the death of Silvester. Surely, says Pecock, this testimony carries more weight than anything to the contrary in any legend of Silvester.

The contrary evidence attributed to Pope Damasus I (366–384), Pecock rejects as inconsistent with the testimony of Eusebius of Caesarea. Pecock did not know—probably no one at the time knew—that this portion of the report credited to Damasus was a forgery. Later in his argument Pecock makes use of the authentic part of the report of Damasus. Only once was Pecock taken in by a spurious document, that attributed to Pope Urban I (222–230), which he accepted as proving that in the times of that pope the church at Rome possessed landed properties. This was a serious blunder.

The text of the *Constitutum Constantini,* as given in Gratian's *Decretum,* Pecock declares, can hardly be the product of Constantine's pen, for it is not consistent with his manner of writing Latin, "for in other epistlis of Constantyn, which he wroot whanne he was in his moost rialte [at the height of his power] is not such a stile of him."

Pecock does not know or he intentionally ignores the fact that the "Donation" was not put into the *Decretum* by Gratian himself. Cusa and Valla both think the point worth making. It seems to the present writer quite possible that Pecock did not think so, since he proposed to demonstrate conclusively that the "Donation" was apocryphal.

St. Ambrose and St. Jerome, he points out, accept the statement of Eusebius of Caesarea that Constantine was baptized shortly before his death; so do Theodoret, Socrates, and Sozomen, continuators of the *Tripartite History;* these authorities outweigh any others.

The endowment of the papacy with extensive territories, Pecock remarks, was made by Pippin, Charles the Great, Louis the Pious, and Matilda of Tuscany. (Cusa speaks of the first two.) Constantine's gifts for the support of churches in Rome were modest. If he had made the immense territorial grant attributed to him in the "Donation," Pope Damasus I would not have failed to say so in the report he made to St. Jerome at the latter's request, for he mentions the small gifts and would himself have been in possession of the territories in question.

No credible history knows anything about the alleged transfer of the West to Silvester; but on the contrary, the *Tripartite History* tells that Constantine, nigh unto death, divided his whole empire among his three sons, giving Rome and the West to his son Constantine. Later on, another son reigned over the reunited empire. Moreover Pope Boniface IV (608–615) asked, and received, from the Emperor Phocas (602–610) the Pantheon at Rome to be made into a church, which he could not have done "if Bonefas hadde be ful lord of al Rome and of alle cuntrees ligging about bi gifte of the First Constantyn." Another proof is the plain record of the chronicles that the emperors at Constantinople reigned over both the East and the West until Charles the Great was crowned emperor by the pope.

Still another proof supported by the chronicles is the fact, which Pecock as a good Churchman regrets, that for many hundred years after Silvester the elections of the popes were reported for confirmation to the emperor at Constantinople. This clearly proves that the latter was lord "of Rome and of alle the cuntrees ligging aboute." (Cusa made this point.) There is no use alleging that Pope Gelasius vouches for the reality of the "Donation," for in his epistle mentioning the legend of Silvester there is not a word about the "Donation." Finally, the *Tripartite History* proves that the account of the foundation of Constantinople recorded in the "Donation" stamps it as fraudulent. "And [t]herefor the seid epistle [the *Constitutum Constantini*]," Pecock concludes, "is an vntrewe apocrife, namelich sithen histories, dwelling in thilk same cuntre and [written] soone after the deede doon, kouthen [could] knowe the treuthe of the deede than othere men dwelling ferther fro thens in rombe [remotely]."

It is clear and plain that the scholastic doctor did a better job on the "Donation" than the Humanist did. Valla's superiority in the use of the linguistic anachronisms and of coins is marked, although Pecock, innocent though he was of philological lore, did recognize that the style of the "Donation" was not Constantine's. In all other respects, Pecock carries off the honors. He knew the sources better, and his one blunder is not so serious as the blunders of Valla. The great Döllinger, unduly depreciative of Cusa, yet praises Pecock for the "accurate handling of the sources in his historical investigation," as against Valla's "artistic production" —"an oratorical declamation rather than a calm historical examination."[24] Eduard Fueter, the chief historian of modern historiography, also awards the palm to Pecock: "the English bishop, Reginald Pecock, entirely untouched by Humanism, who carried through his investigation and findings on the forgery in a much more clean-cut fashion than Valla."[25]

This will not surprise a medievalist. The scholastic discipline, with its training in evidence and its disputations, so similar to the analysis of the decisions of the courts in a legal brief, was no mean preparation for the task presented by the "Donation."[26]

24 *Papst-Fabeln,* p. 118.

25 *Historiographie,* p. 112.

26 *Cf.* Rashdall in *Cambridge Medieval History,* Vol. VI, Chap. XVII, especially pp. 595 ff.

One final word: The reader is reminded that Valla, the Humanist, strove to turn back the clock and re-establish classical Latin as the literary language of his country, while Pecock, the scholastic doctor, wrote on religion for the laity in the vernacular.

CHAPTER X: THE FINE ARTS

The adoption of Christianity and its spread over the Roman empire and the neighboring regions led to fundamental changes in the art language which the Middle Ages inherited from the Greco-Roman world.[1] In the Near East, which took its cue, in the long run, from Constantinople, the new religion and the resurgence of older modes of thought led to the abandonment of the plastic form of the Greeks and to the creation

[1] Morey, *Mediaeval Art.* This chapter leans heavily on Morey's great work.

of the Byzantine style—illustrated by the mosaics—in which Christian emotion found its release in the contemplation of the mysteries. In the West, the descendants of the Roman provincials and the Teutonic invaders elaborated out of the Greco-Roman bequest an art language of their own. God had become man in the person of Jesus, and the Christians of Western Europe were not content with contemplating the mystery; they strove with all the strength of their art to feel their union with the divine. After the passage of centuries the Gothic cathedral finally made this supremely possible. Human interest in the earthly scene asserted its rights in the decoration of the cathedral and in the borders of contemporary manuscripts. Toward the end of the twelfth century, the leaf capitals and the friezes of the cathedrals and the borders of books came to reflect the flora and the smaller fauna that the artists knew at first hand. The incorporation of the beauty of the earth in the house of God, the "grasping of the infinite while rooted in the concrete," was of the same nature as, and preceded by only a brief space of time, the reconciliation of Faith and Reason, with the recognition of the legitimacy of secular interest in natural phenomena, which St. Thomas celebrated in his *Summa Theologiae*.

It was the vaulted space of the Gothic cathedral which best expressed the transcendental element in life with all its mystery and emotion. This space was not confined by the walls, as was the space of St. Sophia, but was only a segregated portion of the vast infinitude of space without the walls, through whose translucent glass of many colors the Light Divine seemed verily to stream.

The realistic evolution of ornament, represented by the use of leaf and flower and bird, was matched by progressive changes in the statuary which encrusted the great edifice. The changes in the carved figures well illustrate the growing humanization of the divine and the saintly. The hieratic Virgin of the west façade of Chartres, the representative of divine wisdom, was followed, a generation later, by the more naturally posed mother and child of the lateral portal of the north transept of Chartres; in the virgin portal of Amiens she is shown as more queenly than divine; in the north transept of Notre Dame of Paris she is an aristocratic marquise with delicate features and grace; in the *Vierge dorée* of Amiens she is "more understandably feminine"; and in the choir of Notre Dame of Paris she is almost a coquette.[2]

The German Gothic which flowered during the thirteenth century in the rugged Thuringian Forest, bordered by the bishoprics of Bamberg in the south and Naumburg in the north, exhibited an even more outspoken interest in the earthly scene. In the cathedral of Naumburg, the walls of the western choir were decorated with a dozen statues—not of the saints which the French would have put in such a consecrated place, but of the benefactors of the bishopric, the

2 *Ibid.,* pp. 353–54.

princes of the Wettin dynasty and their wives, who had lived two hundred years before. These " 'likenesses' are pure evocations, and their strong individuality is therefore even more surprising evidence of German Gothic ability to find its ideal in the concrete."[3] The secular, in short, was beginning to assert its independent claims, as it was soon to do even more emphatically, in the science and logic of William of Ockham and his school.[4]

The evolution of art in medieval Italy differed in some important respects from that in transalpine Europe, which we have in the main been considering. The clearer air of the peninsula, in which individual objects, even trees, stand out with sharper silhouettes than in the transalpine lands, the inherited fondness of the Italians for the ancient cult of the human figure and for the antique forms and habiliments which their Roman ancestors had found congenial, and which surviving monuments recalled, go far to explain the differences from the "North." The Gothic cathedral with its mysterious interior and its walls of translucent glass found little favor in sun-drenched Italy. Some of its features—for example, the pointed windows—were adapted to the ends of external decoration, but the art interest of Italy was concentrated chiefly upon the human figure and the human scene, in harmony with the Latin maxim, "man the measure of all things."

3 *Ibid.*, p. 296.   4 *Cf.* White in *American Historical Review,* LII: 421–35.

The art of Giotto (*ca.* 1300), with his success in the handling of the third dimension, inaugurated the realistic movement in Italian painting. The scientific study of perspective, which engrossed some of the best minds of Florence in the fifteenth century, was obviously of service in promoting stricter realism. Its values can be conveniently observed in the reproductions of the less damaged *Last Supper* of Leonardo. The study of perspective and anatomy, and progressive experiments in the rendering of light and movement, bore their fruits in the art of the *Quattrocento,* commonly known as the "Early Renaissance" in Italy. The preferred subjects of the painters were still biblical and saintly in theme; but they were handled in an intimate human fashion, with a plethora of domestic gear as if the people represented were contemporaries of the artists. On the other hand, the art of the *Cinquecento,* or the "High Renaissance," is selective and aristocratic. Its characteristics and its departures from the more bourgeois art of the *Quattrocento* are systematically and conveniently discussed by Heinrich Wölfflin[5] and will be touched upon here only incidentally.

The art of the High Renaissance in Italy exhibits clearly two inherited features which distinguish it from the art of the same period in transalpine Europe. The first is the interest in idealized human beauty: Art must be selective; nature must be perfected. This necessarily involved a departure from strict realism—to a degree

5 *The Art of the Italian Renaissance.*

a denial of reality— and a weakening of expressiveness in favor of formal beauty. The second is the growing employment of landscape, particularly in the Venetian school, as a backdrop for the figures, but not as a habitat within which the action takes place (*e.g.,* Leonardo's *Mona Lisa*); but the Roman and Florentine schools soon dropped landscape almost completely.

Northern art pursued its independent course of fidelity to fact, parallel with the art developments of Italy. Professor Mather, whose preference for Italian art makes his testimony favorable to the North the more convincing, has said: "Since the zeal for more truthful representation was constant in the Italian Renaissance, and equally so in the North, I do not see how we can deny to the late Gothic painting of the North the quality of a Renaissance of realism."[6]

In the later Middle Ages the most influential artists of the North were the Netherlanders. They shaped the arts in France until Francis I brought in the Italians, and they conquered the Germanies by about 1450 with their superior technique. Claus Sluter (d. 1405) was the Dutch sculptor who "determined the future trend of Burgundian sculpture." The painters of the miniatures of the *Très Riches Heures* of the Duke of Berry (d. 1417), the brother of Duke Philip the Bold of Burgundy, were Dutch. When their art migrated from the miniatures to the panel paintings, the same integration of man in nature was maintained. The *Adora-*

6 Mather, *Western European Painting of the Renaissance,* p. 3.

tion of the Lamb, the masterpiece of the brothers
Hubert and Jan Van Eyck, which was finished by Jan
in 1432, is the noblest illustration of this development.
"The landscape of the *Adoration* envelops the figures;
they belong to it . . . , and the setting thereby imparts
to the spiritual allegory a sense of physical experience."[7] Jan was the more matter-of-fact of the two.
His portrait of the Canon van der Paele, in the
Madonna painted for the Canon, "is the most powerful
physical likeness that art had known since the portraits
of republican Rome."[8]

The greatest French work of the fifteenth century
is the Pietà from Villeneuve-lès-Avignon, now in the
Louvre. It is, Morey declares, "the finest rendering
of the theme in art, not even excepting Michelangelo's
great group in St. Peter's at Rome." Gothic painting,
he adds, "here attains a universal note without the aid
of landscape, without resort to abstraction as in Italy,
and with no relaxation of its hold on concrete and
poignant reality." It "is an achievement of idealism
through the realistic process alone, and independent
of landscape and setting."[9]

In general, however, Gothic (or "northern") painting was distinguished by its belief that the object must
be depicted in its spatial setting if its full reality is to
be made manifest. The togetherness of things, which
impressed the artists of the North, may be explained
in part by the misty character of their homelands—

7 Morey, *Mediaeval Art,* p. 363.   9 *Ibid.,* pp. 384–85.
8 *Ibid.,* p. 365.

misty in comparison with the clear atmosphere of most of Italy. In the North things are seen together. In Italy, it is in a way the separateness of things that strikes the native artist, and his painted groups are in effect made up of separate individuals, juxtaposed, each complete in itself. Landscape, if introduced at all—anywhere outside the School of Venice—is but a background. An analogy from music will make this point clear: In Italy we have a melody and solo with a harmonizing accompaniment; in the North we have an orchestra which determines the mood, and out of the depths of its harmonies the solo rises up and touches the consciousness of the listener.[10]

It was no accident, then, which made landscape the chief interest of the northern painters. "Nature has produced man and raised him to the first place among her children." She, not man, is the real hero of the drama of existence and her moods reflect her cosmic power and mystery.[11] The interior of the Gothic cathedral awakens in the worshiper and even in the casual visitor a sense of the transcendental. Something of the same sense of environing mystery is evoked by the sight of the boundless sea, the mountain ranges, and even "the fruitful plain." Memling's *Madonna of Martin van Nieuwenhove,* Morey remarks, illustrates to per-

10 Neumann, *Rembrandt,* I: 232. The various aspects of this feature of northern art psychology are impressively explained in Professor Oskar Hagen's *Deutsches Sehen* and more briefly, but still clearly, in his first American publication, *Art Epochs and their Leaders,* Chap. III.

11 Hagen, *Deutsches Sehen,* pp. 116–17.

fection "the transcendental atmosphere which landscape gave to northern painting; if one shuts out the vista seen through the window, the Virgin loses half her spell."[12]

Northern painting did not, however, confine all its attention to landscape. It also excelled in portraying homely scenes of middle-class and peasant life, in which honest contentment with the comforts and diversions of everyday existence is made manifest. In the *genre* paintings which thus celebrated the earthly joys, the Netherlanders went into greater detail than did the artists of *quattrocento* Italy, although the two groups have much in common.

In the sixteenth century, the more showy and more beautiful and aristocratic High Renaissance art of Italy, inferior though it was in the deeper realities to the art of the North, threatened not merely to give northern art useful hints in figure drawing and in composition, but to overthrow it utterly. The growth of absolutism in government, which was a marked feature of the sixteenth century, and which was accompanied by increasing deference to and increasing assumption of dignity by the rulers, now the great patrons of art, made the "grand style," the "courtly selectiveness," of the Italian High Renaissance (and of the Mannerism which followed it) the vogue with high society for a century and more. The hauteur of Spanish court etiquette and the ceremonialism of the court of Louis XIV of France seem to be—and not

12 Morey, *Mediaeval Art,* p. 370.

improbably are—elaborations of the manners of the High Renaissance of Italy. In a word, the Gothic tradition was almost overwhelmed by the grandiose and the nude. Only one land resisted stoutly—the Dutch Netherlands, commonly known as Holland. Dutch art did not surrender.

Spanish art in the period of Velasquez, indeed, regained its freedom; Holland, however, promptly rejected Italian art and Spanish control. Holland "continued the honest and penetrating portraiture of men and things its own sons had initiated at the beginning of the fifteenth century," and transmitted to our own time the two contributions of late Gothic: "the candid portrait of person and thing, and landscape in its own right, reflective of mood, wherein the modern soul still seeks to recover the communion with the infinite which was the initial and essential content of mediaeval art."[13]

If the Netherlands was the America of modern art, Rembrandt van Rijn (1606–69) was her Columbus. The heroes of Dutch independence, political and artistic, were William and Maurice of Orange, de Ruyter, and Rembrandt.[14] In the Dutch landscapes it is a matter of indifference whether the individual contents are beautiful or ugly; it suffices that "they are the countenances on which cosmic and psychical powers express and mirror their moods."[15] Rembrandt's holy personages are not the heroized beings of the High Renaissance in Italy; they are the poor and the humble, modelled

13 *Ibid.*, p. 392.
14 Neumann, *Rembrandt*, II: 288–
89.
15 *Ibid.*, I: 210–11.

upon members of the Jewish colony in Amsterdam. Only momentarily, before suffering had refined him, did Rembrandt, seduced by the histrionic charm of Italian art, fail to portray in his paintings nature's cosmic power.

Chiaroscuro, or light and shade, was his principal means in making the human figure derive its life from its spatial setting. (The method was first employed in a forcible manner by the Lombard painter Caravaggio (1569–1609).) The Dutch portrait had been superior in the fifteenth century, the century of the Van Eycks, to the profile of the Italian medal, and with Rembrandt it reached the heights of significance. He started always with the given physical being and added "the other," reversing the sequence in which the architects of the Gothic cathedrals had brought nature into communion with the transcendental. The *Portrait of Nicolaes Bruyningh* is his greatest portrait; the man gazes into the expressive distance and listens to ravishing words.[16] Rembrandt's master painting is the *Return of the Prodigal Son.* The figures are life-size, and the mood is of the utmost quietude, as if all were stilled in contemplation of the miracle of repentance and compassion. "Rembrandt's art," Professor Hagen declares, "is in truth a power in the evolution of our present-day civilization which we can no more imagine away than we can the art of Shakespeare or Goethe. Where would our perception of the human soul be without him?"[17]

16 But *cf.* Hagen, *Art Epochs and their Leaders,* pp. 205 f.

17 *Ibid.,* p. 202.

The contributions of the Middle Ages to modern art are admirably summarized by Professor Morey in his Oberlin address of 1938. He speaks, *inter alia,* of stained glass, of the drama, and of polyphonic music— that great medium for the expression of transcendental emotion (Bach, Beethoven, Brahms). Then he places stress on those "elements of experience which were not realized in [the arts of] antiquity": "(1) the recognition of transcendental values, (2) the establishment of emotion as a valid element of content, (3) the introduction of the realistic point of view."[18]

A minor problem may well be looked at by way of conclusion. Vasari is usually regarded as responsible for the idea that the greatness of the High Renaissance art of Italy was due to the study of antique monuments. The "change to the perfect manner," he says, "was caused by the discovery of ancient marbles . . . the Laocoon, the Hercules, the Great Torso of the Belvedere . . . the Venus, the Cleopatra, the Apollo," etc.[19]

This doctrine was of course harmonized with Leonardo's dictum that art is the imitation of nature. Dolce puts it very well: "One should then choose the most perfect form, imitating nature in part . . . . And partly one should imitate the beautiful marble and bronze figures of the ancient masters. Whereof who so shall taste and possess fully the marvellous perfection, will be able with certainty to correct many defects of

18 *Historical Aspects of the Fine Arts,* pp. 31–41, especially pp. 31–32.

19 Mather, *A History of Italian Painting,* p. 316.

nature . . . . Inasmuch as the ancient things contain the entire perfection of art, and can be the exemplars of all beauty."[20]

Franz Landsberger, deeply convinced though he was of the influence of the antique upon Italian artists, believed that they did not consciously imitate the antique, but were nevertheless in many ways aided by it, that the antique taught them to select from nature.[21] Oskar Hagen, in a review of Landsberger's book which he has generously placed at my disposal, points out that Landsberger's argumentation is throughout hypothetical, and that he overlooks the fundamental fact that antique and Italian Renaissance art both handle Italian materials, in works created by men of relatively the same blood and temperament, on the same soil and under the same climatic conditions. The same problems of the relation of man to nature, Hagen observes, necessarily arose, and no direct knowledge of antique solutions need be conjectured.

Professor Mather is inclined to believe that the antique influence was real although slight and unobtrusive. "All that really happened was that a few very talented young artists who were coming up early in the fifteenth century were alert and sensitive enough to scrutinize and understand certain antique statues and buildings that were being investigated, were perceptive enough to see that the superiority of these antiques rested on much calculation and observation of natural

20 *Ibid.,* p. 446.   21 *Die künstlerischen Probleme der Renaissance.*

appearances, and were sensible enough to measure up the ruins and to study the human form more carefully and enthusiastically than their predecessors had done." There was, he adds, "no definite break with the past."[22] A little later, in the same lecture, Professor Mather seems to make a further qualification: "The Italian artist was, of course, expressing himself, but he was shaping his self-expression in view of noble precedents. Fortunately these ancient exemplars were too rare and too vaguely apprehended to constitute a tyranny . . . . Painting is the great art of Renaissance Italy, possibly because the Italian painter really saw very few antique paintings, but had to work from the native resources of his art and from sensitive influences from the parallel arts of sculpture, architecture, and poetry."[23]

Bernhard Berenson, the great American specialist in Italian art, concludes that the antique was of slight if any importance. Apropos of Mantegna (1431–1506), he remarks: "Englamoured and undiscriminating only as an Italian Humanist could be, Mantegna was blinded to the fact that his [antique] models were, in everything but conception, inferior to the work of his own peers and contemporaries . . . . He was saved from insipidity only by the vigour and incorruptibility of genius . . . . Although he doubtless wasted much of his talent upon the monstrous effort to assimilate an execution inferior to his own, he received no fatal injury. The effort, however, did not advance him. Perhaps but

22 *Historical Aspects of the Fine Arts*, p. 43.   23 *Ibid.*, p. 59.

for this waste of energy his zealous quest of line would have been crowned with far greater success . . . ."[24]

The eminent Heinrich Wölfflin has a right to the last word. "The world of antique monuments which contained the productions of a ripe and of an over-ripe art, far from determining the progress of the modern development of style, did not even conduce to a premature harvest of results . . . . In the sixteenth century art reached such a pinnacle that for a short time it was on a level with the antique. This was a distinctly individual development, and not the result of a deliberate study of the remains of antiquity. The broad stream of Italian art flowed on, and if there had been no antique figures the Cinquecento must have become what it actually became."[25]

"It is safer," Leonardo remarks, "to go direct to the works of nature than to those which have been imitated from her originals with great deterioration and thereby to acquire a bad method, for he who has access to the fountain does not go to the waterpot."[26]

24 *North Italian Painters of the Renaissance,* pp. 43–44. Berenson's discussion of the antique covers pp. 24–52.

25 *The Art of the Italian Renaissance,* p. 363. *Cf.* pp. 361–69.

26 MacCurdy, ed., *The Notebooks of Leonardo da Vinci,* II: 278–79.

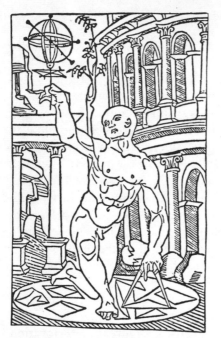

CHAPTER XI:

DISCOVERIES
AND
INVENTIONS

For the purposes of this book it will not be necessary to survey the whole fields of discovery and invention[1] during the Renaissance epoch; it will be enough to consider the outstanding phenomena and their relation, if any, to the revival of antiquity.

Printing.—The greatest invention of the period and probably of all past time was the invention of printing from cast movable type, or the art of typography.[2]

1 Usher, *A History of Mechanical Inventions;* White in *Speculum,* XV: 141–59.

2 Wroth, ed., *A History of the Printed Book;* McMurtrie, *The Book: the Story of Printing and Bookmaking.*

Like most inventions it was not hit upon by a happy inspiration; it was, on the contrary, a work of synthesis, a new combination and adaptation of existing devices and processes. Goldsmiths knew how to cast and carve medals and jewelry; bookbinders were accustomed to stamping with dies the covers and clasps of books with lettering and ornamental figures; weavers of textiles printed patterns upon some of their fabrics with wooden or metal blocks; painters even before the Van Eycks had learned of the superiority of oil paints; vintners and paper-makers had long employed lever or torsion presses, the former to extract the juice of the grape, the latter to squeeze the water out of their product.

Furthermore, production had begun on paper, a relatively inexpensive material upon which to print. The Chinese had invented it, making it from linen rags, early in the second century, and Europe had learned the process from the Arabs via Spain. Toward the end of the thirteenth century paper mills were in production in France and in Italy, and later elsewhere. This invention was fundamental for the large-scale development of typographic printing; for parchment, made from the skins of calves (vellum) and sheep, was too costly for extensive use, and too limited in quantity to meet the growing popular demand for the printed word.

The clever Chinese had also experimented with movable type, made from earthenware, as early as the eleventh century, and their enlightened neighbor, the emperor of Korea, was casting movable type from

bronze about 1400.[3] These oriental inventors of movable type were in the end defeated by the absence of
an alphabet; their ideographic words required thousands of characters, and they found it advisable to be
content with their eighth-century invention of printing
from engraved wooden blocks. (Marco Polo had told
his readers about the printed paper money of his
master, the Great Khan.)

Whether Europe invented block printing—printing
from engraved wooden blocks—for itself or got the
idea from China, over the oriental trade routes, is still
undetermined. In either case the Europeans, from the
fourteenth century on, were using block printing for
playing cards and holy images, later for illustrated
sheets on devotional subjects. From this stage it was
but a step to the production of block-printed books.
This step was taken in the Netherlands and adjacent
Germany by the second quarter of the fifteenth century,
and thereafter the product gained in quality and vogue,
until, about the close of the century, it had to give way
before the advantages of its typographic rival.[4]

Johann Gutenberg of Mainz (*ca.* 1400–1468) was
the man who, shortly before 1450, after prolonged
labors, invented a method of casting movable type
which could be economically employed in the large-
scale production of books. There is no evidence that
he had ever heard of Chinese, Korean, or Japanese

3 Carter, *Invention of Printing
in China and its Spread Westward.*

4 McMurtrie, *The Book,* Chap.
VIII; *cf.* Wroth, ed., *A History
of the Printed Book.* pp. 35-36.

type, although Carter thinks it probable; but, as McMurtrie remarks, "an idea is not an invention." The process was not simple. It required a hard punch for each letter, a matrix in fairly durable metal to receive the impress of the punch, a mold—a two-piece metal mold, capable of easy adjustment for the differing widths (and uniform thickness, for correct alignment) of the type letters of the alphabet—and, for the casting of the type, a metal alloy which would not shrink when it cooled. Ink too had to be devised from linseed oil paint, and the press had to be made into a rigid mechanism with movable bed for the page or pages of type. The surmounting of the many difficulties which the problem presented took much time and much borrowed capital. It is painful to know that Gutenberg was driven into bankruptcy by his principal creditor, Johann Fust, who took over the inventor's tools and supplies and in partnership with Gutenberg's former technical assistant, Peter Schoeffer, proceeded to produce, within two years after the bankruptcy, the earliest typographically printed books. Johann Gutenberg was not the first or the last benefactor of mankind to have such an experience.

The new art was spread over Europe by German printers with great rapidity. It reached Italy, Paris, London, Stockholm, and Madrid—to name only the greater centers—before the end of the century. There were no patent laws to check its progress. The times were ripe. Old knowledge and new knowledge had begun to pour over the continent, and new controversies were ready to enlist the aid of the new art everywhere.

The invention of printing worked a revolution in the intellectual life of mankind. Scholarship received a mighty impetus. Once set up, a book could be reproduced not only in quantities but with uniformity. Careful preparation of copy and revision of proofs ensured hundreds and, if desired, thousands of accurate copies, all exactly alike. Scholars, however widely separated, could join their forces with specific reference to chapter, page, or line of the same edition of a book.[5] Even more important was the chance it gave to all men. It opened the doors of knowledge to layman as well as to cleric, to peasant as well as to peer; it made government by the people not only possible but inevitable. Books, pamphlets, newspapers—Frederic Harrison did not exaggerate when he wrote: "We place Gutemberg amongst the small list of the unique and special benefactors of mankind, in the sacred choir of those whose work transformed the conditions of life, whose work, once done, could never be repeated."[6]

It is superfluous to remark that the revived interest in antiquity contributed nothing to the invention of printing.

The Discovery of America.—When Christopher Columbus of Genoa (1451–1506),[7] probably a com-

5 Allen, *Erasmus: Lectures and Wayfaring Sketches,* pp. 31 ff.
6 *The Choice of Books and Other Literary Pieces,* p. 17.
7 Morison, *Portuguese Voyages to America in the Fifteenth* *Century; Admiral of the Ocean Sea;* Prestage, *The Portuguese Pioneers;* Kimble, *Geography in the Middle Ages;* Nowell in *American Historical Review,* XLIV: 802–22.

mon sailor, had his ship sunk under him, in 1476, off the southern coast of Portugal, in a sea battle which destroyed a Genoese trading fleet, he managed to swim to the land with the aid of an oar. Thus, unexpectedly but luckily, he set foot on the little kingdom of about a million and a quarter inhabitants which was outdistancing all the other countries of west and central Europe in prosperity, energy, and maritime ambition. The Portuguese expansion had begun in 1415, when Prince Henry the Navigator (1394–1460) and two of his four brothers, the sons of King John I and his English wife, Philippa, captured Ceuta in Africa from the Moslems. Soon afterward Prince Henry set up his maritime school at Sagres, on the most southwestern promontory of Europe. Here, with the resources of the rich Order of Christ, of which he was the secular head, he assembled and inspired the best seafaring talent in seamanship, instrument- and map-making, ship-designing, and exploration which the Mediterranean coasts and islands produced; here, in truth, he organized the overseas expansion which was to make Portugal rich.

The achievements which Prince Henry directed from Sagres were in brief these: He colonized the Madeiras, rediscovered and peopled the Azores, and discovered the Cape Verde islands; his captains pushed down the coast beyond Cape Verde, passed the site of modern Dakar and reached almost to Sierra Leone, and opened up a lucrative trade along the Guinea coast in gold dust, negro slaves (purchased principally from negro

slave-traders), pepper almost as good as that of the
Far East, and ivory tusks. By the time of his death or
shortly afterwards the idea of reaching the Indies by
rounding Africa was firmly implanted in Portuguese
minds. The southward drive of the Portuguese captains,
now directed by the monarchy itself, continued until
finally, in 1488, Bartholomew Dias rounded the Cape
of Good Hope and knew the ultimate goal was as good
as in sight.

Meanwhile, the advance down the west coast of
Africa and the discovery of the Azores and the Cape
Verde islands had encouraged adventurous Portuguese
captains to push out into the Atlantic in search of the
mythical islands, Antilia, St. Brendan, and the rest,
with which map-makers had for centuries decorated
their maps; and to search also for the other islands
they believed they had glimpsed through the mists of
twilight or the fogs. The Portuguese crown encouraged
these adventurers with promises to bestow the government of newly found islands upon their discoverers. In
1485, presumably the year after Columbus had asked
the king's patronage for a voyage westward to the Far
East, the king promised even more substantial rewards
to two of his subjects who proposed to find Antilia.[8]
No lists have been preserved of the many westward
searches; their constant failure was undoubtedly due to
the prevailing westerly winds of the North Atlantic.
Voyages to the north were of course feasible; Colum-

8 Morison, *Portuguese Voyages,*   *Ocean Sea,* I: 96–97.
   pp. 43 ff.; *Admiral of the*

bus shipped out on at least one of them and reached Iceland.

What Portuguese sea skill and sea efforts did for Columbus may well be left at this point to the reader's reflections; Morison's seasoned judgment is that without the preliminary work of the Portuguese the first voyage of Columbus would have failed.[9]

Christopher Columbus (1451–1506) was the son of a weaver of Genoa and as a youth helped his father at his craft. But the sea called him, as it called many lads born on the shores of the Mediterranean, and after a time he sailed on a trading voyage of the far-flung Centurione firm of Genoa to Chios in the Levant, an island at that time still a Genoese possession. A little later he took part, probably as a common seaman, in a naval raid against Tunis, and still later in that passage through the straits of Gibraltar which landed him as a castaway on the Portuguese coast in 1476. The Genoese colony in Lisbon came to his aid, and in Lisbon and thereabouts he maintained himself, as did his brother Bartholomew, with map-making and kindred activities.

During the nine years between his coming and his withdrawal from Portugal, Columbus married into a good family, went on a business trip to Madeira for an associate of the Centurioni, resided for a time in one of the Madeiras, sailed to Galway in Ireland, and thence to Iceland, and in 1482–1483 or thereabouts voyaged at least once and possibly twice to the Guinea

9 *Portuguese Voyages*, p. 5.

coast. No doubt whatever, he chatted with the old
sailors about the sea and its wonders. No doubt that he
interested himself in all the newer tricks of navigation.

It is the belief of most of the Columbus experts that
when he reached Portugal he was illiterate. (Joan of
Arc and William the Conqueror, too, were illiterate.)
Columbus thought he needed languages, and he learned
Portuguese and also Castilian, the preferred language
of the upper-class Portuguese, and acquired some com-
petence in Latin, the language of the learned books.
True, his Castilian was sprinkled with Portuguese
spellings, and his Latin was not idiomatic; but he could
read and write both of them understandably a few
years after he went to Spain (1485), perhaps earlier.

We do not know, and it is likely that Columbus himself did not know, when he attained the certainty that
he was going to sail west to the Far East, that he was
going to do what others had so long talked about. His
Christian name took on increasing significance: Christopher, the saint whose lovely legend told how he bore
the Christ child and the weight of the world across the
flood. He, Christopher Columbus, a devout Christian,
was he not to carry the Gospel to the heathen East,
across the Ocean Sea? The conviction, whenever
reached, grew firm and unshakable, and he was also
persuaded that God would not send him to barren
regions, but rather to regions rich in gold, jewels, and
spices, such as Marco Polo described, and "Sir John
Mandeville" too; lands, in short, worthy of such a
great enterprise.

No doubt Columbus's faith in the soundness of his plan was confirmed, or was at least made more capable of defence before critics, by what he found in books: especially in Marco Polo's *Travels;* in Cardinal Pierre d'Ailly's *Imago mundi,* written about 1410, and in the pamphlets of a kindred sort which the Cardinal composed a little later, after he had read Ptolemy's *Geography* (translated into Latin by Jacobus Angelus of Florence in 1406); and thirdly, in the cosmographical work of Aeneas Sylvius, written or at least completed after he became pope in 1458, *Asiae Europaeque elegantissima descriptio.*[10]

These writings of the Cardinal and the Pope were of course little more than compilations of compilations;[11] the Cardinal does not cite Marco Polo; the Pope does. Still, they contained matter which Columbus eagerly grasped as well as matter that he rejected. His own plan was the criterion. His marginal notes to the *Imago mundi,* which number more than a thousand, reveal his own beliefs most fully.[12] He was obviously very happy over the matter in the eighth chapter of the

10 The 1699 edition, printed at Helmstädt as a part of a volume called *Opera Geographica et historica* of Pope Pius II, bears the title, *Cosmographia seu rerum ubique; gestarum historia locorumque descriptio.*

11 Kimble, *Geography in the Middle Ages,* pp. 208 ff.

12 *Ymago mundi de Pierre d'Ailly,* original Latin with French translation of four cosmographical texts and accompanying marginal notes of Columbus, edited by Edmond Buron. The argument of some critics that the marginal notations were made subsequent to the first voyage is properly and brusquely rejected by Morison in *Admiral of the Ocean Sea,* I: 125. Morison's analysis of the postils, *ibid.,* pp. 120–25.

Imago mundi which Buron proves to be an unacknowledged forced loan from Roger Bacon's *Opus majus*. Here is part of what Bacon tells: "Aristotle says that the sea is small between the end of Spain on the west and the beginning of India on the east. Seneca in the fifth book on *Natural History* says that this sea is navigable in a very few days if the wind is favorable. And Pliny teaches in his *Natural History* that it was navigated from the Arabic Gulf to Cadiz . . . therefore the width of the earth through which the Red Sea [the Indian Ocean] extends is very great; from which fact it is clear that the beginning of India in the east is far distant from us and from Spain, since the distance is so great from the beginning of Arabia toward India. From the end of Spain beneath the earth the sea is so small that it cannot cover three-quarters of the earth. This fact is proved by the weight of another consideration. For Esdras [in the Apocrypha] states in the fourth book that six parts of the earth are habitable and the seventh is covered by water . . . therefore, according to these facts the extent of the habitable portion is great and what is covered by water must be small."[13]

Columbus's computations of the size of the world, of the length of a degree, of the length of the land mass from Cape St. Vincent to the eastern edge of Asia, and his selection of material from Ptolemy's *Geography,* all were fitted in to support his thesis that the voyage

13 Burke's translation of *Opus majus* quoted by Kimble, *Geography in the Middle Ages,* pp. 86–87; Pierre d'Ailly, *Ymago mundi,* I: 207–15.

westward from Spain to the Far East would be short and easy. The distance from the Canaries to Japan is now known to be 10,600 nautical miles; Columbus calculated it at 2,400.[14]

Columbus also got some "high-brow backing" for his thesis from the Florentine physician and geographer, Toscanelli, who assured him that the plan was feasible and that he could break his voyage at the well-known Antilia (!). It is a safe conjecture that Toscanelli was merely echoing d'Ailly. Obviously Toscanelli was no expert.[15]

Columbus had also some objective evidence to cite, for from old salts in Portugal and in the islands, he had gathered reports of exotic pine trees blown by a western gale upon the coasts of the Azores, of wood strangely carved, of reeds unknown to Europe, and of the bodies of men with faces of a strange type, which had been thrown up on the shore.[16] Surely the Far East must be near!

The purposes of this chapter do not require a review of the efforts which Columbus made from 1484 on to get the royal backing which the financing of his plan required. Certainly his plan was reasonably mature in 1484 when he sought the patronage of the Portuguese monarch. He *knew* he was right; but others had to be convinced by solid arguments. The experts consulted by Ferdinand and Isabella, by Henry VII of England, by

14 Morison, *Admiral of the Ocean Sea*, I: 87–91.
15 *Ibid.*, I: 57–58, 85–86, 104–5.

16 Nunn, *Geographical Conceptions of Columbus*, pp. 38–39; Morison, *Admiral of the Ocean Sea*, I: 82–83.

Anne of Beaujeu of France, as well as by the Portuguese crown, were not convinced; they did not believe
that the Indies were so near as Columbus tried to
prove. They were of course right. It was not scientific
evidence that persuaded Queen Isabella to champion
Columbus's voyage. Was it her belief in Columbus, the
man, or was it an inexpensive gamble? (The Portuguese were getting results.) We shall never certainly
know. And so Columbus set out with his three caravels,
and sailing southwest from the Canaries in search of
Japan, he caught the easterly trade winds and found
America—and immortality.

The "wonderful truth" is this: "The discovery was
made by a self-educated, emotional, unpopular man,
prone to self-pity, who clung tenaciously and fervently
to a quite mistaken cosmographical theory. Blind chance
determined that his error should prove the key that
unlocked the New World. Where he declared the
hithermost coasts of Asia to lie, there as a matter of
fact lay a quite unexpected America!"[17]

The purposes of this book do, however, require us
to consider what contribution, if any, the revived interest in antiquity made to the discovery of America,
now the hope of the civilized world. Toscanelli was a
Humanist, but his Humanism had nothing to do with
his views as to the nearness of "the hithermost coasts
of Asia," and he was quite as wrong as Columbus. The
Geography of Ptolemy was translated into Latin by a

[17] Miss E. G. R. Taylor in *Select*   *Four Voyages of Columbus*
    Documents Illustrating the   (edited by Jane), II: lxxvi.

Humanist in 1406. It and the *Almagest* won the allegiance of some Humanists "and thereby helped to retard the growth of accurate geographical concepts."[18] "As to the geographical discoveries," George Sarton says, "the humanists not only failed to appreciate their supreme importance, they generally ignored them altogether."[19] Sarton is our chief American historian of science. Charles Raymond Beazley, the justly celebrated English historian of geography, agrees substantially with the conclusion of Kimble that the Revival had no influence, unless a detrimental one.[20]

Copernicus.—Half a century after Columbus discovered the New World, Copernicus published his *De Revolutionibus* [*orbium coelestium*], which disclosed a new, a heliocentric, universe. The results were more than astronomical.[21]

Copernicus (1473–1543) was a Pole and a subject of the Polish crown. His family was well-to-do, and his maternal uncle, made a bishop in 1489, gave him additional support and freed him from all financial cares. In 1491 the youth matriculated in the University of

18 Kimble, *Geography in the Middle Ages,* p. 62.

19 Sarton in *Civilization of the Renaissance,* p. 81.

20 Beazley to the writer, orally, in Madison, Wisconsin, *ca.* 1908.

21 Birkenmajer in *Organon, International Review,* I:111–34; Armitage, *Copernicus, The Founder of Modern Astronomy;* Rosen, trans. and ed., *Three Copernican Treatises;* Stimson, *The Gradual Acceptance of the Copernican Theory of the Universe;* Mizwa, *Nicholas Copernicus, 1543-1943;* Heath, *Aristarchus of Samos, the Ancient Copernicus.*

Cracow, one of the best of the transalpine universities, and there devoted his chief attention to the study of astronomy, a subject in which Cracow enjoyed a well-deserved reputation. It captivated Copernicus and led him to read more widely in it than was customary and to purchase for himself, while at Cracow, among other astronomical books, the standard *Astronomical Tables* of Alfonso X, composed in the thirteenth century, and the *Tabulae directionum* of Regiomontanus (1436–1476), published at Nürnberg in 1475.[22]

In 1496 Copernicus went down to the University of Bologna, ostensibly to study canon law, for which Bologna had a reputation that was centuries old. He took with him the two books just mentioned, and shortly after he arrived at Bologna he purchased the epitome of the *Almagest*—i.e., *the Epitome in Cl. Ptolemaei magnam compositionem,* made by Purbach and Regiomontanus and just published in Venice in 1496. It is plain that the canon law was not extinguishing the young man's interest in astronomy.[23]

The reading of the *Epitome* confirmed the dissatisfaction with the two reigning astronomical systems which Copernicus had felt at Cracow.[24] These were the homocentric system to which Aristotle had lent his name and the so-called Ptolemaic system. According to the former the earth, at rest in the center of the universe, witnesses the daily revolution of the planets

---

22 Mizwa, *Copernicus,* pp. 18 f., 57; Birkenmajer in *Organon,* I: 119 and note.

23 Birkenmajer in *Organon,* I: 114 n., 124.

24 *Ibid.,* pp. 123–24.

about it, each of them wheeling in its own circle at its own immutable distance from the earth. The homocentric scheme was somewhat discredited by the easily observed fact that the planets were at times nearer to the earth—and more brilliant—than at other times, as well as by the appearance of eclipses; but Aristotle's authority was so great, and the homocentric system which he had espoused became so enmeshed in literature, that his system had its followers throughout the Middle Ages.

The criticisms of the homocentric system which ancient astronomers had made had given birth to several other systems.[25] Among these was the one which was accepted by Ptolemy of Alexandria and was expounded by him in the *Almagest* (composed about A.D. 150 and translated into Latin in the twelfth century). The Ptolemaic system, as it came to be called, was one of "eccentrics and epicycles"; the planets still revolved about the motionless earth, but each of them also turned on its own center, which in turn slowly revolved around the circumference of another circle. The advantage of the Ptolemaic scheme, complicated though it was, was that it harmonized fairly well with the observable phenomena of the heavens and enabled astronomical tables to be drawn up which were approximately adequate for the prediction of celestial movements and other calculations. The *Almagest* included tables of this sort. It is therefore not surprising that

25 Heath, *Aristarchus of Samos,*   Chap. I.
   Part I; Armitage, *Copernicus,*

the Ptolemaic system was expounded at Cracow and the other European universities alongside the Aristotelian system. Neither, it was admitted, was perfect; but perhaps it was as nearly perfect as fallible man had a right to expect.

One defect of the Ptolemaic account of the structure of the universe was a subtle one, but it did not escape the scrutiny of the youthful Copernicus. The account violated the metaphysical principle, accepted by all ancient and medieval astronomers and by Copernicus himself, that the celestial orbs revolve with uniform circular movements. Actually, the Ptolemaic system required some of them to turn with movements which were only quasi-uniform; that is, some of them were arranged by Ptolemy to be uniform with reference to some points other than their own centers.[26] The metaphysical principle was erroneous, we know; but the Ptolemaic system accepted it, as did Copernicus.

The reading of the *Epitome* of the *Almagest,* made by Purbach and Regiomontanus, confirmed Copernicus's dissatisfaction with the Ptolemaic scheme. This dissatisfaction became focussed on the strange behavior of the moon. The two German astronomers, Ptolemaists as they were, knew that, according to the system, the quarter moon, or moon at the quarter (completed in imagination to its full circle), ought to appear four times as large as the moon at the full. Purbach and Regiomontanus remarked that "it is surprising that the

26 Birkenmajer in *Organon,* I: 119–24; Rosen, trans., *Three* *Copernican Treatises,* p. 29 and note.

moon does not appear so great in our eyes during its quarters as one should expect," and let it go at that. Copernicus resolved to do something about it.[27]

The test which Copernicus made, 9 March 1497, is known as "the experiment of the cross." It was carefully planned, and the observation and the calculations which completed it proved that the distance between the moon and the earth remains almost constant in the two cases in question. Clearly the Ptolemaic system did not accord with the facts.[28]

The upshot of the matter was that Copernicus turned his full attention to another ancient theory, one which made the sun rather than the earth the center of the universe and treated the earth as one of the planets revolving around it. The idea was not foreign to the Middle Ages, for Ptolemy, in the *Almagest,* had devoted several columns[29] to refuting it. The Ockhamists had been intrigued by it, as we have noted in the chapter on philosophy, and Duhem sweepingly declares that in supposing the earth mobile and the heaven of the fixed stars immobile, they were of the opinion that we should have a more satisfactory astronomical system. Oresme, Duhem goes on to say, "develops the reasons [for this view] with a plenitude, a clarity, and a precision which Copernicus will be far from reaching."[30] In his *Système du monde* Duhem points out,

27 Birkenmajer in *Organon,* I: 124.
28 *Ibid.,* pp. 124–26.
29 Translated in Stimson, *Coper-* *nican Theory,* pp. 107–9.
30 *Études sur Léonard de Vinci,* III: x, 31.

again and again, that the Ockhamist ideas were well known in the Italian centers which Copernicus frequented. Thus Duhem would have us believe that it was the Ockhamists who gave Copernicus the clue out of the astronomical labyrinth.[31]

In 1498 Copernicus was made a canon of Frauenburg by his uncle, the bishop. The canon-elect went home in 1501 to be installed in his new post, and, the installation accomplished, the cathedral chapter promptly authorized him to return to Italy in order to study medicine. He went to the University of Padua, the great medical center, where he spent the years 1501–1503, before assuming his duties at home. It was possibly at Bologna and certainly at Padua that he gave attention to the study of Greek, presumably in order to be able to read untranslated Greek astronomical writings. Whether he did read them and whether they could help him is another matter, for he was already in possession of the heliocentric idea, and his real problem was to study the recorded observations of the heavens, catch their errors, make his own supplementary observations, and determine the mathematical adequacy of the heliocentric hypothesis. The recorded observations of the past were already available in the *Almagest,* in the Alfonsine *Tables,* and in other similar collections in Latin.

The originator and champion of the heliocentric hypothesis in antiquity was Aristarchus of Samos (third

31 See indexes to *Le système du monde,* under "Copernicus."

century, B.C.).[32] Copernicus knew that Aristarchus was reputed to believe in the mobility of the earth,[33] but that is about all. The details of the system of Aristarchus could be learned only from Archimedes, and his writings were not published until 1544.[34] The details would have encouraged Copernicus, for the great Syracusan says that Aristarchus taught that the sphere of the stars is motionless and its apparent daily revolution is due to the diurnal revolution of the earth, and that the sun forms the center of the universe, that is, the center of the sphere of the stars and of the circular orbit in which the earth and all the planets revolve around it.[35] These details would have encouraged Copernicus; but they would not have helped him appreciably, for what he wanted was proofs. If Aristarchus had any, they have not come down to us.[36]

Antiquity had rejected the heliocentric hypothesis of Aristarchus; common sense was against it; religion declined to surrender the privileged position of the centrally located earth; Aristotle would have none of it. The planetary tables of Ptolemy, and of those who followed his lead throughout the Middle Ages and from time to time tinkered with his system, formed such a workable basis for forecasts that they buttressed

32 Heath, *Aristarchus of Samos,* pp. 301–6.
33 Birkenmajer in *Organon,* I: 127 n.
34 *Ibid.*
35 The moon, of course, revolv-

ing around the earth. Heath, *Aristarchus of Samos,* pp. 302–3, 310; Armitage, *Copernicus,* p. 28.
36 Heath, *Aristarchus of Samos,* p. 306.

its credit for centuries.[37] The system was to die hard.

The part which Copernicus ascribed to antique theories in the origin of his system is to be found in the pathetically conciliatory dedication to Pope Paul III which serves as the preface to *De Revolutionibus*.[38] After pointing out the inadequacies and complications of the Aristotelian and Ptolemaic systems as they stood in his day and his search for a more coherent explanation of the mechanism of the universe, he tells of his scrutiny of the ideas of the ancients and his discovery in Cicero and Plutarch of the support given to the idea of the mobility of the earth by Hicetas, Philolaus, Heraclides of Pontus, and Ecphantus.[39] This citation of ancient opinion must have appealed to a Humanist pope. It may, indeed, have been designed to conciliate his good will, for it is pertinent to note that Copernicus does not mention the *Almagest* or the "heretical" Aristarchus.

Copernicus, then, got the idea of a heliocentric universe from the ancients (including Ptolemy). Granted; but as McMurtrie remarked of the invention of printing, "an idea is not an invention." If it were, then Leonardo da Vinci invented the aeroplane. The idea of a heliocentric system was merely a hypothesis. Would

37 Armitage, *Copernicus,* pp. 67–68.

38 Translated in Stimson, *Copernican Theory,* pp. 109–15.

39 Herbert Dingle's conclusion, in *Science and Human Experience,* pp. 31–32, that Copernicus merely sought a simpler scheme and therefore was just a medievalist—"the beginnings of science are not with him"—is fanciful. See Birkenmajer in *Organon,* I: 123.

it stand up? "I found at length," Copernicus goes on to explain to Paul III, "by much and long observation, that if the motions of the other planets were added to the rotation of the earth and calculated as for the revolution of that planet, not only the phenomena of the others followed from this, but also it so bound together both the order and magnitude of all the planets and the spheres and the heaven itself, that in no single part could one thing be altered without confusion among the other parts and in all the universe."[40]

The materials that Copernicus had to work upon were old and new. The old were the records of past observations of the skies, set forth in the *Almagest*, in the *Epitome* of the *Almagest*, in the Alfonsine *Tables*, in the recent *Tabulae directionum* of Regiomontanus, and in similar collections. The new were Copernicus's own observations of the phenomena of the heavens, which he made in the course of his efforts to construct a consistent theory which would account for the facts. These observations totalled sixty, a few in Italy, two or three at Cracow, most of them at home in Warmie.[41] With all this material—testing, checking, and calculating, again and again—Copernicus finally worked out his great discovery of "a systematic planetary theory, capable of furnishing tables of an accuracy not before attained, and embodying a principle whose adoption was to make possible the triumphs of Kepler and Newton in the following century." "In his plane-

40 Stimson, *Copernican Theory*, p. 112; Birkenmajer in *Orga-non*, I:127-29.
41 *Ibid.*, p. 119.

tary theory Copernicus succeeded in numerically relating to a single cause those principal inequalities of the several planets which had always been regarded as just so many unrelated phenomena to be separately explained by the introduction of an *ad hoc* complication into the economy of each planet."[42]

The earth, according to the Copernican scheme, stating the matter simply, has three motions—a diurnal rotation from west to east about the polar axis; an annual revolution about the sun from west to east in the plane of the ecliptic; and a variation in the inclination of the earth's axis, which produces the cyclical changes of season.[43]

It is not necessary to rehearse the defects of detail in the heliocentric system of Copernicus. They were to be corrected by the labors of Tycho Brahe, Kepler, Galileo, Newton—and Einstein. These men built on the foundation which Copernicus had laid. The system, with its supporting data and argument, was given to the learned world in 1543. It promptly met with the condemnation of both Luther and Melanchthon. Luther jeered at "the new astrologer"; "the fool," he said, "will overturn the whole system of astronomy." The Roman Catholic Church was not so precipitate; it was content for over sixty years to follow the lead which St. Thomas had given and leave the human reason free

42 *Ibid.*, pp. 129 ff.; Armitage, *Copernicus*, pp. 90, 162; Duhem, *Système du monde*, III: 332.

43 Armitage, *Copernicus*, p. 91; Rosen, *Three Copernican Treatises*, pp. 147–50.

to explore the physical nature of the universe. Indeed, it was not until Galileo openly supported the Copernican system that the Holy Office, in 1616, condemned it and placed the *De Revolutionibus* on the Index, where it remained until 1835.

It is easy to understand the initial embarrassment of the theologians. The geocentric system fitted Christian theology like a glove. "Isidore of Seville taught that the universe was created to serve man's purposes, and Peter Lombard (12th century) sums up the situation in the definite statement that man was placed at the center of the universe to be served by that universe and in turn himself to serve God."[44] The Copernican system displaced the earth from its central position, reduced it to the status of a planet, and wrecked the consoling Aristotelian—and medieval Christian—belief in the contrast between the transcendental, immutable, and eternal heavens, the home of the blest, on the one hand, and the sublunary sphere of the earth, the scene of birth, change, decay, and death on the other. Some of the Ockhamists had glimpsed the idea. The theologians, of course, finally adjusted theology to the new conceptions. They will continue to do so.

"There is no figure in astronomical history," Simon Newcomb says, "which may more appropriately claim the admiration of mankind through all time than that of Copernicus."[45] With that verdict of the American specialist we may well be content.

44 Stimson, *Copernican Theory*, p. 18.

45 Quoted in Mizwa, *Copernicus*, p. 9.

What of the rôle of the Revival of Learning in the achievement of Copernicus? It reduces itself, it is safe to say, to the ability which he acquired in Italy to read Greek. Yet he does not cite at firsthand any Greek work; it is Cicero and Plutarch (almost certainly in Latin translation) that he cites to the pope in the preface to the *De Revolutionibus*. Brudzewski of Cracow, a man with Humanistic interests, probably instructed Copernicus in astronomy; but he had no heliocentric leanings that we know of. Novara, the astronomer of Bologna, with whom Copernicus, as a junior colleague, made two or three observations, notably "the experiment of the cross," was a Ptolemaist, and Guido D'Arturo, who is professor of astronomy at the modern University of Bologna, explicitly declares that "we do not know if any incentive to heliocentric ideas came [to Copernicus] from Novara or others."[46] "Others" may refer to Nicholas of Cusa; if this is so, his help was worthless.[47] The great authority on Copernicus, Ludwik A. Birkenmajer, father of the author of the article in *Organon,* in his investigations of the notes Copernicus made in his books—carried off, fortunately, to Sweden by Gustavus Adolphus—and of the original manuscript of the *De Revolutionibus,* with its multiple emendations, discovered certain evidence that Copernicus, while a student at Cracow, found both the Aristotelian and the Ptolemaic systems out of harmony

46 Article, "Copernico," in *Enciclopedia Italiana.*

47 *Cf.* Thorndike, *Science and Thought in the Fifteenth Century,* Chap. VII.

with the facts and then turned to the study of the heliocentric theory,[48] the theory which Ptolemy had described and condemned in the *Almagest,* and which, as a consequence, had been known for centuries. Thus it is plain that the rôle of the Revival of Learning in the achievement of Copernicus was negligible.

The Growth of Science.—The problem with which this book is concerned does not require us to consider in any detail the development of scientific interests in the era of the Renaissance. For the Humanists repeatedly make the point that they do not seek to be innovators, but rather restorers of that which had already existed in the Golden Age of the past. How very different the view of the natural scientists! They regarded themselves as radical innovators, challenging the authority of the past, and they located their "Golden Age" in the future.[49]

The hypotheses of evolution and the atomic theory conceived by the Ionian Greeks were brilliant divinations; but they failed to discover how to use them as guides to the collection of new observational and experimental facts to establish their truth. This failure was primarily due to the general lack of contact between speculative thinkers and manual workers. These observations of J. G. Crowther[50] are amply supported by

48 Birkenmajer in *Organon,* I: 113 f. *Cf.* Armitage, *Copernicus,* index, under "Birkenmajer."

49 Varga, *Das Schlagwort vom* "*Finsteren Mittelalter,*" p. 97; Slichter, *Science in a Tavern,* pp. 127–36.

50 Crowther, *The Social Relations of Science,* p. 59.

others. Vesalius, the author of the fundamental work on anatomy, the *De Fabrica* (1543), ascribed the decline of Greek science to the Greco-Roman contempt for manual work. He knew that his own discoveries were a result of his combination of theoretical study and his own practical work in dissection.[51] George Sarton has broadened the generalization: "Much of our experimental knowledge—and with few exceptions the best of it—developed almost naturally together with the instruments which human hands had built and used. It is truly essential to exhibit this interdependence of intellectual processes and handicraft, of minds and tools."[52] Wilhelm Dilthey writes with conviction of "the creative union of industrial labor with learned reflection," which "brought nearer the age of the autonomy and supremacy of reason."[53] The achievements of Gutenberg, Columbus, and Copernicus obviously rest on the same foundation.

"To illustrate the lack of scientific interest of the Humanists, it will suffice to recall their cold reception of the two greatest events of the age: the development of printing and the geographical discoveries."[54] With these words of Sarton we may leave the topic.

---

51 *Ibid.*, pp. 123, 125.
52 Sarton, *The History of Science and the New Humanism*, p. 166.
53 *Gesammelte Schriften*, II: 257–60. *Cf.* Wolf, *A History of Science, Technology, and*
Philosophy in the Sixteenth and Seventeenth Centuries, pp.5–6.
54 Sarton in *Civilization of the Renaissance*, pp. 80–81. And see his eulogy of Leonardo—a craftsman, not a Humanist —*ibid.*, p. 82–85.

CHAPTER XII: CONCLUSION

The conclusion which the preceding survey foreshadows
and compels can easily be stated: The Revival of
Learning or, to phrase the matter more inclusively, the
revived knowledge of antiquity, cannot have been the
creative force which ushered in modernity. The real

seminal force was the natural effort of men to achieve
a more abundant life on this earth by applying their
wits to problems which required, and admitted of,
solution. Alfred North Whitehead touches the heart
of the matter: "From the very beginning of critical
thought, we find the distinction between topics susceptible of certain knowledge, and topics about which
uncertain opinions are available. The dawn of this distinction, explicitly entertained, is the dawn of modern
mentality. It introduces criticism."[1]

The medieval communes of Italy and of the Netherlands, and the people of later urban centers, may not
have "explicitly entertained" the distinction in question;
but they led the van in solving problems "susceptible
of certain knowledge." Dilthey and other wise men
believe that it was the union of manual labor with the
investigative spirit which brought nearer "the age of
the autonomy and supremacy of reason."[2]

It is, in a certain sense, permissible to speak of this
fruitful increase of attention to the concerns of this
world as a growth of secularism. Thus Bréhier says that
in the Renaissance the contemplative and speculative
people had to yield the center of the stage to practical

1 Whitehead, *Adventures of
Ideas,* p. 208.

2 Dilthey, *Gesammelte Schriften,*
II:257–60, 321 ff., 416 ff. Hefele ascribes all the achievements of the Italian Renaissance to the freedom and patriotism of the communes after the
defeat of Frederick Barbarossa,

Historisches Jahrbuch, XLIX:
444–59. Groethuysen, *Origines
de l'esprit bourgeois en France,*
Vol. I, explains at length the
realistic nature of the bourgeois
mind. The bourgeois said: "I
am," not "I dream, therefore I
am"; he said: "I act; therefore
I do not dream, therefore I
am." *Ibid.,* p. viii *et passim.*

men, men of action, artists and artisans, technicians of all sorts;[3] but it may be questioned whether the contemplative persons as such really occupied the center of the stage for any substantial period except in the sphere of religion. The common ascription of special religiousness to the Middle Ages is doubtless due for the most part to the quasi-monopoly of the medieval pen by the clergy.

It has probably been much the same with the germinal power ascribed to the Revival of Learning. The repute which a classical Latin style and the ancient classics had acquired in Renaissance Italy was perpetuated among individuals of a literary bent by the classical type of education which replaced the scholastic type for students of the Liberal Arts, was later erected into a dogma by the writings of Burckhardt and Voigt, and by and large held its place until forced to give ground before the advance of natural science.[4]

The abandonment of the theory—mostly a *post hoc*

3 Bréhier, *Histoire de la philosophie,* I: 742.

4 It is not without interest in this connection to recall the opinion which Rashdall, the classically educated historian of the medieval universities, expressed toward the close of his life: "It may be questioned," he wrote, "whether the intellectual exercise involved in the study of Aristotle, in familiarity with the technicalities of scholastic Logic and in the practice of scholastic disputation, was not at least as valuable a training for the intellectual work of practical life as the later education which consisted in intimate acquaintance with a very small number of Latin classics, a much slighter study of Greek, and unlimited practice in the art of writing Latin verse." Rashdall also pointed out "how largely the superiority of the educated man to the uneducated is independent of the subject-matter on which the education is based." *Cambridge Medieval History,* VI: 599–600.

ergo propter hoc—that the revival of interest in and increased knowledge of antiquity ushered in modernity, leaves us, as we have intimated, with something much more real and more significant as the true cause of the advance of civilization in the era of the Renaissance, namely, the life energies, hopes, and activities of vigorous people all over Western Europe. A little detail will be useful at this point.

The organization of life in the communes and capitals of the West (including all the inheritance from ancient times which had passed into customary use), its adornment with art and literature, and its integration with philosophy and history; the expansion of industry and of commercial enterprise, involving contact with other civilizations and lands; the growth of geographical knowledge and maritime skill from Marco Polo to Diaz and Columbus; the inventions of printing, the microscope, the telescope, and artillery; the demonstration of the heliocentric conception of our universe; the investigations into the nature of political authority which are marked by the insight of Marsilius of Padua and by the challenge to papal omnipotence—and, in truth, to all "supreme authority"—by the Councils of Constance and Basel; the growing share of the laity in all the activities of learning—these are the main constituent elements of the true Renaissance. *The Renaissance did not cause these phenomena; these phenomena constituted the Renaissance.*[5]

5 Various scholars have attempted to account for the energy and drive which produced the phenomena, and the partisans

The Renaissance was the achievement of the more advanced people in various parts of Europe, Italy of course included. Siciliano may be right in his contention that Italy outclassed the other regions of the West in the number and importance of outstanding men in the earlier part of the era.[6] If so, surely this pre-eminence was unstable! Copernicus, Vesalius, Tycho Brahe, Descartes, Kepler, Galileo, Harvey, Newton, Montaigne, Rabelais, Shakespeare, Francis Bacon, and Grotius—how many of these men can be credited to Italy, the frustrated Italy of the despots and of Spanish control? France led the forces of civilization in the epoch 1100–1300 and again in the "age of Louis XIV"; England, from Elizabethan times onward, gathered her strength for leadership, in rivalry with Spain, the Dutch Netherlands, and France; Germany challenged the world in science and then, alas, in arms; and France remained, and remains, the land of that taste and logical clarity which Siciliano claims as the birthright of Italy. Surely, it is indubitably true that the civilization of the West—now guarded and promoted chiefly

of the Vikings and of the Arabs are still occasionally heard from. But if agreement were reached along this line, it would be regarded as necessary, would it not, to account for the energy and drive of the Vikings, the Arabs, or the others? And so on. Let us rather, following Leonardo and Goethe, investigate the investigable and pay *das Unerforschliche* the calm tribute of respect. *Cf.* Farinelli, *Michelangelo e Dante,* p. 416 n.

6 The University of Padua, as a center of scientific activity—and also of rampant Averroism, which was clearly an "incompatible" — attracted some notable men from beyond the Alps: for example, Copernicus, Vesalius, and Harvey; but it is safe to say that these three brought at least as much with them as they received.

by the people of the United States of America, on the only possible basis, of liberty—has been evolving for centuries, with now one nation, now another, leading the advance.

That does not mean that we are to regard the Revival of Learning as a negligible factor in the *evolution* of our civilization. It had a part in the development and elaboration of some forms of literature; it furnished subjects for painters and sculptors; it indirectly shaped an architectural style; above all, it paved the way for that sound and fruitful knowledge of antiquity which culminated in the eighteenth century and after; and there must have been some leakage from the ivory towers of the Italian Humanists into the surging life of the Italian people, although it is hard to trace it. The greatest gift of antiquity was the art of clear thinking, the recognition of the dependence of fact upon fact, of "a causality independent of fears and hopes,"[7] and this gift the scholastic doctors, not the Humanists, inherited from the Greeks, via Rome, and transmitted to future generations.

Nevertheless, the Revival of Learning, although it did not usher in the modern age, did, *in the long run,* fertilize it with clearer conceptions of the breadth and richness of ancient times than the Middle Ages knew, heavily indebted though the latter were to the "classical tradition" (H. O. Taylor's phrase). This enrichment began to show its fruits when Leon Battista Alberti and

7 Whitehead, *Adventures of Ideas,* p. 107; Slichter, *Science in a Tavern,* p. 127.

Lorenzo the Magnificent in Italy, renouncing the dogma that Latin was the literary language of Italy, began to write in Tuscan Italian, and when Sir Thomas More and other northern Humanists of the early six-teenth century began to write in their mother tongues. The progress these Humanists initiated was, however, seriously interrupted by the outbreak of the revolts against the ancestral Church and the so-called religious wars and the repressions which followed. These may be regarded as lasting until the close of the Thirty Years War. Thereafter, in France, England, Germany, and elsewhere, especially in the North, the onward march of classical scholarship was resumed. Its values are incontestable and should never be allowed to perish.

Henry Seidel Canby's warning—that the champions of the cultural inheritance of beauty and wisdom which men have received from Greece and Rome and Pales-tine must see to it that it is vitally related to the en-vironmental climate of the modern age, if it is to be a vital factor in contemporary civilization[8]—might, *mu-tatis mutandis,* have profited many of the Humanists of the period of the Renaissance, if they could have but grasped its import. It is, unfortunately, the bitter truth that most of them, in their aristocratic eyries, with their scorn of the vernacular and their indifference toward science, were unable to share vitally in the life of the people, in the deep emotional and creative cur-rents that produced the Renaissance.

[8] Editorial, *Saturday Review of Literature,* 10 February 1945.

BIBLIOGRAPHY

Acton, John E. E. D. *Lectures on Modern History*. New York, 1906.

Adams, George Burton. *Civilization during the Middle Ages*. Revised edition. New York, 1914.

Ailly, Pierre d'. *Ymago mundi de Pierre d'Ailly*. Ed. Edmond J. P. Buron. Original Latin and French translation with the marginal notes made by Columbus. 3 vols. Paris [1930].

Allen, Percy Stafford. *Erasmus: Lectures and Wayfaring Sketches*. Oxford, 1934.

Aquinas, Thomas. *Summa Theologiae*. English translation by the Fathers of the English Dominican Province. 22 vols. London, 1918–30.

Ariosto, Lodovico. *Orlando Furioso*. Trans. William Stewart Rose. 2 vols. London, 1913.

Armitage, Angus. *Copernicus, the Founder of Modern Astronomy.* London [1938].

Augustinus, Aurelius. *Confessions.* Trans. J. G. Pilkington. New York, 1942.

Balzani, Ugo. *Le cronache italiane nel medio evo.* Milano, 1900.

Bédier, Joseph and Hazard, Paul, edd. *Histoire de la littérature française illustrée.* 2 vols. Paris [1923–24?].

Benoist, Charles. "L'Influence des idées de Machiavel," *Académie de droit internationale, Recueil des Cours, 1925,* IV (Paris, 1926), 131–301.

Berenson, Bernhard. *North Italian Painters of the Renaissance.* New York, 1907.

Besant, Walter. "Froissart." Article in *Encyclopaedia Britannica* 11th edition, New York, 1010–11.

Birkenmajer, Aleksander. "Comment Copernic a-t-il conçu et réalisé son oeuvre?" *Organon, International Review,* I (Warsaw, 1936), 111–34.

Blau, Joseph Leon. *The Christian Interpretation of the Cabala in the Renaissance.* New York, 1944.

Boccaccio, Giovanni. *Decameron.* Trans. Richard Aldington. 2 vols. New York, 1930.

————. *The Filostrato of Giovanni Boccaccio.* Trans. with parallel original text by Nathaniel Edward Griffin and Arthur Beckwith Myrick. Philadelphia, 1929.

Brandi, Karl. "Das Werden der Renaissance," *Deutsche Rundschau,* CXXXIV (1908), 416–30.

Bréhier, Emile. *Histoire de la philosophie:* Vol. I, *L'antiquité et le moyen âge.* Paris [1927].

Burckhardt, Jacob Christoph. *Civilisation of the Renaissance in Italy.* Trans. by S. G. C. Middlemore from Geiger's revision of the third edition. London, 1904.

————. *Die Kultur der Renaissance in Italien. Neudruck der Urausgabe.* Ed. Walter Goetz. Stuttgart, 1922.

Burton, Edwin. "Pecock." Article in *Catholic Encyclopedia.* New York, 1911.

Carter, Thomas Francis. *The Invention of Printing in China and its Spread Westward.* Revised edition. New York, 1931.

Cassirer, Ernst. *Die Platonische Renaissance in England und die Schule von Cambridge.* Leipzig, 1932.

Cervantes Saavedra, Miguel de. *Don Quixote*. Trans. John Ormsby. 2 vols. New York, n. d.

Charles, Émile Auguste. *Roger Bacon*. Paris, 1861.

Chaucer, Geoffrey. *The Poetical Works of Chaucer*. Ed. Fred Norris Robinson. Boston [1933].

Cheyney, Edward Potts. *The Dawn of a New Era, 1250–1453*. New York, 1936.

Chubb, Thomas Caldecot. *Life of Giovanni Boccaccio*. London [1930].

Chute, Marchette Gaylord. *Geoffrey Chaucer of England*. New York, 1946.

Clagett, Marshall. *Giovanni Marliani and Late Medieval Physics*. New York, 1941.

Clapham, John Harold. "Commerce and Industry in the Middle Ages," *Cambridge Medieval History*, VI (New York, 1929), 473–504.

Coleman, Christopher Bush. *Constantine the Great and Christianity*. New York, 1914.

———, ed. *The Treatise of Lorenzo Valla on the Donation of Constantine*. Text and trans. New Haven, 1922.

Commines, Philippe de. *The History of Commines*. Trans. Thomas Dannett (1596). In Tudor Translations, vols. XVII–XVIII. London, 1897.

———. *Mémoires de Philippe de Commynes*. Ed. B. de Mandrot. 2 vols. Paris, 1901, 1903.

Compagni, Dino. *La cronica di Dino Compagni delle cose occorrenti ne' tempi suoi*. Ed. Isidoro del Lungo. Firenze, 1902.

———. *The Chronicle of Dino Compagni*. Trans. E. C. M. Benecke and A. G. F. Howell. London, 1906.

Cornford, Francis Macdonald. *Plato's Cosmology*. New York, 1937.

Coulton, George Gordon. *The Chronicler of European Chivalry*. London, 1930.

Croce, Benedetto. *The Theory and History of Historiography*. London [1921].

Crowther, James Gerald. *The Social Relations of Science*. New York, 1941.

Crump, Charles George, and Jacob, Ernest Fraser, edd. *The Legacy of the Middle Ages*. Oxford, 1926.

Dante Alighieri. *The Convivio of Dante Alighieri*. Trans. Philip H. Wicksteed. London, 1903. Other trans.

——. *Divine Comedy*. Prose trans. C. E. Norton. 3 vols. Boston, 1891–92. Many other trans. in verse and prose.

——. *De Monarchia*. Trans. Aurelia Henry. Boston, 1904.

——. *The New Life (Vita nuova)*. Trans. C. E. Norton. Revised edition. Boston, 1892. Other trans.

——. *De vulgari eloquentia*. Trans. A. G. F. Howell. London, 1890.

D'Arturo, Guido Horn. "Copernico." Article in *Enciclopedia Italiana*. Milano–Roma, 1931–39.

Della Torre, Arnaldo. *Storia dell' Accademia Platonica di Firenze*. Firenze, 1902.

Denifle, Heinrich, and Châtelain, Émile. *Chartularium Universitatis Parisiensis*. 4 vols. Paris, 1889–97.

De Sanctis, Francesco. *History of Italian Literature*. 2 vols. New York [1931].

Dickinson, Goldsworthy Lowes. *Appearances*. London, 1914.

Dilthey, Wilhelm. *Gesammelte Schriften*. 11 vols. Leipzig, 1921–36.

Dingle, Herbert. *Science and Human Experience*. New York, 1932.

Dixon, William Macneile. *The Englishman*. London, 1938.

Döllinger, Johann Joseph Ignaz von. *Die Papst-Fabeln des Mittelalters*. Second edition. Stuttgart, 1890.

Dublin Review. "Bishop Pecock, His Character and Fortunes," LXXVI (New Series, Vol. XXIV, 1875), 27–55.

Dubois, Pierre. *De Recuperatione Terre Sancte*. Ed. Charles Victor Langlois. Paris, 1891.

Duhem, Pierre Maurice Marie. *Études sur Léonard de Vinci*. 3 vols. Paris, 1906–13.

——. *Le système du monde, histoire des doctrines cosmologiques de Platon à Copernic*. 5 vols. Paris, 1913–17.

Edwards, Ernest Woods. *The Orlando Furioso and its Predecessor*. Cambridge, Eng., 1924.

Farinelli, Arturo. *Michelangelo e Dante*. Torino, 1918.

Firmin-Didot, Ambroise. *Alde Manuce et l'Hellénisme à Venice*. Paris, 1875.

Fisher, Herbert Albert Laurens. *A History of Europe*. 3 vols. Boston, 1935–36.

Fitzmaurice-Kelly, James. *Chapters on Spanish Literature*. London, 1908.

——. *A New History of Spanish Literature*. Oxford, 1926.

Foligno, Cesare. *Epochs of Italian Literature*. Oxford, 1920.

Ford, Jeremiah Denis Matthias, ed. *Romances of Chivalry in Italian Verse*. New York, 1906.

Froissart, John. *The Chronicle of Froissart*. Trans. Lord Berners (1523–25). Ed. W. P. Ker. 6 vols. London, 1901–1903.

——. *The Chronicles of England, France, Spain, etc.* Condensed from the Johnes translation. Everyman's Library. London [1930].

Fueter, Eduard. *Geschichte der neueren Historiographie*. München-Berlin, 1911.

——. "Guicciardini als Historiker," *Historische Zeitschrift*, C (1908), 486–540.

Gairdner, James. *Lollardy and the Reformation in England*. 4 vols. London, 1908–13.

Gardner, Edmund Garrett. *The Arthurian Legend in Italian Literature*. London [1930].

——. *The King of Court Poets . . . Ariosto*. New York, 1906.

Gilson, Étienne Henry. *Études de philosophie médiévale*. Strasbourg, 1921.

——. *La philosophie au moyen âge*. Paris, 1930.

——. *Reason and Revelation in the Middle Ages*. New York, 1938.

——. *Spirit of Mediaeval Philosophy*. New York, 1936.

——. *Le Thomisme*. Paris, 1927.

Goetz, Walter Wilhelm. *König Robert von Neapel (1309–1343), seine Persönlichkeit und sein Verhältnis zum Humanismus*. Tübingen, 1910.

——. "Mittelalter und Renaissance," *Historische Zeitschrift*, XCVIII (1907), 30–54.

Gooch, George Peabody. *History and Historians in the Nineteenth Century*. Second edition. London, 1913.

Green, Vivian Hubert Howard. *Bishop Reginald Pecock*. Cambridge, Eng., 1945.

Greswell, William Parr. *Memoirs of Angelus Politianus* . . . . London, 1805.

Groethuysen, Bernard. *Origines de l'esprit bourgeois en France.* Third edition. Paris, 1933.

Guicciardini, Francesco. *Counsels and Reflections of Francesco Guicciardini.* Trans. Ninian Hill Thomson. London, 1890.

———. *Storia d'Italia.* Ed. Costantino Panigada. 5 vols. Bari, 1929.

———. *Storia fiorentine dal 1378 al 1509.* Ed. Roberto Pal-morrochi. Bari, 1931.

Hagen, Oskar. *Art Epochs and Their Leaders.* New York [1927].

———. *Deutsches Sehen.* Third edition. München, 1938.

Halphen, Louis. "Les universités au xiii° siècle," *Revue Historique,* CLXVII (1931), 1–15.

Harnack, Adolf. "Neoplatonism." Article in *Encyclopaedia Britannica,* 11th edition. New York, 1910–11.

Harrison, Frederic. *The Choice of Books and Other Literary Pieces.* London, 1891.

Haskins, Charles Homer. *The Renaissance of the Twelfth Century.* Cambridge, 1928.

———. *Studies in the History of Mediaeval Science.* Cambridge, 1927.

Hauser, Henri. *La Modernité du xvi° siècle.* Paris, 1930.

———, ed. *Les sources de l'histoire de France, 1494–1610.* 4 vols. Paris, 1906–15.

Hauvette, Henri. *Boccace, étude biographique et littéraire.* Paris, 1914.

———. *Littérature italienne.* Paris, 1906.

Hearnshaw, Fossey John Cobb, ed. *Mediaeval Contributions to Modern Civilisation.* London [1921].

———. *Social and Political Ideas of some Great Mediaeval Thinkers.* London [1923].

Heath, Thomas Little. *Aristarchus of Samos, the Ancient Copernicus.* Oxford, 1913.

Hefele, Hermann. "Zum Begriff der Renaissance," *Historisches Jahrbuch,* XLIX (1929), 444–59.

Hollway-Calthrop, Henry Calthrop. *Petrarch, His Life and Times.* London, 1910.

Holtzmann, Robert. *Wilhelm von Nogaret.* Freiburg, 1898.

Hutton, Edward. *Giovanni Boccaccio, a Biographical Study.* London, 1910.

Jacob, Ernest Fraser. "Changing Views of the Renaissance," *History,* New Series, XVI (1931–32), 214–29.

———. "Innocent III," *Cambridge Medieval History,* VI (New York, 1929), 1–43.

Jane, Cecil, ed. *Select Documents Illustrating the Four Voyages of Columbus.* 2 vols. London, 1930–33.

John of Salisbury. *Policraticus.* Ed. Clemens C. I. Webb. 2 vols. Oxford, 1909.

Johnstone, Hilda. "France, the Last Capetians," *Cambridge Medieval History,* VII (New York, 1932), 305–39.

Jusserand, Jean Jules. *The School for Ambassadors and Other Essays.* New York, 1925.

Ker, William Paton. *Essays on Medieval Literature.* London, 1905.

Kimble, George H. T. *Geography in the Middle Ages.* London [1938].

Kristeller, Paul Oskar. *The Philosophy of Marsilio Ficino.* New York, 1943.

Landsberger, Franz. *Die künstlerischen Probleme der Renaissance.* Halle, 1922.

Laski, Harold J. "Political Theory in the Late Middle Ages," *Cambridge Medieval History,* VIII (New York, 1936), 620–45.

Lewis, Dominic Bevan Wyndham. *François Villon.* New York, 1928.

Lippmann, Walter. *A Preface to Morals.* New York, 1929.

Little, Andrew George, ed. *Roger Bacon Essays.* Oxford, 1914.

Livingstone, Richard Winn, ed. *The Legacy of Greece.* Oxford, 1923.

Loomis, Louise Ropes. "The Greek Renaissance in Italy," *American Historical Review,* XIII (1908), 246–58.

———. *Medieval Hellenism.* Lancaster Pa., 1906.

Lowes, John Livingston. *Essays in Appreciation.* Boston, 1936.

———. *Geoffrey Chaucer and the Development of His Genius.* Boston, 1934.

Luchaire, Achille. *Innocent III.* 6 vols. Paris, 1905–1908.

Luciani, Vincent. *Francesco Guicciardini and his European Reputation*. New York, 1936.

Lungo, Isidoro del, ed. *Le più belle pagine di Dino Compagni e di Giovanni Villani*. Milano, 1924.

MacCurdy, Edward, ed. *The Notebooks of Leonardo da Vinci*. 2 vols. New York, 1938.

Machiavelli, Niccolò. *The Historical, Political, and Diplomatic Writings of Niccolò Machiavelli*. Trans. Christian Edward Detmold. 4 vols. Boston, 1882.

——. *The Prince and The Discourses*. The Modern Library, New York [1940?].

Madariaga, Salvador de. *Don Quixote*. Oxford, 1935.

Maitland, Frederic William. *English Law and the Renaissance*. Cambridge, Eng., 1901.

Mancini, Girolamo. *Vita di Lorenzo Valla*. Firenze, 1891.

Mandonnet, Pierre. *Dante le théologien*. Paris [1935].

——. *Siger de Brabant et l'Averroïsme latin au xiii° siècle*. Revised edition. 2 vols. Louvain, 1908, 1911.

Manly, John Matthews. "Chaucer and the Rhetoricians," *Proceedings of the British Academy*, XII (London [1926]), 95–113.

Marsilius of Padua. *Defensor Pacis*. Ed. Richard Scholz. 2 vols. Hannover, 1932–33.

Marzials, Frank Thomas, trans. *Memoirs of the Crusades by Villehardouin and de Joinville*. Everyman's Library [1908?].

Masefield, John. *Chaucer*. New York, 1930.

Mather, Frank Jewett, Jr. *A History of Italian Painting*. New York, 1923.

——. "The Spirit of the Renaissance," *Historical Aspects of the Fine Arts*. Oberlin, 1938.

——. *Western European Painting of the Renaissance*. New York [1939].

McIlwain, Charles Howard. *The Growth of Political Thought in the West*. New York, 1932.

McKeon, Richard Peter, ed. *Selections from Mediaeval Philosophers*. 2 vols. New York [1929].

McMurtrie, Douglas Crawford. *The Book: The Story of Printing and Bookmaking*. New York [1943].

Merriman, Roger Bigelow. *Suleiman the Magnificent, 1520–1566.* Cambridge, 1944.

Mizwa, Stephen Paul. *Nicholas Copernicus, 1543–1943.* New York, 1943.

Molinier, Auguste, ed. *Les sources de l'histoire de France.* Vols. I–VI on the Middle Ages. Paris, 1901–1906.

Monnier, Philippe. *Le Quattrocento.* 2 vols. Paris, 1901.

Monroe, Harriet, and Henderson, Alice Corbin, edd. *The New Poetry: An Anthology.* New York, 1918.

Montaigne, Michel Eyquem. *Essays.* Trans. Jacob Zeitlin. 3 vols. New York, 1934–36.

More, Thomas, trans. *The Life of Pico della Mirandola.* Ed. J. M. Rigg. London, 1890.

Morey, Charles Rufus. *Mediaeval Art.* New York [1942].

——. "The Middle Ages," *Historical Aspects of the Fine Arts.* Oberlin, 1938.

Morison, Samuel Eliot. *Admiral of the Ocean Sea.* 2 vols. Boston, 1942.

——. *Portuguese Voyages to America in the Fifteenth Century.* Cambridge, 1940.

Morley, John. *Machiavelli.* The Romanes Lecture. London, 1897.

Munro, Dana Carleton, and Sellery, George Clarke, edd. *Medieval Civilization.* New York, 1907.

Neumann, Carl. *Rembrandt.* 2 vols. München, 1924.

——. "Byzantinische Kultur und Renaissancekultur," *Historische Zeitschrift,* XCI (1903), 215–32.

Nordström, Johan. *Moyen âge et Renaissance.* Translation of the Swedish text of 1929 by T. Hammar. Paris, 1933.

Nowell, Charles E. "The Columbus Question," *American Historical Review,* XLIV (1939), 802–22.

Nunn, George Emra. *The Geographical Conceptions of Columbus.* New York, 1924.

Osgood, Charles Grosvenor. *Boccaccio on Poetry.* Princeton, 1930.

Pecock, Reginald. *The Book of Faith.* Ed. J. L. Morison. Glasgow, 1909.

——. *The Donet.* Ed. E. V. Hitchcock. London, 1929.

————. *The Folewer to the Donet.* Ed. E. V. Hitchcock. London, 1924.

————. *The Reule of Crysten Religioun.* Ed. W. C. Greet. London, 1927.

————. *The Repressor of Over Much Blaming of the Clergy.* Ed. Churchill Babington. 2 vols. London, 1860.

Petrarch, Francesco. *Letters to Classical Authors.* Trans. M. E. Cosenza. Chicago, 1910.

————. *Petrarch, the First Modern Scholar and Man of Letters.* Translations, James Harvey Robinson and Henry Winchester Rolfe, edd. Revised edition. New York, 1914.

————. *Petrarch's Secret; or, the Soul's Conflict with Passion.* Trans. William Henry Draper. London, 1911.

————. *The Sonnets of Petrarch.* Verse trans. Joseph Auslander. New York, 1931.

Picard, Émile. *La vie et l'oeuvre de Pierre Duhem.* Paris, 1922.

Pirenne, Henri. *Economic and Social History of Medieval Europe.* New York, 1937.

————. *Medieval Cities, Their Origins and the Revival of Trade.* Princeton, 1925.

————. "Northern Towns and their Commerce," *Cambridge Medieval History,* VI (New York, 1929), 505–27.

Power, Eileen. "Pierre Dubois and the Domination of France," *The Social and Political Ideas of some Great Mediaeval Thinkers,* ed. F. J. C. Hearnshaw. London [1923].

Prestage, Edgar. *The Portuguese Pioneers.* London, 1933.

Previté-Orton, Charles William. "Marsilius of Padua," *Proceedings of the British Academy* (1935), 137–83.

Pusino, Ivan. "Ficinos und Picos religiös-philosophische Anschauungen," *Zeitschrift für Kirchengeschichte,* XLIV (1925), 504–43.

Rajna, Pio. *Le fonti dell'Orlando Furioso: ricerche e studi.* Firenze, 1900.

Ramsay, William Mitchell. *The Imperial Peace.* Oxford, 1913.

Rashdall, Hastings. "The Medieval Universities," *Cambridge Medieval History,* VI (New York, 1929), 559–601.

Read, Conyers. *The Tudors.* New York, 1936.

Reade, W. H. V. "Philosophy in the Middle Ages," *Cambridge Medieval History,* V (New York, 1926), 780–829.

Robert of Clari. *The Conquest of Constantinople.* Trans. Edgar Holmes McNeal. New York, 1936.

Rosen, Edward, trans. *Three Copernican Treatises.* New York, 1939.

Rossi, Vittorio. *Il Quattrocento* (*Storia letteraria d'Italia*). Milano, n. d.

Rostovtzeff, Mikhail. *A History of the Ancient World.* 2 vols. Oxford, 1926–27.

Ruiz, Juan. *The Book of Good Love.* Verse trans. Elisha Kent Kane. Privately printed, 1933.

Saintsbury, George Edward Bateman. "Chaucer," *Cambridge History of English Literature,* II (New York [1908]), 179–224.

———. *The Earlier Renaissance* (*Periods of European Literature*). New York, 1901.

———. *A History of Criticism.* 3 vols. Edinburgh, 1900–1904.

Sandys, John Edwin. *A Short History of Classical Scholarship.* Cambridge, Eng., 1915.

Santayana, George. *The Genteel Tradition at Bay.* New York, 1931.

Sarton, George. *The History of Science and the New Humanism.* New York [1931].

———. *Introduction to the History of Science.* 3 vols. in 5. Baltimore, 1927–48. (In progress.)

———. "Science in the Renaissance," *Civilization of the Renaissance,* by James Westfall Thompson, George Rowley, Ferdinand Schevill, and George Sarton. Chicago [1929].

Schevill, Ferdinand. *History of Florence.* New York, 1936.

Scholz, Richard. *Die Publizistik zur Zeit Philipps des Schönen und Bonifaz VIII.* Stuttgart, 1903.

Shears, Frederick Sidney. *Froissart, Chronicler and Poet.* London, 1930.

Shorey, Paul. *Platonism Ancient and Modern.* Berkeley, 1938.

Siciliano, Italo. *François Villon et thèmes poétique du moyen âge.* Paris, 1934.

———. *Medio Evo e Rinascimento.* Milano, 1936.

Slichter, Charles Sumner. "Science and Authority," *Science in a Tavern.* Madison, Wis. [1938].

Stewart, John Alexander. *The Myths of Plato.* London, 1905.

Stimson, Dorothy. *The Gradual Acceptance of the Copernican Theory of the Universe.* Hanover, N. H., 1917.

Stoll, Elmer Edgar. *Shakespeare and Other Masters.* Cambridge, 1940.

Symonds, John Addington. *Renaissance in Italy.* 7 vols. London, 1875–86.

Taylor, Alfred Edward. *Plato.* London, 1911.

Taylor, Henry Osborn. *The Mediaeval Mind.* Second edition. 2 vols. London, 1914.

———. *Thought and Expression in the Sixteenth Century.* 2 vols. New York, 1920.

Thatcher, O. J., and McNeal, E. H., edd. *Source Book for Mediaeval History.* New York, 1905.

Thode, Henry. *Franz von Assisi und die Anfänge der Kunst der Renaissance in Italien.* Third edition. Berlin, 1926.

Thorndike, Lynn. *History of Magic and Experimental Science.* 6 vols. New York, 1923–41.

———. *Science and Thought in the Fifteenth Century.* New York, 1929.

Tomlinson, Henry Major. *The Sea and the Jungle.* New York, 1920.

Torraca, Francesco. *Per la biografia di Giovanni Boccaccio.* Milano, 1912.

Trachtenberg, O. V. "William of Occam and the Prehistory of English Materialism," *Philosophy and Phenomenonological Research,* VI (1945–46), 212–24.

Turberville, A. S. "Changing Views of the Renaissance," *History,* New Series, XVI (1931–32), 289–97.

Ullman, Berthold Louis. "Leonardo Bruni and Humanistic Historiography," *Medievalia et Humanistica,* IV (1946), 45–61.

Usher, Abbott Payson. *A History of Mechanical Inventions.* New York, 1929.

Varga, Lucie. *Das Schlagwort vom "Finsteren Mittelalter."* Wien, 1932.

Villani, Giovanni. *Cronica di Giovanni Villani.* Ed. Francesco Gherardi Dragomanni. 2 vols. Firenze, 1844–45.

———. *Villani's Chronicle, Being Selections.* . . . Trans. Rose E. Selfe and Philip H. Wicksteed. London, 1906.

Villari, Pasquale. *The Life and Times of Niccolò Machiavelli.* 2 vols. New York, 1891.

Villon, François. *Oeuvres.* Ed. Auguste Longnon, revised by L. Foulet. Paris, 1923.

————. *Oeuvres.* Ed. Louis Thuasne. Paris, 1923.

————. *The Complete Works of François Villon.* Verse trans. John Urban Nicolson. New York, 1931.

Vinogradoff, Paul. *Roman Law in Medieval Europe.* Second edition. Oxford, 1929.

Voigt, Georg. *Die Wiederbelebung des classischen Alterthums.* 2 vols. Berlin, 1893.

Volpi, Guglielmo. *Il Trecento (Storia letteraria d'Italia).* Milano [1907].

Wechssler, Eduard. *Das Kulturproblem des Minnesangs.* Halle, 1909.

White, Lynn, Jr. "Natural Science and Naturalistic Art in the Middle Ages," *American Historical Review,* LII (1947), 421–35.

————. "Technology and Invention in the Middle Ages," *Speculum,* XV (1940), 141–59.

Whitehead, Alfred North. *Adventures of Ideas.* New York, 1933.

Wolf, Abraham. *A History of Science, Technology, and Philosophy in the Sixteenth and Seventeenth Centuries.* London [1935].

Wölfflin, Heinrich. *The Art of the Italian Renaissance.* New York, 1913.

Wroth, Lawrence Counselman, ed. *A History of the Printed Book.* New York, 1938.

Zingarelli, Nicola. *Dante (Storia letteraria d'Italia).* Milano [1901?].

ACKNOWLEDGMENTS

The author wishes to thank the following publishers:

EDITIONS STOCK, for permission to quote from *Moyen âge et Renaissance*, by Johan Nordström.

R. OLDENBOURG, for permission to quote from *Geschichte der neuren Historiographie*, By Eduard Fueter.

THE KOSCIUSZKO FOUNDATION, for permission to quote from *Nicholas Copernicus, 1543-1943*, by Stephen Paul Mizwa.

DOTT. FRANCESCO VALLARDI, for permission to quote from *Il Quattrocento*, by Vittorio Rossi; and *Il Trecento*, by Guglielmo Volpi.

CLARENDON PRESS, for permission to quote from *The Legacy of the Middle Ages*, edited by Charles George Crump and Ernest Fraser Jacob; *Epochs of Italian Literature*, by Cesare Foligno, and *A History of the Ancient World*, by Mikhail Rostovtzeff.

WILLIAM HEINEMANN, LTD., for permission to print the lines from Swinburne's translation of Villon's "Ballade of the Hanged," which are quoted on page 105.

OXFORD UNIVERSITY PRESS, for permission to quote from *Don Quixote*, by Salvador de Madariaga; *The Legacy of Greece*, edited by Richard Winn Livingstone; and John Matthews Manly's article in *Proceedings of the British Academy*.

G. P. PUTNAM'S SONS, for permission to quote from *North Italian Painters of the Renaissance*, by

Bernhard Berenson; and *The Art of the Italian Renaissance*, by Heinrich Wölfflin.

CAMBRIDGE UNIVERSITY PRESS, for permission to quote from *English Law and the Renaissance*, by Frederic William Maitland; and from articles by George E. B. Saintsbury in the *Cambridge History of English Literature*, and by W. H. V. Reade and Hastings Rashdall in the *Cambridge Medieval History*.

THE HAKLUYT SOCIETY, for permission to quote from *Select Documents Illustrating the Four Voyages of Columbus*, edited by Lionel Cecil Jane.

PRESSES UNIVERSITAIRES DE FRANCE, for *La modernnité du XVIᵉ siècle*, by Henri Hauser.

G. C. SANSONI, for permission to quote from *Le fonti dell'Orlando Furioso*, by Pio Rajna.

OBERLIN COLLEGE, for permission to quote from *Historical Aspects of the Fine Arts*.

A. COLIN, for permission to quote from *François Villon*, by Italo Siciliano; and *Littérature italienne*, by Henri Hauvette.

APPLETON-CENTURY-CROFTS, INC., for permission to quote from *Medieval Civilization*, by Dana Carleton Munro and George Clarke Sellery.

ALLEN AND UNWIN, LTD., for permission to quote from *Copernicus, the Founder of Modern Astronomy*, by Angus Armitage.

E. P. DUTTON AND COMPANY, INC., for permission to quote from *The Sea and the Jungle*, by Henry Tomlinson; *The King of Court Poets*, by Edmund

Garret Gardner; and the Everyman's Library edition of Froissart's *Chronicles*.

HOUGHTON MIFFLIN COMPANY, for permission to quote from *Geoffrey Chaucer and the Development of His Genius* and *Essays in Appreciation*, by John Livingston Lowes; and *A History of Europe*, by H. A. L. Fisher.

CHARLES SCRIBNER'S SONS, for permission to quote from *Art Epochs and Their Leaders*, by Oskar Hagen; *Civilization during the Middle Ages*, by George Burton Adams; and *Selections from Mediaeval Philosophers*, edited by Richard P. McKeon.

HENRY HOLT AND COMPANY, for permission to quote from *A History of Italian Painting*, by Frank Jewett Mather; and *The Tudors*, by Conyers Read.

W. W. NORTON AND COMPANY, INC., for permission to quote from *Medieval Art*, by Charles Rufus Morey.

MACMILLAN COMPANY, for permission to quote from *Chaucer*, by John Masefield; *The Choice of Books and Other Literary Pieces*, by Frederic Harrison; *Adventures of Ideas*, by Alfred North Whitehead; *Lectures on Modern History*, by John E. E. D. Acton; and *A Preface to Morals*, by Walter Lippmann.

DOUBLEDAY AND COMPANY, INC., for permission to quote from *Appearances*, by Goldsworthy Lowes Dickinson.

LIBRAIRIE ACADÉMIQUE PERRIN, for permission to quote from *Le Quattrocento*, by Philippe Monnier.

WILLIAM BLACKWOOD AND SONS, LTD., for permission to quote from *A History of Criticism*, by George E. B. Saintsbury.

EDWARD ARNOLD AND COMPANY, for permission to quote from *The Englishman*, by William Macneile Dixon.

GEORGE G. HARRAP AND COMPANY, LTD., and BARNES AND NOBLE, INC., for permission to quote from *Social and Political Ideas of some Great Mediaeval Thinkers*, by F. J. C. Hearnshaw.

A. ET J. PICARD ET Cⁱᵉ, for permission to quote from *Les sources de l'histoire de France*, edited by Auguste Molinier; and the Louis Thuasne edition of the *Oeuvres* of François Villon.

COWARD-McCANN, INC., for permission to quote from *François Villon*, by D. B. Wyndham Lewis.

THE ENCYCLOPAEDIA BRITANNICA, for permission to quote from articles by Walter Besant and Adolf Harnack in the eleventh edition.

HARVARD UNIVERSITY PRESS, for permission to quote from *The Mediaeval Mind* and *Thought and Expression in the Sixteenth Century*, by Henry Osborn Taylor; *Sulieman the Magnificent*, by Roger Merriman; and *The Renaissance of the Twelfth Century*, by Charles Homer Haskins.

SOCIETÀ ANONIMA EDITRICE DANTE ALIGHIERI, for permission to quote from *Medio Evo e Renascimento*, by Italo Siciliano.

In addition, the author would like to thank George Peabody Gooch, for permission to quote from his

History and Historians of the Nineteenth Century; Ferdinand Schevill, for permission to quote from his book, *A History of Florence,* and the editors of *The American Historical Review, History, The Nation, Atlantic Monthly,* and *The Saturday Review of Literature,* for permission to quote from those magazines.

INDEX